Theater of the Word

To Susie, most
awesome colleague
+ chair. Thank
you so very much
for all you have
done for me!
   Live free!
with love +
respect + gratitude :)
         Julie

Reformations: Medieval and Early Modern

SERIES EDITORS: DAVID AERS, SARAH BECKWITH,
AND JAMES SIMPSON

RECENT TITLES IN THE SERIES

*Writing Faith and Telling Tales: Literature, Politics, and
Religion in the Work of Thomas More* (2013)
Thomas Betteridge

*Unwritten Verities: The Making of England's Vernacular
Legal Culture, 1463–1549* (2015)
Sebastian Sobecki

Mysticism and Reform, 1400–1750 (2015)
Sara S. Poor and Nigel Smith, eds.

*The Civic Cycles: Artisan Drama and Identity in
Premodern England* (2015)
Nicole R. Rice and Margaret Aziza Pappano

Tropologies: Ethics and Invention in England, c. 1350–1600 (2016)
Ryan McDermott

*Volition's Face: Personification and the Will in
Renaissance Literature* (2017)
Andrew Escobedo

*Shadow and Substance: Eucharistic Controversy and
English Drama across the Reformation Divide* (2017)
Jay Zysk

*Queen of Heaven: The Assumption and Coronation of the
Virgin in Early Modern English Writing* (2018)
Lilla Grindlay

*Performance and Religion in Early Modern England:
Stage, Cathedral, Wagon, Street* (2019)
Matthew J. Smith

JULIE PAULSON

Theater of the Word

SELFHOOD IN THE ENGLISH MORALITY PLAY

University of Notre Dame Press
Notre Dame, Indiana

Published in the United States of America

Library of Congress Cataloging-in-Publication Data

Names: Paulson, Julie C., 1970- author.
Title: Theater of the word : selfhood in the English morality play /
Julie Paulson.
Description: Notre Dame, Indiana : University of Notre Dame Press, [2019]
| Series: Reformations : medieval and early modern |
Includes bibliographical references and index. |
Identifiers: LCCN 2019002933 (print) | LCCN 2019007021 (ebook) |
ISBN 9780268104634 (pdf) | ISBN 9780268104641 (epub) |
ISBN 9780268104610 | ISBN 9780268104610 (hardback : alk. paper) |
ISBN 0268104611 (hardback : alk. paper) | ISBN 9780268104627
(paperback : alk. paper) | ISBN 026810462X (paperback : alk. paper)
Subjects: LCSH: Self in literature. | Moralities, English—
History and criticism.
Classification: LCC PR635.S38 (ebook) |
LCC PR635.S38 P38 2019 (print) | DDC 822/.051609—dc23
LC record available at https://lccn.loc.gov/2019002933

For my parents.

CONTENTS

ACKNOWLEDGMENTS

This book is in large part about the role of community in shaping the self. I have been very fortunate in the course of my life to be shaped by wonderful intellectual and educational communities, accumulating numerous debts along the way. I trace my interest in premodern selfhood to the storied "Hum 110" course required of all first-year students at Reed College and wish to acknowledge the inspiring teachers there, particularly Nathalia King, Gail Sherman, and Ellen Stauder. Good fortune landed me at Duke University for graduate work with Sarah Beckwith and David Aers, who helped me shape the central premises of this book at its earliest inception, many years ago. It is my sincere hope that the richness, rigor, and generosity of their instruction is felt by my own students today. I am also grateful for the contributions of Meg Greer, Toril Moi, and Laurie Shannon and to the many others who formed my intellectual community at Duke. Thank you, Sarah, for encouraging me to submit the book to the ReFormations series.

My wonderful colleagues at San Francisco State University have been indispensable to the development of this project. Steve Arkin, Dean Paul Sherwin, and Sugie Goen-Salter provided crucial support early and late in its development, and I am grateful for the leaves and assigned time that allowed me time for research. I would particularly like to thank the core members of my writing group—Sara Hackenberg, Gitanjali Shahani, Lynn Wardley, and Lehua Yim—for their astute comments and companionship in the writing process. Sara Hackenberg has read and reread every chapter of this book, always with great assiduousness and invaluable suggestions. Lara Bovilsky, Sarita Cannon, Jody Enders, Jason Gleckman, Robert Hornback, Erin Kelly, Shirin Khanmohamadi, Maura Nolan, Margaret Pappano,

Melissa Sanchez, Summer Star, and Andrew Tumminia also provided helpful feedback on pieces of this project at various stages in its progress. Dorrie Armstrong, Kathy Ashley, Katie Little, and the late Claire Sponsler reviewed the manuscript in full, and I have greatly benefited from their insights and encouragement.

I wish to thank Stephen Little, Matt Dowd, Susan Berger, and Wendy McMillen at the University of Notre Dame Press for shepherding this book toward publication and Scott Barker for his skilled copy editing. This is a far better book for the perceptive and thorough commentary received from Kate Crassons and an anonymous reader for the press—I deeply thank them both. All errors and shortcomings are my own.

An earlier version of chapter 2 appeared as "A Theater of the Soul's Interior: Contemplative Literature and Penitential Education in the Morality Play *Wisdom*" in the *Journal of Medieval and Early Modern Studies* 38.2 (Spring 2008). Likewise, an earlier version of chapter 4 appeared as "Death's Arrival and *Everyman*'s Separation" in *Theatre Survey* 48.1 (May 2007). Thank you to the Folger Shakespeare Library for permission to use the image of the stage plan of *The Castle of Perseverance*.

This book is dedicated to my parents, Leon and Pearl Paulson, whose abundant love and support over the years I cannot even begin to describe. This book only exists because of the countless hours of childcare my parents and husband provided, and the many family outings and trips I missed so I could write. I especially thank my husband, Ben Wallace, and my children, Zachary and Adeline, for the sacrifices they made to make this book possible. I am immeasurably thankful for the love and companionship they give me every day.

INTRODUCTION

One and the same man perceives himself both to understand and to have sensations. Yet sensation involves the body, so that the body must be said to be part of man.
—Thomas Aquinas, *Summa Theologiae*

"Man," writes Augustine in the *City of God*, "is neither the soul alone, nor the body alone, but body and soul together."[1] Invoking Augustine's definition, Aquinas likewise argues that a human being is a compound of a soul and a body where the "intellectual soul" is the "form of the human body."[2] Human beings cannot be a soul or mind without a body. It will be such conceptions of the human and the Aristotelian metaphysics they imply that Descartes will reject in his famous formulation of the *cogito* with its radical separation of mind and body and attendant privileging of the interior life as the guarantor of the self. Descartes's influence, despite much critical debate, continues to be felt today in the privileging of a private, hidden interiority—and the associated categories of inwardness, self-recognition, subjectivity, introspection, self-consciousness, and the like—as the defining criteria of what we mean by a "self." Such privileging is also operative in histories of the self that seek to establish when the modern individualist "subject," however variously defined, first emerged. This book, by turning away from Cartesian conceptions of the self as subject, offers a new way of understanding medieval representations of the self. I propose Wittgenstein, rather than Descartes, as the philosopher who can best help us understand the joined body and soul of medieval conceptions of selfhood.[3]

1

For much of the twentieth century (and earlier), scholars identified the dawn of modernity with the emergence of an individual self-
consciousness.[4] In response to a spate of Marxist-inspired histories
of subjectivity produced in the 1980s, David Aers and Lee Patterson
wrote a set of influential essays that rightly sought to correct the view
that interiority in the Middle Ages did not exist. "The dialectic between an inward subjectivity and an external world that alienates it
from both itself and its divine source," Patterson pointed out, "provides the fundamental economy of the medieval idea of selfhood."[5]
Although it importantly redirects critical attention to medieval anthro-
pologies of the self, Patterson's formulation nonetheless leaves the bi-
nary between an inward subjectivity and the external world in place.
Notably, at the same critical moment that medievalists were defending
the very existence of interiority in the Middle Ages, other critics, most
prominently Judith Butler, were insisting on the performative nature
of identity, where the self is variably constructed in and through its
acts.[6] In this book, I reconsider our privileging of internal subjectivity
and the language of self-revelation as the defining category of what it
means to be a self. I look anew at how medieval constructions of selfhood emerge from a sacramental culture in which penitential ritual
and other social performances play a formative role in the shaping of
Christian selves. I focus on the form of drama known as the morality
play, a dramatic form that explicitly addresses the question of what it
means to be human and that takes up a ritual tradition long associated
with medieval "interiority" — confession and penance — as its primary
subject.

The morality play is allegorical drama, a theater of the word, that
typically follows a penitential progression in which an everyman figure
falls into sin and is eventually redeemed through penitential ritual. Because of their use of dramatic personification and penitential themes,
the plays are regularly described as didactic or instructional dramas
that dispatch easily discerned moral truths using "flat" abstract types
and predictable stories of temptation, fall, and regeneration. My argument is that the opposite is true. Rather than seeking to impart static
moral lessons, the plays instead demonstrate the pedagogical and performative power of penance where the meanings of words develop
through participation in penitential ritual. Dramatic personification—
by representing words as human beings and human beings as words—

foregrounds the relation of language to human embodiment. The morality plays present a model of language, theater, and self in which the human body is not a site of obfuscation but of revelation, and where the meaning of the words we use to describe our relations to one another is the product of those very relations. The initial innocence of the plays' protagonists is characterized not by sinlessness but by a lack of self-knowledge, and the character will only gain self-knowledge—which in the morality plays is inextricable from an understanding of one's relationship to God—through the temporal experiences of sin, repentance, and forgiveness. Shown in performance, penance is revealed to be itself performative. As the ritual that places a demand upon penitents to acknowledge their responsibility to God and community, penance shapes one's understanding of the meanings of words central to moral selfhood.

Produced during the same era as the great urban biblical cycles of Chester and York, the five extant works commonly seen to define the medieval morality play as a dramatic form were all written sometime between the late fourteenth and early sixteenth centuries. The earliest, *The Pride of Life*, is a fragmentary Anglo-Irish text of 502 lines probably composed in the late fourteenth century.[7] The play describes the efforts of its protagonist, the King of Life, a representative of human pride, to deny his mortality and defeat death.[8] The three plays of the Macro manuscript (Folger MS V.a.354)—*The Castle of Perseverance* (ca. 1400–25), *Wisdom* (ca. 1465–70), and *Mankind* (ca. 1465–70)—were originally transcribed as three separate paper manuscripts and were bound together sometime in the early nineteenth century; a second, incomplete copy of *Wisdom* exists in Bodleian MS Digby 133.[9] Although no performance records of any of the plays remain, all three plays include stage directions and other internal evidence that strongly suggest they were intended for performance.[10] The *Castle* is a play of 3,649 lines that has thirty-five parts and, in the tradition of the early fifth-century poet Prudentius's *Psychomachia*, dramatizes a protracted struggle between virtue and vice for the soul of Humankind. Its manuscript includes a detailed stage plan, the first of its kind in England, for an elaborate outdoor "place and scaffold" performance. A much shorter play of 1,163 lines, *Wisdom* recounts the temptation of the soul and its faculties, represented by the female Anima and her three male "mights," by Lucifer. The play's lavish costuming, liturgical chants and processions, masked dances, and contemplative themes suggest it was intended for performance in the great hall of an aristocratic or ecclesiastical household. The staging and casting requirements of *Mankind*, a play of 914 lines that has seven parts, one of which can be doubled, are comparatively modest. The play describes Mankind's efforts to follow the directives of a sententious figure named Mercy and his eventual capitulation to the wiles of the play's witty and foul-mouthed vice figures. The vices' energetic efforts to collect money from the play's audience have led scholars to believe the play was intended for a professional touring troupe, but its actors may equally have been raising money for a town or parish.[11] *Everyman* (ca. 1500), a play of 921 lines, is a translation of the Dutch play *Elckerlijc* and portrays the relentless stripping away of everyone and everything around Everyman as he approaches death.[12] It is extant in four printed editions, all dating between ca. 1510 and ca. 1535: two printed by John Skot, and two, extant only as fragments, by Richard Pynson. Although modern productions have proved *Everyman* to be a powerful play in performance, the headnote of the Skot edition advertises itself as a "treatyse . . . in maner of a morall playe," suggesting that *Everyman* may have been originally intended to be read rather than played.[13]

All written in East Midlands dialect, the three Macro plays were part of the rich dramatic tradition of late medieval East Anglia.[14] East Anglia in the fifteenth century was a prosperous, densely populated region of small towns and villages with a thriving cloth trade and was, as the variety and volume of surviving records witness, a center of dramatic activity.[15] The region was home to a biblical cycle play, the *N-Town Plays* (Cotton MS Vespasian D. viii), as well as a number of other plays and fragments, including the only surviving English host (Eucharistic) miracle play, the Croxton *Play of the Sacrament*; the Brome *Abraham and Isaac*; the Norwich Grocer's *Play of the Fall of Man*; and a fragmentary incest tale, *Dux Moraud*. In addition to the *Wisdom* fragment, Digby 133 includes two saint plays, *Mary Magdalene* and the *Conversion of Saint Paul*, as well as a biblical drama copied by the same scribe of the *Wisdom* fragment, the *Killing of the Children*. The Macro manuscript has strong ties to Bury St. Edmunds in Sussex, prompting some scholars to propose that the powerful Benedictine abbey of Bury St. Edmunds was a direct or indirect sponsor of the plays.[16] A scribe identifying himself as a monk named Hyngham wrote identical verses at the end of the Macro *Wisdom* and *Mankind* (and may have also been the scribe who copied the texts themselves); both Richard Beadle and Jeremy Griffiths have identified the monk as Thomas Hyngham, who lived at the Bury abbey in the 1470s.[17] Another inscription in the Macro *Wisdom*, in what appears to be in a sixteenth-century hand, identifies the writer as "Rychard Cake of Bury." The Macro plays themselves are named for their eighteenth-century owner, the Bury antiquarian Cox Macro (1683–1767). In addition to these links, the name or initials of Myles Blomefylde, a physician and alchemist born in Bury in 1525, are written in three of the Digby plays, including the *Wisdom* fragment.[18] Because this book investigates the role of penance and performance in late medieval constructions of the self, I examine the four complete extant medieval morality plays that explicitly dramatize penitential ritual: *The Castle of Perseverance*, *Wisdom*, *Mankind*, and *Everyman*, in chapters 1 to 4, respectively. In chapter 5, I consider two post-Reformation plays indebted to the morality play tradition, John Bale's *King Johan* (ca. 1538) and Lewis Wager's *The Life and Repentance of Mary Magdalene* (ca. 1547–66).[19]

In examining the representation of penance in the morality play, this book argues for the centrality of performance to late medieval understandings of the self. The plays demonstrate that the meanings of words, including the language used to describe the self, are bound up in human interactions and material practices, and in particular those structured by penitential ritual. Because of the influence of Michel Foucault's *History of Sexuality*, most theories of medieval selfhood emphasize the interaction between penitent and priest as an initiatory site of self-revelation, and stress the importance of the confessional subject as the locus of emerging forms of modern subjectivity.[20] In contrast, the morality plays do not dramatize the penitent's detailed itemization of his or her particular sins. Private confession is pushed out of the performance; in *Wisdom*, Anima's confession takes place offstage entirely (ll. 981–1082). The self does not emerge through the self-scrutiny demanded by confession but rather through the material practices and interpersonal relations structured by penance.[21] The centrality of such communal practices to the self can be difficult to see, because a Cartesian privileging of the interior subject persists as an abiding anachronism in our attempts to understand medieval selfhood. By looking to nonmentalist models, we can better understand the relation between the medieval and early modern. Wittgenstein's philosophy of language suggests an alternative to the standard Cartesian view of the self by demonstrating the embodied, public nature of the meanings of words, including those words we use to describe our inner lives. As in Wittgenstein, in the morality play one's vocabulary for describing a "self" arises not through introspection but through human interaction.

According to a Wittgensteinian view of language, the meanings of words such as "mankind," "mercy," or "mischief" are only discovered through our use of them, in the specific exchanges of human beings with each other. Sarah Beckwith has recently drawn attention to the affinities between the understanding of language in the morality play *Mankind* and ordinary language philosophy, where—like Wittgenstein and ordinary language philosophy more broadly—the morality play understands "language as act, as event in the world."[22] Rather than "inviting us to recognize abstract virtues that exist outside of the world of the play, and independently of any particular agency," Beckwith argues, *Mankind* instead describes a "process of recognition" in which "meanings are opened out through relations," that is, through the characters' encounters with one another.[23] Building on this work, my present study shows the sophistication with which the morality plays engage contemporary religious debates about the sacraments by providing an account of how dramatic personification in the plays fosters an understanding of the communal bases of language and the performative nature of the self. Mankind will understand his need for God's Mercy (both the character and the concept)—and thus what it is to be "mankind"—only by painfully experiencing the need at the hands of the vices. In other words, to understand the meaning of "mercy" is to understand it as a social virtue where mercy is never self-contained but requires two or more beings in order to exist. It is therefore always already socially performed. Mercy is meaningless in the mouth of Mankind until he cries out for it; by the end of the play, Mankind no longer understands "mercy" simply as doctrine but acknowledges mercy as it manifests itself through his relationships with other people.

Emerging in the late fourteenth and fifteenth centuries, a period of orthodox reform when the ritual life of the Catholic Church was under scrutiny, the medieval morality plays imagine a self that is first and foremost *performed*: constructed, articulated, and known through communal performances. In doing so, they present a sophisticated defense of penance that counters Wycliffite (or lollard) arguments that challenged the necessity of oral confession to a priest. They press beyond a simple, dogmatic assertion of the necessity of auricular confession, instead demonstrating the centrality of penitential ritual to the formation of Christian subjects. In the sixteenth century, the morality play continued to be a locus of larger cultural debates over the ritual life of the church, as Tudor playwrights reimagined the medieval plays' content and form to navigate the enormous religious and cultural changes that accompanied the Reformation. Protestant playwrights in particular embraced the form, looking to the figure of the vice masquerading as virtue as a potent means of excoriating the very rituals the morality play had previously celebrated. In seeking to sort out the "false actors" of the old religion from the "true spectators" of the new, the Reformation dramas create a theater of recognition and misrecognition and a moral selfhood that remains forged in performance.

PENANCE AND REFORM

Penance gives the medieval morality plays their basic form. The penitential trajectory of fall and redemption structures their action; its language establishes their central concepts and vocabulary. The plays' dual penitential and pedagogical themes can be seen ultimately to derive from the twenty-first canon of the Fourth Lateran Council of 1215, known as the *Omnis utriusque sexus* decree, which required all Christians to confess their sins at least once a year to their parish priest. When, in *Wisdom*, the soul's disfigurement by sin is literalized in Anima's shocking physical transformation (902sd) or when, in *Everyman*, Good Deeds advises Everyman that penance will "hele the of thy smarte [pain]" (528), the plays reflect the decree's imagery of the sinner as wounded soul: "The priest shall be discerning and prudent, so that like a skilled doctor he may pour wine and oil over the wounds of the injured one. Let him carefully inquire about the circumstances of both the sinner and the sin, so that he may prudently discern what sort of advice he ought to give and what remedy to apply."[24]

The requirement of annual auricular confession produced a large body of pastoral literature in both Latin and the vernacular to help priests prepare parishioners for the confessional, including academic *summae* of moral teaching, practical handbooks for priests on how to hear confessions, general manuals on pastoral care, compendia of virtues and vices, and collections of sermons and sermon exempla. Like this literature, the morality plays give penance an important role in lay religious education and highlight the healing power of penance, representing penance according to its traditional three-part structure in which the forgiveness of sins requires penitents to feel sorrow for their sins, confess their sins to their priest, and perform the acts of satisfaction the priest enjoins. Yet, unlike contemporary confessional manuals, the plays do not focus on the interaction between penitent and priest and thus avoid staging aspects of penitential ritual upon which reformers were putting considerable pressure. Instead, by showing how the experience of penitential ritual activates the soul's self-knowledge, the plays present penance, the sacrament that reforms of the soul of *mankind*, as itself the instrument of individual and collective reform.

The confessional manuals that followed the publication of the *Omnis utriusque sexus* decree were designed to help priests fulfill their role as diagnostician and assist their parishioners in a full examination of their conscience. For instance, the *Summula* of the diocese of Exeter (1240) directs that a penitent should reveal "all his inner wounds to his spiritual doctor" and disclose "all those circumstances and everything which could aggravate the sin in any way," providing priests with the mnemonic "who, what, where, by whose aid, why, how, and when" (*quis, quid, ubi, quibus auxiliis, cur, quomodo, quando*) to help them do so.[25] Such an emphasis on the detailed itemization of sin persisted into the fifteenth century: John Mirk's *Instructions to Parish Priests* (ca. 1400) similarly directs that, once the penitent has confessed all his sins, the priest should ask him to "grope hys sore" to ensure that the penitent has not left anything out, inquiring whether he has broken any of the Ten Commandments, participated in any of the seven deadly sins, or engaged in any number of lesser offenses.[26]

Post–Lateran IV pastoral literature also strongly aligns the soul's reformation with its education where, as Marjorie Curry Woods and Rita Copeland note, "the confessional . . . operates in the manner of the classroom: the priest-confessor, as teacher, instructs and examines the penitent, to produce in him or her an internalized system of self-regulation."[27] *The Lay Folks' Catechism* (1357) explicitly instructs that parsons, vicars, and parish priests should "enquere diligently of thair sugettes, in the lentyn tyme" when "thai come to shrift" whether they know the "sex thinges" every Christian should know: the articles of faith, the commandments, the sacraments, the deeds of mercy, the virtues, and the deadly sins.[28] Mirk's *Instructions to Parish Priests* similarly directs confessors to ask penitents if they know their Pater Noster, Ave, and Creed, noting that if a parishioner "con hyt not," the priest should "make hym hyt to lerne" as penance (28/917–22). Insofar as such a practice called upon penitents to affirm their knowledge of the fundamentals of Christian teaching, such a practice would have ritualized parishioners' association between the confession of sins and the confession of faith.

The morality plays draw on the tropes, directives, and categories of this pastoral literature. *Mankind*'s lead devil, Titivillus, for instance, appears in numerous penitential manuals and sermons as the demon who collects the dropped words of priests who garble the Mass or records the idle words of gossiping congregants.[29] Or, in the *Castle*, when Humankind confesses his sins, he describes them using classificatory schemes outlined in countless confessional manuals. However, in taking up the decree's language of the sick soul, the morality plays downplay the priest's role as diagnostician, instead emphasizing the restorative work of the performance of penance itself. Absent is the "minute analysis of conscience" encouraged by vernacular confessional texts.[30] *Wisdom*'s stage directions indicate that Anima's confession occurs offstage. In *Mankind*, the confessional scene emphasizes Mankind's recognition of God's mercy rather than the itemization of sin. In *Everyman*, Everyman asks Confession for mercy, but the dramatic action underscores penitential purgation of sin and the revival of Everyman's Good Deeds rather than detailed self-examination. Of the morality plays, the *Castle* includes the most extended dramatization of auricular confession, but even then its central character confesses only in general terms. Penance and Shrift do not "carefully inquire about the circumstances of both the sinner and the sin"; instead, Humankind only broadly acknowledges that he has committed all seven of the deadly sins "many a þrowe [time]" both "in home and halle," broken the Ten Commandments, misspent his "fyue wyttys" (five senses), and failed to give money to the poor (1474–86).

The plays are also not primarily catechistic in nature. In fact, as I argue in the chapters to follow, they often foreground the pedagogic limitations of dogmatic exposition of doctrine. Instead, they present the penitential acknowledgment of sin as itself a generative act that produces new forms of self-knowledge. As Robert Potter notes in his 1975 study of the morality play, the plays describe sin itself "as a necessary stage in the education of Mankind."[31] In linking the experience of sin with the soul's self-knowledge, the morality plays resonate with contemporary devotional, literary, and pastoral texts that likewise understand sin and suffering to produce new ways of seeing God and the self. For instance, an understanding of the pedagogic value of sin and suffering can be discerned in late medieval commentaries on the Penitential Psalms, which, Lynn Staley contends, "adumbrate a drama that begins in abject self-consciousness and ends in the acceptance of God's merciful sovereignty."[32] In William Langland's *Piers Plowman*, the narrator's experience of periods of sinful abandon and adversity are key to preparing him for reform.[33] Notably, the *Speculum Sacerdotale* suggests that the experience of auricular confession itself transforms the soul's self-knowledge. Presenting penance as "a nedeful thyng vnto a synner þat desireþ for to recouere heleþ of his soule," the *Speculum Sacerdotale* indicates that the pedagogical work of confession extends beyond reinforcing parishioners' knowledge of the rudiments of the faith:[34]

> Alle this is to be schewid and to be sorowed that he may after siche verrey knoweliche of his synne fynde God merciful to hym. For in knowlegynge of his synne, he shall fynde ekynge [increase] of grace. For-thi knowe the maner and qualite of thy synne as I now rehercy, and clense it with the teris of thy yȝen, and sorowe for the vertu þat þou vsid noȝt in alle that tyme, for it is noȝt onely to sorowe for the synne, but also for the vertue þat was therfore depriuyed. (65/33–66/1)

Through acknowledging their sins, the *Speculum* writer suggests, sinners will discover God's mercy and grace. Moreover, to acknowledge fully the damage done by one's sins, one must recognize not only the harm done by the sins themselves but the opportunities for virtue that have been lost.

By foregrounding the pedagogical and performative importance of penance, the morality plays present a sophisticated defense of penance that, by seeking to recuperate penance as a ritual form, deflects contemporary reformist concerns about the materialism of contemporary penitential practices and counters lollard arguments that challenged the necessity of oral confession to a priest. Geoffrey Chaucer's famous depiction of the Pardoner in the *Canterbury Tales* reflects broader concerns about abuses associated with the system of indulgences, and his Friar, who in the *General Prologue* gladly accepts penitents' silver in lieu of "wepynge and preyeres," reflects contemporary unease about the denigration of the sacrament into financial transactions between penitent and confessor that threatened to undermine penance by compromising contrition.[35] Such anticlerical sentiments are explicitly given voice in *Everyman*. When Everyman leaves the stage to receive last rites, Five Wits lauds the priesthood, arguing that, as ministers of the sacraments and God's earthly representatives, priests "excedeth all other thynge" and are set "aboue aungelles in degree" (732–49). Knowledge, however, is more skeptical: "If preestes be good, it is so, suerly," he replies, going on to denounce priests who "theyr Sauyour do by or sell," whose children "sytteth by other mennes fyres," and who live an unclean life rife with "lustes of lechery" (750–63). Five Wits dismisses Knowledge's remarks, saying, "I trust to God no suche may we fynde" (764–65). Although their exchange introduces doubts about the virtue of the priesthood and thus their ability to fulfill their pastoral role, the play nonetheless overwhelmingly confirms the absolute necessity of penitential confession by demonstrating the profound changes the ritual produces in Everyman.

Whereas Chaucer's *General Prologue*, *Everyman*, and the genre of ecclesiastical satire from which they draw take aim at the sins of individual ecclesiasts, Wyclif and his followers extended this critique and challenged the notion of confession itself as an office of judgment. Emphasizing that God alone forgives sins, Wyclif denied that auricular confession to a priest was necessary to forgiveness, a view also held by many of his followers.[36] Most lollards, like Wyclif, acknowledged that a good priest could help a sinner move toward contrition and did not reject oral confession completely.[37] However, Wyclif and his followers raised concerns about the legally enjoined nature of confession and the juridical apparatus that surrounded it that rendered the notion of confession as a voluntary action of the will highly dubious. As the author of one lollard treatise observes: "whenne a man is constreyned by bodily peyne to telle his gilte, he confesseþ not"; instead "confession mut be wilful, or ellis it is not medeful to man."[38] Also of concern was the secrecy of confession, which made parishioners vulnerable to dishonest priests.[39]

Although many lollards acknowledged the benefit of, and even endorsed, auricular confession, some condemned the practice as one that both misconstrues the role of the priesthood and subjects the laity to a host of misconceptions about the process through which sins are forgiven. In his account of his 1407 testimony before Archbishop Arundel, the lollard preacher William Thorpe emphasizes that priests who take it upon themselves to absolve men of their sins "blasfemen God."[40] Instead, priests should concern themselves with living a holy life and teaching their parishioners the word of God, restricting themselves "to counseile men and wymmen for to leue here synne, confortynge hem þat bisien hem þus to done for to hope stidefastly in þe merci of God" (82/1888–90). For Thorpe, the priest's legitimate office is in his role as teacher and counselor: he should preach the gospel, model its principles, and encourage sinners to leave their sins. The author of the *Lanterne of Liȝt* condemns priests who falsely usurp the power of forgiveness in still stronger terms: "Art not þou þanne a wickid man, a foultid schepard, a cruel beest, þe sone of perdicioun & anticrist him silf þat pretendist in þee & in þi membris to bynde & lose, to blesse & curse, biside þis name Iesu?"[41] Instead, invoking Psalm 118:105, the author stresses that the faithful should look to God's word as "þe lanterne of liȝt" that "schineþ so fer derkness of synne & cloudis of þe fendis temptaciouns vanischen awey & moun not abide" (4/11; 4/14–15). In dwelling on the corruption of the priesthood and the problems associated with auricular confession, such polemical statements arguably gloss over the difficulty and intricacy of coming to contrition. If penance is the means through which one ultimately recognizes his or her own sinfulness, how might one come to selfknowledge in absence of such rituals?[42]

Recent scholarship has helped to uncover the variety of lollard beliefs and complexity of lollard spirituality, drawing attention to the permeability of the boundary between lollard and mainstream writing.[43] Many scholars have also noted that trial records, as inherently adversarial and biased documents, are poor gauges of lollard views.[44] Yet lollard trial records amply demonstrate that, regardless of what defendants in fact believed, their persecutors were enormously concerned about the circulation of heretical views about the efficacy of the sacraments and the necessity of auricular confession. In his recantation to Archbishop Arundel in 1402, Lewis Clifford attributed to the lollards the view that the seven sacraments are but "dead signs" (*signa mortua*).[45] The records of Bishop Alnwick's persecution of William White in Norwich and the proceedings against the brothers William and Richard Sparke of Somersham, Huntingdonshire, attribute to later East Anglian lollards similarly antisacramental views, portraying the accused to hold such rites to be at best a distraction and at worst idolatrous. According to the record of her 1430 confession, Hawisia Moone of Loddon, a follower of White, said that baptism is "but a trufle" as all of Christ's people are sufficiently baptized in the blood of Christ, that the sacrament of confirmation is of "noon availe" because a child who has reached the age of discretion and can understand the word of God is sufficiently confirmed by the Holy Ghost, and that confession should be made only to God.[46] In 1457, William and Richard Sparke were accused of, among other things, holding that "a priest has no more power to make 'the body of Christ' than the wheat-stalk has," confession to a lollard is "more soul-healing than confession made to a priest," the marriage service "was brought in solely to provide fees for priests," and the only effect of extreme unction is "to dirty and make vile the person's body."[47]

Unlike other texts of the period, the morality plays do not explicitly counter lollard views of the sacraments as we see articulated in trial documents or other sources. Although *Everyman*'s Five Wits pronounces that the "preest byndeth and vnbyndeth all bandes" (740), *Everyman* and the earlier morality plays' broader response to contemporary critiques of penance is far less dogmatic. By showing penance in performance, the plays reveal penance itself to be performative, dynamic, and capable of changing its central characters' understanding of both themselves and their relation to others. Rather than insisting upon the doctrinal necessity of auricular confession, the plays address contemporary critiques of the sacrament by foregrounding its pedagogical importance and demonstrating the vital role penance plays in introducing parishioners to the forms of life that define the Christian faith.

Performance and the Pardoner

When discussing the intersecting categories of penance, performance, and self, medievalists often invoke Chaucer's Pardoner, a figure whose association with abuses of the penitential system put him at the center of contemporary controversies surrounding the sacrament. Famously, the Pardoner hawks his illegitimate indulgences to an audience he openly scorns. He both illicitly adopts the sacerdotal offices of preaching and absolution and brazenly declares his only concern is material gain. Yet, I submit that the Pardoner's "confession" that he is a fraud does not indicate the hiddenness and privacy of his interior but the importance of performance to late medieval understandings of the self. Rhetorical and material success, he seems to suggest, resides in the drama of his presentation:

> I stonde lyk a clerk in my pulpet,
> And whan the lewed peple is doun yset,
> I preche so as ye han herd bifoore
> And telle an hundred false japes moore.
> Thanne peyne I me to strecche forth the nekke,
> And est and west upon the peple I bekke [nod],
> As dooth a dowve sittynge on a berne [barn].
> Myne handes and my tonge goon so yerne
> That it is joye to se my bisynesse.
>
> (6.391–99)[48]

In his carefully choreographed performance, the Pardoner, authoritatively perched "lyk a clerk" above the "lewed people" he addresses, coordinates flapping body parts and wagging "tonge" in a bravura display of rhetorical power. His straining neck and nodding, oscillating head present an absurd image of Holy Spirit turned barnyard dove, the substitution of letter for spirit, where material gain replaces preaching's proper motive and end. His "entente," as he repeatedly insists, is "nat but for to wynne, / And nothyng for correccioun of synne" (403–4). He is, by his own report, "a ful vicious man" (459). At once supercilious and self-loathing, he delights in the spectacle of "false japes" (393) he has created while despising the crowds that flock to see him. He is, to borrow a term from Clifford Geertz, a master of his own "thick description" for the other pilgrims' consumption.[49] The Pardoner's defiant and paradoxical self-disclosure exposes himself as a fraud and suggests that preaching is narcissistic display.[50] Ever an actor, he is an "impenitent man [who] performs a penitential act," the human embodiment— the personification, if you will—of the fraudulent indulgences he sells.[51]

The Pardoner's paradoxical self-disclosure and his ambiguous sexuality have been interpreted as seeming signs of a complex and turbulent "inner life," long captivating scholars interested in medieval interiority and the history of subjectivity. Spurred by the narrator's tantalizing remark in the *General Prologue*, "I trowe he were a geldyng or a mare" (1.691), scholars have sought to uncover the "secret" of the Pardoner's sexuality, a critical preoccupation that has in turn made him attractive to psychoanalytic criticism in particular.[52] More recently, scholars have been critical of such attempts to psychologize the Pardoner.[53] Derek Pearsall denies the Pardoner an inner life altogether: "There is no inner consciousness, because there is no 'within'. . . . It is as if he exists only in the act of performance."[54] The Pardoner's performance, Pearsall suggests, is simply empty. Scholars' fascination with the Pardoner's interior life—or its absence—is indicative of the continuing power of the Cartesian subject to interfere with critical attempts to describe and analyze a premodern self in medieval texts.

Chaucer's Pardoner is regularly read in relation to Faux Semblant (False Seeming) of *Le Roman de la Rose*, a religious figure who, like the Pardoner, openly admits his own hypocrisy: "Whatever place I come to, no matter how I conduct myself," Faux Semblant boasts, "I pursue nothing except fraud."[55] Faux Semblant as an allegorical figure embodies the false, a function he consistently and continuously ("whatever place . . . no matter how") performs. As Stephen Knight notes, an association between Faux Semblant and the Pardoner can easily be aligned with a comfortably liberal humanist notion of the self: "If you follow the usual modern course and conceive of the pardoner as an individual, then you can easily talk or write in a facile way about his assumption of a bogus role as preacher in order to make a lot of money for his real acquisitive self. . . . False exterior, real interior, that is a pattern which ratifies a dominant modern concept of the personality."[56] Knight puts pressure on reading either text through such individualist constructs, but I want to draw attention here to Chaucer's emphasis upon the allegorical and performative processes through which the Pardoner cuts himself off from the life of the spirit.

In a passage of *Le Roman de la Rose* that surely influenced Chaucer's depiction of the Pardoner, the character Reason describes the processes through which the false preacher, motivated by material gain, becomes locked into a pattern in which the more wealth he gains, the more he burns for more:

> When they preach in order to acquire honors, favors, or riches, they acquire, in addition, hearts torn by such anguish. They do not live lawfully. But, above all, those who pursue vainglory buy their souls' death. Such a deceiver is himself deceived, for you know that however much such a preacher profits others, he profits himself nothing; for good preaching that comes in fact from evil intention is worth nothing to the preacher, even though it may save others. (106/5198–12)

Reason's formulation links an insatiable desire for the material with both hearts torn by anguish (*cuers en teus destreces*) and, most importantly, the death of the soul (*la mort de lor ames*), a soul deprived of sanctifying grace and alienated from God. Whereas Reason describes a process through which a preacher's misplaced desires leads to his spiritual death, Chaucer's Pardoner shows us this process in action.

Strikingly, the Pardoner's own self-dramatization of his sins points not to a self defined by hidden depths—or the lack of them—but to a self defined in performance. The Pardoner's speech, in which he self-consciously relates his performance as a preacher, is itself a performance that both describes and reenacts his alienation from God. Those performances are central to the Pardoner's self-production where the performative process of substituting letter for spirit is a foundational act of self-(un)making. That act of substitution both happens in performance and is itself performative: his words are themselves an act of self-alienation. The process is shown brilliantly and compactly in the Pardoner's image of the dove, the traditional icon of the Holy Spirit. The image enacts the danger inherent in allegory that readers will take the letter for the spirit and read literally what should be taken allegorically. When the Pardoner compares himself to the "dowve sittynge on a berne," he both invokes and impedes proper use of the dove's iconic referent as Holy Spirit. In its traditional formulation, preaching is itself an act of substitution where the preacher's own voice is subsumed by that of the Spirit: "For it is not you that speak, but the Spirit of your Father that speaketh in you" (Matt. 10:20).[57] Or, as Augustine advises the orator: "When the hour in which he is to speak approaches, before he begins to preach, he should raise his thirsty soul to God in order that he may give forth what he shall drink, or pour out what shall fill him," a sentiment parodied by the Pardoner when he insists that, before beginning his tale, he needs to stop and "drynke" some corny ale while he thinks up "som honest thyng" on which to speak (6.328).[58] For Augustine, preaching is an act of self-abnegation that is finally an act of self-realization, where the self finds its true voice in its manifestation of and participation in the divine.

The processes through which the preacher is transformed by the Spirit, however, are blocked by the Pardoner's insistent literalism.[59] What is substituted is not flesh for spirit, but flesh for flesh, where the somatic flourishes of his homiletic performance ("I beke") are likened to ("as dooth") the adamantly material "dowve sittynge on a berne." The performative substitution of the material for the material *produces* a self alienated from God, for in his attachment to the material and his insistence on the letter, the Pardoner enacts the Pauline formulation "the letter killeth, but the spirit quickeneth."[60] The Pardoner's participation in the hollowing out of homiletic and penitential performance results in a corollary hollowing out of the self. Moreover, by publicly declaring his own depravity, the Pardoner jeopardizes the salvation of his hearers. Alastair Minnis has demonstrated that, according to standard Scholastic teaching, as long as they remain a secret, a preacher's private sins only harm himself; they only endanger his audience's spiritual welfare when they become publicly known and thus subject to scandal.[61] Or, to put it in J. L. Austin's terms, the perceived insincerity of the speaker interferes with the smooth and happy functioning of his performative utterances.[62] But in the case of the Pardoner, the problem is not simply that the audience will not take the good words of a bad man to heart. The real danger lies in that by openly declaring that he offers but empty stagecraft, pretty words, and easy absolutions as a point of pride, the Pardoner travesties—threatens to render empty and void—the spiritual practices and ritual performances central to the formation of Christian selves. In this way, Chaucer's Pardoner suggests a premodern complexity of self that is first constructed through communal performances, and then, only secondarily, deprived (privated) from that community. When Pearsall denies the Pardoner an inner consciousness, saying the Pardoner appears to exist "only in the act of performance," his suggestion that the Pardoner's interiority is not at issue begins to address such premodern complexity. However, his implication that the Pardoner's performance is simply empty falls short of a full engagement with what that performance actually does to constitute a self, to construct a self defined by the pursuit of the material, alienated from God, and in that sense only understandable as hollow or empty.

As has often been observed, Chaucer makes the processes through which "the letter kills" still more concrete in the hilarious parodies of spiritual metaphors that pepper the *Pardoner's Tale* itself. The three revelers unwittingly give the Trinity material form when they swear on "Goddes digne bones" that "we thre been al ones" and would seemingly seek to usurp Christ's redemptive role in vowing "we wol sleen this false traytour Deeth" (6.695–96; 699). Their insistent literalism will finally result in their literal deaths when "the love of money," which is the "root of all evil," appears as a fatal pot of gold at the base of a tree. The bread and poisoned wine that cause their demise parody the Eucharist, where the ultimate signifier of Christ's life-giving grace, when made literal, proves deadly. Yet, even here, in the apparent triumph of the literal, allegory—the spiritual implication of their deaths—prevails: as Pearsall emphasizes, "The death that the rioters find is no more than the physical correlative, an allegorical enactment, of the death that they (and the Pardoner) have already undergone."[63] If the *Pardoner's Tale* finally serves to confirm the presence of the spirit in the letter, the inescapability of the spirit is similarly reconfirmed in the interactions that follow between the Pardoner and his fellow pilgrims.

Critics continually wonder why, after confessing he is a fraud, the Pardoner attempts to sell his false pardons and relics to the Host (Harry Bailey) and the other pilgrims. It is a mistake, however, to look for a psychological motive. Rather, his attempt is the necessary conclusion to his performance: the Pardoner only becomes a pardoner in the *act* of selling his false pardons and relics, an act that serves to make him a pardoner even as it alienates him from both God and the other pilgrims, as the violence of the ensuing exchange—culminating in the Host's threat to cut off the Pardoner's "coillons" (balls) and enshrine them in a hog's turd—suggests (952–55). Yet if, in the Pardoner, Chaucer demonstrates the spiritually disastrous consequences of such hollowing out of the sacred, he simultaneously shows the tenacity of such rituals to carry meaning. For, significantly, if the Pardoner's invitation to the Host to come and kiss his false relics has been met with violence, the *Pardoner's Tale* ends with another reconciliation ritual, the ritual of "kissing and making up," an interaction itself modeled on the liturgical ritual of kissing the Pax board during Mass as a sign of the restoration of peace among congregants. By asking the Host to kiss the Pardoner, the Knight puts a stop to their altercation and brings the Pardoner, if silenced, back into the community of pilgrims. In the end, the ineluctable power of ritual performances both to signify the spirit and to reconstruct the self through fellowship is confirmed.

In his proclivity for self-dramatization, Chaucer's Pardoner resembles another figure from medieval literature, Margery Kempe, who in her *Book* (1435–40) likewise presents a self defined by penitential performance. For Kempe, penance is a continuous interactive performance that happens in the everyday world. Early in her narrative, Kempe recounts her response to a group of Canterbury monks and laymen who have been ridiculing her for her loud outbursts of pious weeping. She tells her detractors the story of a man who had "synned gretly a-ȝens God" whose confessor commands him to hire men to chide and reprove him for his sins, instructing him to give them silver for their labor.[64] When some time later the man finds himself in the midst of a group of "many gret men" who deride him, he responds with obvious delight. One of the man's detractors asks why he laughs when he is so roundly despised, and he replies, "A, ser, I haue a gret cause to lawh, for I haue many days put syluer owt of my purse & hyred men to chyde me for remyssyon of my synne, & þis day I may kepe my syluer in my purs, I thank ȝow alle." With her characteristic pluck, Kempe explains that while she was at home in Norfolk, "day be day wyth gret wepyng & mornyng, I sorwyd for I had no schame, skorne, & despyte as I was worthy," and duly thanks them all for "what forenoon & aftyr-noon I have had resonably þis day" (28/13–27). Through her story, Kempe's detractors become unwitting actors in a devotional theater in which penance suffuses all she says and does. Her story attempts to incorporate even the most hostile of her oppressors into a spiritual economy where her suffering at their hands becomes yet another token of her sanctity. By demanding that they view their own behavior through her penitential framework, she envelops all those who surround her into a mode of reform that is realized in performance and happens from the outside in.

Kempe's *Book* stands as a reminder of the public, theatrical, and material nature of the late medieval period's devotional practices. Such practices not only provide a counterstory to the ways in which scholars often incorporate medieval religion into a progressive narrative that privileges private introspection and independent initiative on the part of the laity, but her *Book* also serves to remind us of the institutionally situated nature of those practices.[65] Notably, even as Kempe challenges the religious and secular authority represented by the "gret men" of Canterbury, that challenge relies upon the ecclesiastically regulated penitential imperatives overseen by her confessor. In these ways, Kempe's narrative can be aligned with the explicit theater of *The Castle of Perseverance*, another East Anglian cultural production that imagines a world suffused by penance and concerns the role of institutionally mediated performances in the production of Christian selves. Written in Norfolk dialect and thought to have been performed during the same period her book describes, the *Castle* likewise imagines the life and world of its central character in penitential terms.[66] However, whereas Kempe's *Book* seeks to *describe* a life defined by nearly incessant acts of penitential satisfaction, the *Castle*, as I argue in chapter 1, exploits its theatrical resources to incorporate its audience into an all-encompassing penitential performance that is constitutive of a Christian self. Through a playing space that is simultaneously a *mappa mundi*, church, and penitential trajectory, the *Castle* describes the power of institutions to construct the landscape in which Humankind discovers himself.

WORDS MADE FLESH

Unlike the Pardoner, the morality plays, with their "flat" characters and reliance on personification, are not regularly pointed to as complex expressions of medieval interiority.[67] However, together the morality plays suggest that something is at stake in the shaping of the self that is quite different than psychological complexity as we are used to thinking about it. In the moralities, it is impossible to split an interior self from the exterior practices and institutions that define it. Other medieval allegories that engage questions of selfhood—such as *Piers Plowman* (where individual, communal, and institutional reform prove inseparable) or the figurative "castles of the mind" (where building metaphors are used to describe the human psyche) recently described by Christiania Whitehead—similarly suggest an inwardness inextricable from outward forms. In the moralities, by contrast, that interdependence is conveyed through the plays' performative mode. By dramatizing their protagonists' fall and recovery through penance, the plays suggest how the experience of penitential ritual shapes penitents' understandings of the social and moral concepts central to the formation of Christian subjects.

Dramatic personification allegory is central to this process. The meanings of words such as "mankind" or "mercy" do not derive from a static, objective abstraction that the play then personifies, where meaning is correlated with a word in a simple way. The fact of theater, the presence and interactions of actors, is central to the way the meanings of words are constituted. As Richard Emmerson has convincingly argued, the characters of the morality play act as "complex signs whose significance develops as they act out their meaning in relation to other signs and throughout the course of the play's action."[68] In *Mankind*, for instance, the title character's self-understanding fluctuates as different personified characters appear on stage and activate different aspects of his identity. Whereas the play's vices seek to define Mankind according to the mutability of his will, the character Mercy counters by seeking to redefine Mankind according to his ability to resist temptation. The play shows how the meanings of terms such as "mankind" or "mercy" develop through the interactions of characters onstage and through penitential ritual. In Wittgensteinian terms, the plays provide within their actions and to their audiences a kind of *training*; they do not didactically pronounce received church doctrine but instead demonstrate how penitential ritual shapes one's understanding of the meanings of words central to one's understanding of God and self.

Allegory is traditionally defined as a mode of reading or writing in which one thing is said and another is meant, where the operative distinction is between a word and its meaning.[69] Citing Galatians 4:24, Augustine defines allegory as "a trope wherein one thing is understood from another."[70] Rabanus Maurus (ca. 780–856) defines it as "a technique of grammar" that "alleges one thing in words, and signifies another thing in meaning."[71] Both Isidore of Seville (560–636) and Hugh of Saint Victor (1096–1141) describe allegory as a kind of "other-speaking" (*alieniloquium*) in which, in Hugh's words, "one thing is said and another thing is signified."[72] In personification allegory, the allegorical content of a narrative is made explicit: the characters bear the names of the things they represent.[73] Jon Whitman observes that whereas other forms of fictional writing conceal their implied meanings, allegory is "outspokenly reticent, proclaiming that it has a secret."[74] Personification can be seen as an intensification of such outspokenness. Rosemond Tuve calls personification "a most natural form" of allegory.[75] Personification allegory, in naming its characters the concepts they represent, might seem to close the gap between what is "said" and what is "signified"; however, allegorical divergence still occurs between the human *character* on the one hand and the *word* he or she represents on the other.[76] The word "wisdom itself," Whitman points out, "has no shape, no clothing, and no activity."[77] Rather than closing the gap between signifier and signified, in giving a word such as "wisdom" or "mankind" a body and a voice, personification allegory instead returns us to the lived experiences and particular circumstances that give those words their meanings.[78] As I describe in chapter 3, the play *Mankind*, in imagining those circumstances as a linguistic battle between Mercy's "predycacyon" (47) and the vices' "derysyon" and "japyng" (349), foregrounds the multivocal and contested nature of that process.

Ever since the Romantics, allegory has often been seen as a threatening and even inherently violent literary mode. Goethe describes allegory using images of confinement and constriction: in allegory "the concept always remains bounded in the image, and is entirely to be kept and held in it, and to be expressed by it."[79] Even as it enjoyed a rehabilitation at the hands of poststructuralist theorists, it retains the same coercive associations. For Paul de Man, allegory remains "a language that submits the outside world entirely to its own purposes."[80] In de Man's metaphors, personification, or *prosopopoeia*, literally "to confer a mask or face," is still more menacing, carrying the threat of bodily mutilation. "Our topic deals with the giving and taking of faces," de Man writes, "with face and deface, *figure*, figuration and disfiguration."[81] Because of its potential reversibility, personification participates in the danger inherent in reification: When I have rhetorically made a human being into an object, I can conceptually treat it as one.[82] Imagined as a trope by which a human being becomes a mere container for a pregiven abstraction, personification allegory becomes a grizzly thing indeed.

Lawrence Clopper points out that medieval writers, unlike the Romantics, do not define allegory in terms of an opposition between the abstract and the concrete.[83] According to medieval definitions, performance does not undermine personification; instead, it is its essential gesture. Isidore of Seville defines personification as a rhetorical device in which "personality and speech are invented for inanimate things."[84] Through the embodied signs of theater, dramatic personification embeds words in human activity and exchange. Tellingly, in contrast to the images of containment that characterize post-Romantic models, the English rhetorician Geoffrey of Vinsauf (fl. 1200) describes personification in much more positive terms. For Geoffrey, personification is a trope defined by empowerment and emancipation: it is an aid to the poet that gives "power of speech to that which has in itself no such power," granting "poetic license [to] confer a tongue."[85]

Wittgenstein provides a more promising model than those of the Romantics or poststructuralists for understanding personification in the medieval morality play. Both Wittgenstein and dramatic personification foreground the embodied, social nature of language. Wittgenstein's remarks about the way signs take on meaning in the *Philosophical Investigations* (§432) provide a striking contrast to both Goethe and de Man's formulations: "Every sign *by itself* seems dead. *What* gives it life?—In use it is *alive*. Is life breathed into it there?—Or is the *use* its life?"[86] For Wittgenstein, the way a sign takes on meaning only becomes a problem if we isolate the sign and look at it from the outside. The sign appears dead only when it is considered "by itself," away from our life with signs, the whole of the circumstances that give the sign meaning. Wittgenstein suggests that what gives a sign its "life" is the way that signs figure in the lives of living beings.

Wittgenstein's description in section 432 of how a linguistic sign takes on meaning looks something like medieval definitions of personification wherein "life" is similarly "breathed" into an "inanimate" word. His observations allow us to see that personification so defined, like linguistic signs more broadly, does not necessarily presuppose a gap or gulf between a concrete signifier and an abstract signified. In section 432, Wittgenstein's immediate concern is to address his Platonist interlocutor, who has just insisted that "there is a gulf between an order and its execution. It has to be filled by the act of understanding." The order itself "is nothing but sounds, ink-marks," the Platonist observes. "Only in the act of understanding is it meant that we are to do THIS."[87] Wittgenstein asks: What bridges the gulf between the order "Raise your arm!" and its execution? How do you know when I say those words that you should make that particular movement? No amount of explaining, pointing, or modeling bridges the gulf between my words and your understanding of them. (If I try to explain my command by raising my own arm and gesturing that you should to do the same, you still need to understand the meaning of my gestures.) Rather than trying in vain to bridge that gulf, Wittgenstein instead resists the idea that "the ultimate thing sought by the order" remains "unexpressed."[88] In other words, he tries to free us of the burden of having to provide such an account: "If it is asked: 'How do sentences manage to represent?'—the answer might be: 'Don't you know? You certainly see it, when you use them.' For nothing is concealed."[89] If we want to understand how signs take on meaning, Wittgenstein suggests, we must start by stopping thinking about the meaning of our words in isolation, outside of our everyday use of them and independently of how they function in our lives and our activities. Personification allegory likewise does not necessitate a gulf or gap between a word and its meaning; instead, in the morality play, as in language more broadly, the meanings of the personified words are unfolded and revealed through human activity and interaction, particularly those interactions structured by penitential ritual. They are dialectical and processual rather than fixed and "containing."

PERFORMANCE AND THE SELF

This study turns, in its investigation of the performative construction of self in the morality plays, to Wittgenstein because his later philosophy helps dispel post-Cartesian pictures of self and the nature of language that impede our understanding of medieval notions of selfhood. Perhaps more than any other, Wittgenstein is the modern philosopher who has shown that any notion we might have of an "interior" is bound up with our exterior activities, and specifically our interactions with others. A central project of the *Investigations* is to challenge a post-Cartesian mentalist picture of the self and a corresponding picture of language that imagines a gulf between a word and its meaning. Wittgenstein's insight that our understanding of the meanings of the words we use—including language that is central to our concepts of the self—is bound up with our interactions with others provides a helpful framework for understanding the representation of selfhood in the morality play.[90] Through its use of dramatic personification, the morality play exploits its theatrical medium to foreground, as Wittgenstein does, the embodied, public nature of meaning.

Wittgenstein begins his *Investigations* by quoting a passage from Augustine's *Confessions* that (for Wittgenstein) represents a picture of human language—and a proto-Cartesian picture of the self—he will go on to challenge.[91] In the passage, Augustine imagines learning a language as a process of attaching labels to things: an adult shows an infant different objects and names them. Gradually, according to Augustine, the infant learns to associate the names with the objects and, eventually, to express his own desires.[92] Wittgenstein objects that such a picture presents a much too restrictive understanding of human language—one that is at best only applicable to nouns, people's names, and perhaps a limited range of actions and properties. More importantly, he argues, it gives rise to a misleading picture of the essence of human language as a process in which words are aligned with meanings. According to this picture, Wittgenstein explains that "every word has a meaning" and "this meaning is correlated with the word" that is "the object for which the word stands."[93] Wittgenstein contends that such a picture obscures the different aims and functions of words and thus leads to a mistaken understanding of how language works. If I yell "Stop!" for example—whether to prevent you from lurching recklessly into traffic or in an attempt to get you to desist from telling more bad jokes—to what physical or mental object does the word "stop" refer? Wittgenstein further observes that Augustine's picture of how an infant learns language rests on a problematic picture of the self. In the passage, Wittgenstein stresses, Augustine assumes his infant self was already fully aware of both itself and the world *prior* to learning a language: "Augustine describes the learning of human language as if the child came into a strange country and did not understand the language of the country; that is, as if it already had a language, only not this one. Or again: as if the child could already *think*, only not yet speak. And 'think' would here mean something like 'talk to itself.'"[94] Wittgenstein makes the paradox of such a picture obvious. According to Augustine's model, in order to learn to talk, an infant must already know how to do so. Wittgenstein points out that in Augustine's account, to be an infant is (strangely) to be like a stranger in a foreign country. As James Wetzel remarks, Augustine describes a picture of language learning in which "the infant child, infancy itself, seems to belong to no one."[95] For Wetzel, Wittgenstein's critique of Augustine lies in his sense of the impoverished nature of such a picture: "The sober truth may be that I cannot have the experience of others, not even the ones I love intimately and raise from infancy, but the more supple realization is that a parented life is never unambiguously bounded. We tend to spill into our parents as they spill into us, all the way back to Adam and his father."[96] To dispel such a picture, Wittgenstein will return repeatedly to the idea that the meaning of a word is not in the solitude of the human mind but in its *use*, in our shared life with others.[97]

Wittgenstein suggests that teaching a language is instead better described as a kind of training. By way of illustrating that Augustine's picture of language in fact only describes a small part of how language functions, Wittgenstein imagines a primitive language for which, he says, "the description given by Augustine is right." Notably, that primitive language includes the activities into which such a language would be woven:

The language is meant to serve for communication between a builder A and an assistant B. A is building with building-stones:

there are blocks, pillars, slabs and beams. B has to pass the stones, and that in the order in which A needs them. For this purpose they use a language consisting of the words "block," "pillar," "slab," "beam." A calls them out;—B brings the stone which he has learnt to bring at such-and-such a call.—Conceive this as a complete primitive language.[98]

However, even in learning a language as limited as this one, he goes on to argue, "ostensive teaching"—the pointing Augustine described—is of limited use. One only shows one knows what a word like "Slab!" means, Wittgenstein contends, through one's actions:

Don't you understand the call "Slab!" if you act upon it in such-and-such a way?—Doubtless the ostensive teaching helped to bring this about; but only together with a particular training. With different training the same ostensive teaching of these words would have effected a quite different understanding.[99]

When we teach a child to speak, we provide not explanations about what a word means but training in how to use them.[100] Wittgenstein observes that if the child was taught to act differently when he heard the word "Slab!" he would understand the word differently. Wittgenstein concludes part I of his *Investigations* by declaring, "And nothing is more wrong-headed than calling meaning a mental activity!"[101] Instead, our understanding of the meaning of a word emerges out of conversation and human exchange.

For Wittgenstein, even our understanding of the meaning of the words we use to describe our most inner, presumably "private" experiences comes out of such exchanges. When we describe a concept such as "remembering," Wittgenstein holds, a picture of an "inner process" does not give us the correct idea of our use of that word.[102] Most famously, he argues that our understanding of what "pain" is does not arise out of psychological introspection, by identifying an object inside ourselves. Rather, Wittgenstein holds, an infant cries out and others teach it to call that pain:

How do words *refer* to sensations?—There doesn't seem to be any problem here; don't we talk about sensations every day, and give them names? But how is the connexion between the name and the thing named set up? This question is the same as: how does a human being learn the meaning of the names of sensations?—of the word "pain" for example. Here is one possibility: words are connected with the primitive, the natural, expressions of the sensation and used in their place. A child has hurt himself and he cries; and then adults talk to him and teach him exclamations and, later, sentences. They teach the child new pain-behavior.[103]

This view of how we connect the word "pain" to "the pain itself" is in some ways obvious, as simple and as everyday as an adult consoling a crying child. Such explanations, however, do not satisfy Wittgenstein's imagined interlocutor, who asks: "So you are saying that the word 'pain' really means crying?"[104] The interlocutor's worry here seems to be that Wittgenstein subscribes to a form of behaviorism. Is he suggesting that our inner experiences are in fact merely descriptions of outward behaviors, that everything but human behavior is a fiction?[105] "On the contrary," Wittgenstein says, "the verbal expression of pain *replaces* crying and does not describe it" (emphasis mine).[106] Wittgenstein does not deny the existence of sensations. Instead, he suggests that one learns the name of a sensation such as "pain" not through introspective reference to the "pain itself" but through a process in which one *expression* of that pain replaces another. This insight helpfully illuminates how language is allegorical: allegory can be said to likewise be governed by a structure in which one expression or narrative *replaces* or *stands in* for another rather than describing or representing it.

The picture of language in which "every word has a meaning" gives rise to the idea that there is a gap between a word and its meaning, a sign and its referent, that must somehow be bridged, perhaps by still more language or an "interpretation." Wittgenstein follows his assertion that the word "pain" does not mean crying, but he replaces it by asking: "For how can I go so far as to try to use language to get *between* pain and its expression?" (emphasis mine).[107] The grammar of Wittgenstein's question suggests the problematic nature of such an endeavor. Stanley Cavell reads the question as "an attempt on Wittgenstein's part to express a frame of mind in which one feels that in order to insure the connection between a sensation and its name one has to get to the sensation apart from its expression, get past the merely outward expression, which blocks our vision as it were."[108] Rather than seeking to bridge the gap between a sign and its referent—the expression for pain and the pain itself—however, Wittgenstein seeks to free us from such a picture of language by returning our words to the circumstances that give them meaning.[109]

The behaviorist anxiety—that what we refer to as our inner life might not exist at all, or perhaps exist only in a deeply inferior state—is one very familiar to medievalists still chafing under Jacob Burckhardt's characterization of the Middle Ages as a period in which "human consciousness . . . lay dreaming or half awake beneath a common veil." In Burckhardt's Middle Ages, certain habits of mind—"faith, illusion, and childish prepossession"—obscured recognition of one's particularity: "Man was conscious of himself only as a member of a race, people, party, family, or corporation—only through some general category."[110] Here, seemingly, overidentification with abstract categories of self-definition compromises both one's sense of oneself as an individual and consciousness itself. Indeed, the medieval morality play, with its Mankinds and Everymans, would seem the perfect illustration of Burckhardt's view. However, such a "behaviorist" picture of the Middle Ages, where human "consciousness" is profoundly compromised if not completely absent, is predicated on a glaringly Cartesian picture of the self. Mankind's and Everyman's communal identities can only be imagined to efface their individual ones if mind and body, self and world are first understood to be in opposition. Rather than obscuring the particularity of the individuals that make up the more general category "mankind," the use of personification in the morality play—by making words human beings and human beings words—embeds words in human activity and exchange.

A person's understanding of his or her particularity, in the sense of an understanding of oneself as an individual distinct from others, would seem to have little if anything to do with the quality of one's inner life. Herbert McCabe argues that, for Wittgenstein and also Aquinas, what makes people—or animals for that matter—distinct individuals is not anything that can be said or understood about them but "simply that we pick them out separately":

"This is one and that is the other" is not to describe either of them, not to attribute to either of them any meaningful feature, not to predicate anything of them. "One" and "other" do not function that way: they are words that accompany some kind of bodily behaviour, they belong to the job of pointing out.[111]

In this view, our particularity is not something essential about us but something discovered or recognized through our activities in the world, such as "picking things out" or "pointing." If, as Aquinas argues, our individuality is a matter of our particular determinate dimensions, we best recognize the individuality of others through the activities that acknowledge their dimensional particularity.[112] The "individualist subject" only becomes necessary when the body is rejected as part of the self.

We are in the habit of thinking of our words, our bodies as sites of obfuscation. Words conceal meanings. The body veils the mind. Theater is similarly understood. If I accuse you of being "always the actress," I mean that I do not trust the sincerity of your words, that I believe you to be hiding your true thoughts and feelings.[113] By contrast, for Wittgenstein—and, I argue, in the morality plays—the human body is understood as the vehicle of meaning. "The human body," Wittgenstein declares, "is the best picture of the human soul."[114] For Wittgenstein, the things we habitually think of as "exterior"—our words, our bodies—do not hide our minds or our souls but reveal them. If we are in the habit of thinking the opposite, as Cavell has remarked, it is only because the body is the very condition of their revelation: "The mythology according to which the body is a picture implies that the soul may be hidden not because the body essentially conceals it but because it essentially *reveals* it" (emphasis mine).[115] In medieval depictions of death, the soul is often depicted as a small human body, departing the dead body of the deceased. Though one might conclude that medieval artists imagined the soul as a miniature version of the self, a homunculus (literally, "little person"), residing within, the fourteenth-century contemplative Walter Hilton explicitly warns his readers against seeing the soul as a physical object: "Thou schalt not torne thi thought to thi bodi for to seken and feelen it, as it were hid withinne in thi fleschli herte as thyn herte is hid and hoolden withinne thi bodi."[116] The soul, according to Hilton's Augustinian formulation, is not hidden within the body but a "lyf invisible" that animates it. Yet if the soul is a life invisible, medieval representations of death suggest that the human body nonetheless remains its best picture.

Scholars have long remarked the affinities between Wittgenstein's later philosophy and Aquinas's "non-subject-centred conception of the self" and his view that knowledge is a collaborative process between objects in the world and the mind that perceives them.[117] However, it is Augustine, despite any role he might play in the *Investigations* as Wittgenstein's proto-Cartesian strawman, rather than Aquinas to whom I wish to point as the premodern theologian who paves the way for the morality play's performative version of the self.[118] Augustine articulates a self whose embodied presence is the necessary instrument of the full realization of that self through acts of devotion. Michael Hanby persuasively argues that the Augustinian self is best understood as *doxological*, constituted by acts of worship. Throughout his work, Augustine recuperates the pedagogical capacity of temporal experience where knowledge of God (and therefore of the self) is the product of a material existence.[119] When properly viewed, the created world returns us to the creator: "Indeed, if you regard them carefully and piously, every kind of creature and every movement that can be considered by the human mind speaks to us for our instruction. Their diverse movements and dispositions are like so many voices crying out to us, telling us to recognize their Creator."[120] For Augustine, human action is only intelligible as an expression of love for and delight in God. In contrast to Descartes, Hanby emphasizes, the will in Augustine is not autonomous; instead, "the Augustinian self is only completed doxologically, by participation in the love and beauty of the Trinity through the mediation of Christ and his Body."[121] We become more human, more ourselves, as we approach the beauty of Christ. Hanby points to Augustine's Ninth Homily on the First Epistle of John as encapsulating the aesthetic soteriology at the core of the Augustinian self, where divine beauty both draws us in and transforms us into its image:

"Let us love, because he first loved us." . . . He first loved us, Who is always beautiful; and what were we when He loved us, but foul and ugly? But not to leave us foul; but to change us, and from deformity make us beautiful. How shall we become beautiful? By loving Him who is always beautiful.[122]

It will only be through such "delight in Christ, a gift of the mutual delight between the Father and the Son," Hanby contends, that for Augustine "'I' can finally be myself."[123] Hanby shows us an Augustinian self that, as it is constituted through the acknowledgment of divine gift, is the product of a material existence unfolded in time and realized through performative acts of worship.

Augustine's emphasis on the pedagogical potential of temporal experiences is also articulated in the more general assumption of medieval sacramental theology that humans can only apprehend invisible realities through our experiences with visible ones. Hugh of Saint Victor specifically identifies instruction as one of the three reasons the sacraments were instituted:

> For man who knew visible things and did not know the invisible could by no means have recognized divine things unless stimulated by the human. And on this account while the invisible good which he lost is returned to him the signification of the same is furnished him without through visible species, that he might be stimulated without and restored within; so in that which he handles and sees he may recognize of what nature that is which he received and does not see.[124]

According to Hugh, the visible is the means by which we apprehend the invisible, divine realities, where the pedagogical capacity of the sacraments lies in the tension between the visible elements of the sacrament and that which is believed "invisibly" and received. For Hugh as for Augustine, knowledge of God is best understood as an act of recognition, "so in that which he handles and sees he may recognize of what nature that is which he received and does not see."

The medieval morality play likewise implies a self that is only fully realized through its participation in the rituals and other devotional performances, which, in demanding one recognize oneself as sinner and creature, places that self in right relation to God. More recently, McCabe has pointed to the transformative power of such acts of recognition. In seeking to show the inadequacy of Protestant notions of the consecrated elements as standing only in symbolic relation to Christ's body, McCabe asks: "Who is closer to Christ, Peter touching him in Galilee before his crucifixion or ourselves celebrating the Eucharist?"[125] McCabe's question suggests that proximity to Christ is not measured in inches and feet (in which case Christ's presence in the Eucharist could indeed only be symbolic) but is instead achieved through the ritual activities that, in glorifying Christ, put worshippers in relation to him. For Augustine, it is through such acts of worship that both Christ and self are made most fully present. Similarly, in the morality play, the self is constituted through the performative acts—and in particular through penance as the ritual that reforms the soul to God's image—through which one recognizes oneself as a created being.

The morality plays display a similar confidence in the pedagogical potential of temporal experience and emphasis on the constitutive role of ritual in Christian selfhood. If there appears to be little exploration in the morality play of the interior life or mental processes of its characters, it may be simply because such an exploration is beside the point to the plays' investigation of language, meaning, and self. In the morality play, the self is not discovered through confessional self-revelation. Instead, the plays illustrate how penance provides penitents with a particular kind of training that shapes their understanding of the meanings of moral and ethical words central to a conception of a Christian self. The chapters that follow elaborate this dynamic, showing how the morality plays of the fifteenth and sixteenth centuries engage contemporary religious debates about the sacraments and the ceremonial life of the church.

The first three chapters show how the version of the self presented in the three Macro plays emerges out of the plays' engagement with contemporary religious debates. In chapter 1, I read *The Castle of Perseverance* as a response to early fifteenth-century debates about ecclesiology and the role of the sacraments in the forgiveness of sin. I argue that, through a plot and set design that allegorically merges physical space and moral action, the *Castle* aligns itself with contemporary calls for reform while underscoring the importance of the institutional church and its rituals in the soul's reformation and the shaping of Christian selves. Chapter 2, on *Wisdom*, elucidates the morality plays' conceptualization of the "interior" by showing how the play reimagines contemplative instructional models in order to demonstrate how the performance of penitential ritual activates the soul's self-knowledge. Looking to Augustinian models of the soul, *Wisdom* dramatizes the inward transformations that occur through outward ritual actions, showing how penance educates the soul experientially to understand its own meaning and identity. Chapter 3 shows how *Mankind* enters into contemporary pastoral debates about clerical authority, the quality and purposes of preaching, and the most effective means of educating the laity on the principles of Christian faith. I contend that *Mankind* seeks to demonstrate the limitations of didactic pedagogical models by proposing an alternative sacramental pedagogy that demonstrates, rather than declares, Mankind's need of God's mercy.

The final two chapters consider the morality play in the context of the radical religious and cultural changes that accompanied the English Reformation. Chapter 4, on *Everyman*, reads the play in relation to medieval penitential practices surrounding death as a means of illuminating the play's representation of the relationship between an individual and his or her community. I argue that, in contrast to the prevailing critical narrative that sees a progression toward more individualized and interiorized forms of devotion in the years leading up to the English Reformation, *Everyman* describes a spiritual selfhood that emerges through neither confessional self-scrutiny nor the cultivation of an inward piety, but through the communal practices and performances established by penitential ritual.

In the course of the English Reformation, Protestants turned to the morality play as a means of vilifying the rituals that had defined the Catholic Church. Whereas the medieval moralities, by showing penance in performance, show the performative nature of sacramental ritual, Protestant polemicists used the dramatic form to show that such Roman rites were nothing but empty, insidious theater. In chapter 5, I suggest that, as their medieval predecessors did, the morality plays of the sixteenth century manifest the performative nature of language and self. I focus in particular on two morality plays that both adapt the medieval trajectory of fall and repentance and explicitly reject Roman ritual: John Bale's *King Johan* and Lewis Wager's Calvinist morality *The Life and Repentance of Mary Magdalene*. My reading of *King Johan* describes how Bale continues the medieval morality play's investment in the role of performance in the creation of linguistic meaning. In a world where vice disguises itself as virtue, moral selfhood depends on the ability of dramatic performances to cultivate acts of perspicuous spectatorship revelatory of God's Veritas. My reading of *Mary Magdalene* shows how Wager, through the figure of Mary, presents a Protestant exemplar of reformed worshipful performance that intersects with Calvin's own theatrical metaphors in surprising ways. Portraying Mary as a Calvinist "true spectator" of Christ, Wager follows Calvin in embracing theater's potential to forge a new relation between drama and Protestant forms of selfhood. Defining performance primarily as an act of witnessing, theater becomes for Wager a mirror of self-contemplation able to create virtuous spectators.

My conclusion briefly weighs the implications of the arguments I have developed here about the performative nature of the self for our reading of a much more recent incarnation of the morality play: Pixar's 2015 computer-animated film *Inside Out*.

By turning away from Cartesian conceptions of the self, this study reads the morality plays not as literary artifacts—the uncomplicated moralistic allegories of a bygone era—but instead shows the plays to have existed as communal performances interwoven into the social fabric of medieval life. Such an approach allows us to see both the capaciousness with which the plays articulate what it means to be human and the sophistication with which they engage in contemporary religious debates about the sacraments, pastoral care, the education of the laity, and the role of the church in salvation. Moreover, by presenting penance as a cultural practice that transforms a soul's self-knowledge, the plays offer theater historians a premodern consideration of both the performative aspects of ritual and the transformative capacity of performance.

Finally, as a dramatic form that persists into the sixteenth century, the morality play proves to be a particularly provocative lens for understanding of the continuities and ruptures between the medieval and early modern. Whereas the dominant critical narrative characterizes the early modern as a period defined by its distrust of outer appearances and the value it places in "that within which passes show," I argue that medieval understandings about the performative dimensions of language and the self—understandings that were deeply informed by the Catholic ceremonial culture of which reformers were so suspicious—endured in even the most iconoclastic moral dramas of the sixteenth century.[126]

CHAPTER ONE

The Castle of Perseverance and Penitential Platea

Non est ecclesia ubi non est confessio vera.
(Where there is no true confession, there is no church.)
— Thomas Netter, *Doctrinale* (1426–30)

Worldis good nes not holichirche,
Richesse and worschep Y ȝow forbede,
Þe folk is cherche, in hem ȝe worche,
Here noo oþer to don þy dede.
— Poem 8 of Bodleian MS Digby 102
(ca. 1413–14)

The Castle of Perseverance is the earliest surviving play in English to make "mankind" its primary object of investigation.[1] Written during the first quarter of the fifteenth century, the play was composed at a time when both orthodox and heterodox calls for reform had moved the material dimensions of the practices of the English church to the center of contemporary religious controversies.[2] By allegorically merging place and action—where the "castle of perseverance" represents both a physical location *and* human activity—the play foregrounds the material as the condition of human knowledge of the spiritual, and physical space as the setting of moral action. In the *Castle,* the investigation of the role of penance in the shaping of Christian selves takes the form of a critique of the ritualized differentiation of physical space. Creating a theatrical world that superimposes geographic, ecclesiastical, and moral space, the play advances a version of "holichirche" that is inseparable from the performance of forgiveness and the penitential activity of its "folk."

The *Castle* was written and performed in the midst of debates that included the legitimacy of the established church and that extended to the physical edifices that were its most visible manifestation. For instance, in the course of his discussion of the nature of the church, the author of the polemical lollard treatise *The Lanterne of Li3t* (ca. 1409–15) seeks to correct what he views as a particularly foolhardy notion about sacred space. The true church on earth, the writer contends, consists of the body of the elect, the congregation of the faithful souls "þat lastingli kepen feiþ & trouþe in word & in dede" (25/3–4). Human beings guarantee the sanctity of a place, not the other way around:

> Man bi vertu of Goddis word halowiþ þis place but þis place mai not halowe man. . . . Alas what woodnes [insanity] is þis to boost [boast] of hooli placis & we oure silf to be suche viciouse foolis! Lucifer was in heuene & þat is moost hooli place but for his synne he fel to helle: þe place my3t not holde him. Adam was in paradise, þe moost miriest place, & for his synne he was dryuen out: þe place mi3t not defende him. þou þat art neiþir in heuene ne in paradise, but in þis wrecchid world where wenest þou to fynde a place to halowe þee þat leuest not þi synne? (36/17–37/1)[3]

Heaven could not hold Lucifer; paradise could not hold Adam. It is therefore foolish to think that the physical spaces of holy places themselves bestow any special sanctity. For the author of the *Lanterne*, a misguided sense of the spiritual benefits conferred by material objects leads to an unsound understanding of the nature of the church and its authority. The physical spaces of holy places themselves bestow no special sanctity, as the examples of Lucifer and Adam attest. To think otherwise is absurd. Likewise, in his *Treatise on Civil Dominion* (1375–76), Wyclif uses an architectural metaphor that similarly seeks to revise common understandings of sacred space, a strategy that would be picked up by his followers.[4] The church, Wyclif asserts, is built from the three theological virtues: "The house of the spiritual church has for its foundation faith in Christ, its walls are a life of hope, and its roof is *caritas*."[5] The church is "invisible" insofar as it is impossible to know who is among the predestined; however, that church is nonetheless also made visible through the virtues of its members. Notably, these authors show exceptional faith in visibility when the domain in question is the human, even as they vilify the church for sacralizing its visible institutional spaces.

The *Lanterne* author's skepticism of the spiritual benefits conferred by holy places reflects a much broader concern among reformers about the corruptibility of the visible and material dimensions of contemporary spiritual practices and in particular the idolatrous worship of sacramental and other sacred signs. The most prominent example of this critique is the Wycliffite rejection of the doctrine of transubstantiation and condemnation of the "cult of the Eucharist" and what they saw as its idolatrous attention to the elements of bread and wine.[6] For the author of the polemical *Twelve Conclusions of the Lollards* (1395), the misguided understanding of the role of the clergy in the forgiveness of sin was of a piece with the commodification of penitential practices: "Þei seyn þat [þ]e[i] han þe keys of heuene and of helle, þei mown cursyn and blissin, byndin and unbyndin at here [their] owne wil, in so miche þat for a busschel of qwete [wheat] or xii. be ȝere [þ]e[i] welen selle þe blisse of heuene be chartre of clause of warantise [warranty], enselid [sealed] with þe comown sel."[7] Such distrust of the visible and material dimensions of popular devotion extended to theater: the *Tretis of Miraclis Pleying* lambastes popular drama for turning Christ's life and works into an amusing spectacle that provides viewers with "miraclis of oure fleyss [flesh], of oure lustis, and of oure five wittis [senses]" inimical to a penitential mortification of the flesh driven by interior contrition.[8]

Skepticism about the sanctifying power of physical space was not limited to lollard polemic. The twenty-third of the twenty-four "Digby poems" (ca. 1413–14), the series of short lyric poems included in Bodleian MS Digby 102, emphasizes that Holy Church is not constituted by its physical edifices but by the virtues of its members. The material manifestation of the church is not a building but human bodies:

I wole be mendid ȝif Y say mys:
Holychirche nes noþer tre ne stones;

Þe hous of preyers God nempned [named] þys—
Boþe goode men and wikked ressayueþ [receives] at ones.
Þere as gadryng of goode men ys,
Is holychyrche of flesch and bones;
Prestes are lanterne hem to wysse
Þe wise weyes to heuene wones.[9]

Here the poet seeks to substitute one image of the material church for another: a church not of "tre ne stones" but "flesch and bones." The poet will go on to make an emphatic defense of the doctrine of transubstantiation.[10] Unlike the *Lanterne* author, the Digby poet aims to reconfirm rather than challenge mainstream religious practices. As Helen Barr notes, although the poet's denial in Digby 23 that the church is made of trees and stones "sails close to Wycliffite dismissals of the materiality of the church on earth," the poet does so in service of locating a defense of the orthodox Eucharistic theology within a church that already has been established "as a congregation of the spiritually upright."[11] Rather than challenging the authority of the institutional church, the "holychyrche of flesch and bones" the poem advances is guided by the wise "lanterne" of the priesthood and defined by its liturgy and sacraments. The Digby poems as a whole, Barr suggests, serve to rebut Wycliffite views by insisting upon the reforming power of penance and reconfirming the institutional authority of the church and its priesthood as the essential mediators between God and the body of the faithful.

Like the Digby poems, *The Castle of Perseverance* is concerned with defending mainstream spiritual practices. The *Castle* provides a powerful response to lollard critiques of the sacraments and the ritual life of the church by advancing the potential of *performance* as a place of communal meaning-making. Although, as a play, it does not engage directly with lollard polemic (as do other modes of contemporary religious writing), it indirectly engages contemporary fears about the circulation of antisacramentalist views by showing how material practices and ritual performances produce spiritual knowledge. By creating an interactive theatrical space that is at once a penitential trajectory, a map of the world, and a church, the play presents its audience with a version of "holychyrche" that is resoundingly "of fleshe and bones," determined by human activity. The Digby poet, like the author of the *Lanterne*, replaces a church defined by its walls with one produced by human actions, but the *Castle* as performed allegory necessarily *merges* place and action. Insisting that church, world, and penitential practice are mutually productive, the play demonstrates the power of religious institutions and human actions to shape one another. Through its use of dramatic personification, it makes a case for the essential role of penance, as a ritual that manifests divine grace through the performance of forgiveness, in defining what it means to be "humankind." It thus presents a version of human selfhood produced by, and utterly dependent upon, the institutions and social performances in which it participates.

Drawing upon the shared ability of theater and ritual to model a world, the *Castle* presents penitential ritual as *the* shaping power in the life and world of humankind. Penance in the play provides humankind with a fundamental epistemological and soteriological narrative of sin, repentance, and divine forgiveness. Totalizing in its sweep, its plot imagines the entirety of the life of Humankind beginning with his birth and ending with his death—according to a penitential trajectory of temptation, fall, and reconciliation.[12] Its staging, outlined in the remarkable stage diagram appended to the end of the play's text in the Macro manuscript, is equally comprehensive in its scope. The diagram describes a large outdoor playing area divided between *loci*, specific locations designated by scaffolds, and the *platea* or "place," the surrounding acting area, and its features (figure 1). Presenting a landscape divided between *loci* representing worldly temptation and "perseverance" in virtue, the staging materially realizes Humankind's trajectory by projecting the penitential language of virtue and vice onto the world he inhabits.

By representing virtue and vice as physical features, the play describes a physical space that is also a conception of moral action. Clifford Davidson observes that the set design makes Humankind's central predicament—as one suspended between virtue and vice—spatially and iconographically manifest from the first scenes of the play.[13] In the diagram, the center of the *platea* is dominated by a drawing of a large crenellated stone tower identified as "þe castel of perseuerraunse." "Mankyndeis bed"—where Humankind is born at the beginning of the play and dies at its conclusion—is pictured under the tower.[14] The castle is in turn surrounded by a double circle representing a moat or other barrier. Captions written outside the double circle indicate the various *loci*: God's scaffold lies to the east (to the far left on the diagram

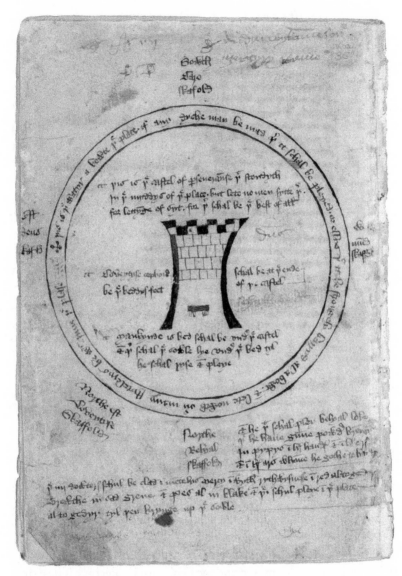

Figure 1. The stage plan for *The Castle of Perseverance*, Folger MS. V. a. 354, f. 191v. Courtesy of the Folger Shakespeare Library.

itself) and the scaffolds of World, the Devil, Flesh, and Covetousness lie to the west, north, south, and northeast respectively.[15] Drawing heavily from contemporary penitential literature and imagery, the scaffolds that surround the castle in the stage diagram house the seven deadly sins, categories parish priests employed to help penitents identify their sins and to determine their penance. As indicated in the play's opening speeches, the scaffolds of Flesh and the Devil house the deadly sins of Gluttony, Lechery, and Sloth and the sins of Pride, Wrath, and Envy, respectively. Covetousness, the deadly sin to whom Humankind proves most vulnerable, has his own scaffold.

The theatrical space described by the play's diagram is both symbolic of and continuous with the world outside it. The diagram itself resembles medieval world maps that placed the walled city of Jerusalem at the center of a huge round landmass—representing the continents of Asia, Europe, and Africa—which was in turn surrounded by a ring-shaped ocean.[16] God's scaffold in the east reflects the location of the *Christus triumphans* that occupied the apex of a *mappa mundi*, while the Devil's scaffold occupies the traditional location of hell, the north. The playing space's alignment with the cardinal directions would have been especially apparent as the sun moved across the sky in the course of a performance, a movement that would itself have been dramatic, given the play's 3,649 lines. In placing God's scaffold to the east, the playing area also resembles the layout of English churches, which faced east toward Jerusalem. Humankind's movement toward God's scaffold in the east, as Davidson notes, thus recalls parishioners' movement eastward under the chancel to receive communion and orientation "toward the salvation symbolized by the heavenly Jerusalem"; by contrast, Humankind's wandering trajectory early in the play from scaffold to scaffold "suggests the vicissitudes of human life as it is lived between the polarities of evil and good."[17]

The play dissolves firm boundaries between place and action, play world and real world, presenting the penitential trajectory it describes as the audience's own. The play presents in microcosm the world of the audience; the audience's world equally becomes part of the play. As Erika Fischer-Lichte remarks, in medieval theater "there is no clear-cut division between the sphere of those who act and of those who observe; for they are all related in the same way to the history of mankind as the history of religious salvation."[18] As an allegorical figure, Humankind acts as an avatar for each member of the audience, and through him the audience iconically enters the play. The permeability of the boundary between actor and audience member is further reinforced by the play's *platea* and *loci* set design where, as Pamela King observes, "barriers between different spaces within the playing space are more carefully and consistently maintained than [the] assumed barrier between audience and play."[19] Both the play's diagram and action strongly suggest that spectators would have entered the playing space. The character World, for instance, refers to audience members who are "þorwe þis propyr pleyn place" (160) and invites them to join his retinue. If spectators followed Humankind's path as he moved from scaffold to scaffold in the course of the play's action, as a reference to "styteleryrs" or crowd marshals on the stage diagram suggests, their nominal identification with Humankind would have been strengthened further still.[20] Unlike a modern theater in which spectators remain silent observers fixed in their seats, King notes, the *Castle*'s open *platea* and *loci* structure creates "constantly changing interstitial relationships between the audience and the play," encouraging spectators to have a "social rather than personal" response.[21] The play thus not only visualizes the moral life, to borrow Davidson's phrase, but incorporates its audience into it.

Through its all-encompassing vision, the *Castle*, like the other moralities of the Macro manuscript, suggests the degree to which lollard critiques of mainstream practices forced their more orthodox contemporaries to reimagine and reframe the central ritual practices and pedagogies of the established church. In emphasizing the necessary coordination of sanctified space and virtuous action, the *Castle* aligns itself with contemporary calls for reform. However, the play resists the antisacramental elements of Wycliffite polemic. It reasserts the necessity of penance in a way that does not rely primarily upon scriptural or doctrinal arguments or on the anticlerical arguments focused on dominion that are standard in lollard critiques of penance. Instead, the play highlights the transformative, rather than the merely mimetic or spectacular, nature of performance. Reinscribing the landscape Humankind and his audience inhabit with the traditional teachings and practices of the English church, the *Castle* investigates—and ultimately affirms—the power of theatrical and ritual experiences to manifest divine mercy and reform humankind. In this way, the play reinvests performance and the shared communal experiences of the body of the faithful with new spiritual authority, revealing a much more capacious conception of the sacrament and more open conception of the church and its sources of authority than that allowed by lollard polemic.

The earliest fully extant morality play, the *Castle* establishes the key features of the morality play as a dramatic form in which penance happens primarily in the world rather than exclusively in a church, and transformative self-knowledge happens through penitential community. That foundational outlook is in turn built upon by later morality plays, which, just as the *Castle* does, present a self that is above all performed. Like the *Castle*, the later moralities present a self shaped interactively and collectively through church-mediated rituals rather than privately and individually. Whereas the later plays define "mankind" primarily according to a temporal progression of fall and redemption, in the *Castle* that progression, and thus the version of the self it presents, is primarily understood spatially, through Humankind's negotiation of theatrical *place*.

REFORM AND THE ENGLISH CHURCH IN THE EARLY FIFTEENTH CENTURY

The *Castle*'s dramatic reimagination of penitential ritual can be seen to participate in the English church's much broader contemporaneous project to reinvigorate public religion and sacramental practice. Recent scholarship has done much to enrich our understanding of the impact of both orthodox and heterodox calls to reform on fifteenth-century English literature and spirituality. In his influential 1995 *Speculum* article, Nicholas Watson argued that the promulgation of Archbishop Thomas Arundel's anti-Wycliffite *Constitutions* (1407–9), prohibiting the unauthorized translation of scripture, all but stifled religious writing in the vernacular for nearly a century.[22] Watson excludes drama entirely from his discussion, and his conclusions about the impact of the *Constitutions* on religious writing more broadly have not gone unchallenged.[23] Jeremy Catto and Vincent Gillespie have drawn critical attention to the efforts of Arundel and his successor, Henry Chichele, archbishop of Canterbury from 1414 to 1443, to promote a positive program of orthodox reform that sought "to renew the religious life of the nation though the traditional sacraments, ceremonies, and doctrines of Catholic Christianity." And Gillespie further argues it was Wyclif rather than Arundel who had the more lasting impact on the English church in the fifteenth-century.[24] Played outdoors "on the green" and presumably directed toward a largely lay audience, the play's vivid dramatization of key tenets of church doctrine were in keeping with the church's renewed commitment to pastoral teaching. However, the *Castle*'s most important contribution to early fifteenth-century debates surrounding penance is its reaffirmation of the tangible, institutional, and above all *performative* dimensions of faith.

The *Castle* can be seen as part of a much broader effort in the early fifteenth century to reinvigorate and reaffirm the ceremonial culture of the institutional church. Catto points out that, in addition to measures designed to curtail the circulation of lollard ideas, Arundel's *Constitutions* contained positive provisions to encourage popular devotions, stipulating that

> the adoration of the glorious Cross, the veneration of images of the saints, and pilgrimages to their shrines or relics . . . are to be commonly taught, and the Cross and Image of Christ is to be preached, and also the images of Saints . . . with processions of the relics, genuflexions, bowing the head, incensing, making offerings, kissing [the relics], and burning lights before them, and with pilgrimages, and in whatever forms and modes have been customary in our time and those of our predecessors.[25]

Arundel's successor, Henry Chichele, continued to encourage and augment public forms of worship. Chichele and his bishops instituted new saints' feasts, standardized the English liturgy according to the Sarum Use, and worked to refine and elaborate church rites:

> The forms of worship practised in fifteenth-century churches can only be reconstructed indirectly. . . . The general direction of the changes, however, is clear: more ceremonies, the introduction of new feasts and cults, more elaborate music and emphasis on public processions, such as the Corpus Christi day procession at Lincoln from Wykford to the Cathedral in which Bishop Repingdon insisted all local clergy should take part "for increase of devotion."[26]

Gillespie notes that the new emphasis on the ceremonial culture of the institutional church paradoxically owed much to Wyclif and lollard calls to reform.[27] The great ecumenical Council of Constance (1414–18) condemned Wyclif as a heretic, decreeing that his bones be exhumed and burned along with his writings, but it also left the English church with a palpable sense that they needed to address the corruption that had spawned schism and heresy and, more importantly for the purpose of understanding the morality plays, to reinvigorate pastoral care. The *Castle* reflects the reformist emphasis within the established church on the care of souls insofar as it educates its audience in the tenets of the faith and on proper procedure for a full and complete confession, and a significant portion of its dialogue and action is drawn directly from contemporary penitential manuals.[28]

In its positive reevaluation of the orthodox practices of the church, the *Castle* also reflects a recurrent theme in early fifteenth-century religious writing: the necessity of traditional rituals, especially auricular confession to a priest. Nicholas Love, in his immensely popular devotional text the *Mirror of the Blessed Life of Jesus Christ*, finds in the Luke 7 gospel story—in which Christ pronounces (in the absence of oral confession) a "sinful woman" at the house of Simon the Pharisee forgiven of her transgressions—an opportune moment to correct "þe fals opinyon of lollardes" that "shrift of mouþe is not nedeful" but that "it sufficeþ onely in herte to be shriuen to god."[29] Lest readers mistakenly think that one need only admit one's sins *inwardly*, Love reminds them that sin offends both Christ's "godhede" and his "manhede." Restitution must therefore address Christ in both his divine and human natures: "And siþen we do haue not here [Christ's] bodily presence as Maudleyn hade þerfore in his stede vs behoueþ to shewe to þe preste by worde, þat we haue offendet him as man, as we shewen to him by repentance in herte, þat we haue offendet him as god."[30] The visible, tangible acts of the priest serve as an extension of, and thus are necessitated and justified by, Christ's human nature.

Such an emphasis upon the visible and institutional dimensions of faith is also evident in the Carmelite friar and theologian Thomas Netter's *Doctrinale Antiquitatum Fidei Catholicae Ecclesiae contra Wiclevistas et Hussitas* (1426–30), written, as its title implies, for the explicit purpose of correcting heretical views.[31] Like Love, Netter grounds his defense of the bodily, material nature of orthodox practices in the dual nature of Christ. However, whereas Love invokes Christ's dual nature in order to defend sacerdotal authority, Netter foregrounds the role of sacramental community in the act of salvation. In opposition to Wyclif's view that the true church consists of the invisible body of the elect, Netter asserts that the church is defined by its visibility and by the embodied penitential practices of the body of the faithful in particular. "Where there is no true confession," he proclaims, "there is no Church."[32] The church is inseparable from the rituals that make divine forgiveness manifest. Netter does not view sacramental ritual to be external to the church but to be constitutive of it. Kevin Alban observes that for Netter, "just as the single person of Christ has two natures, God and man, so . . . the Church possesses not only an inner life but also external features which are equally important and essential to its nature"; Alban further contends that "it follows then that the Church cannot be solely an idea or a concept, but must be visible in order to show that it is the body of Christ."[33] Netter's ecclesiology, Alban emphasizes, is inseparable from his Christology and the congregation's configuration as the body of Christ: faith is inextricable from the performance of it.

Unlike Love or Netter, the *Castle* refrains from engaging directly with lollard views. Instead, the play introduces an altogether different response to the lollard movement than other modes of orthodox writing. Including an extended dramatization of Humankind's confession, it underscores the priest's powers of absolution. Yet, when Humankind falls back into sin, no priest arrives to help usher his soul to heaven. In the end, he will be saved through the intervention of the Four Daughters of God rather than a priest. Ultimately, the play decentralizes the priest's role. Rather than reconfirming the absolute necessity of confessing to a priest, it reveals a Christian selfhood unfolded in performance, presenting a soteriology, ecclesiology, epistemology, and anthropology grounded in one's participation in the practices of the church where the congregation of the faithful and participation in orthodox practices are mutually defining. Notably, in defending the necessary visibility of the church and its material practices, the author of the *Castle* turns to theater, the genre of human embodiment. In seeking to reimagine the relation between physical space and moral action, the play's author looks to romance, aligning moral space with the walls of a castle, rather than the walls of a church, and amoral space with the larger world.

"Þe folk is cherche"

In the *Castle*, self-knowledge is a continual process attained through embodied practices. Humankind's self-knowledge does not emerge through a single epiphany but through a constant, lifelong unfolding. That process is reflected in the very form in which it happens, dramatic personification, which describes how the meaning of a word (whether "greed" or "mankind") only emerges through the manifold and complex human relationships in which we participate. The plot of the *Castle* traces a penitential pattern of fall and regeneration in which a youthful Humankind falls into sin when, through the machinations of his Bad Angel (Malus Angelus) he comes under the sway of a feudal ruler named World (Mundus) and is eventually redeemed through the material intervention of his Good Angel (Bonus Angelus) and the figures of Shrift (Confessio) and Penance (Penitencia), who call upon Humankind to confess. Once he confesses and is absolved of his sins, Humankind "perseveres" in virtue for a time in the protection of the castle. The virtues throw red roses, symbolizing the blood of Christ's passion and the promise of Christian redemption to fend off the vices' attack, and, in the tradition of Prudentius's *Psychomachia*, each of the seven deadly sins are successively repulsed by the virtue that is its opposite. Finally, the physical and financial vulnerability of old age makes Humankind susceptible to vice once again. Fearing poverty in old age, he leaves the castle accompanied by Covetousness.[34] From his deathbed, he cries out for God's mercy with his dying breath. But the cry is too little too late, and his Bad Angel ushers him to hell. However, the final fate of his soul becomes uncertain when the Four Daughters of God—Mercy, Truth, Justice, and Peace (Misericordia, Veritas, Justicia, and Pax)—appear, and Mercy and Peace advocate on his behalf. The debate—which dramatically enacts how Christ's redemption reconciles the competing demands of God's justice, mercy, truth, and peace—is ultimately decided in Humankind's favor, and the Four Daughters escort his soul to heaven. Humankind's penitential and moral trajectory is physically mapped out across the playing space, as he moves between the vices' scaffolds, the castle of perseverance, and finally to God's scaffold. In stark contrast to lollards, who held the public rituals of the church to be extrinsic to salvation, the *Castle* underscores the material world and its institutionally situated practices as the condition of human apprehension of divine grace. Such knowledge in turn has to be itself materialized, realized through one's behavior in the world: it must encourage the practice of virtue by directing penitents in moral and virtuous ways. Places and institutions condition human actions; virtue, in order to exist, must be *performed*.

In projecting Humankind's penitential trajectory across its theatrical *platea*, the *Castle* does not simply illustrate the obligation to and challenges of pursuing a life of virtue. Instead, the stakes of the play are epistemological: the play suggests that human knowledge of virtue and vice is *itself* materially, temporally, and institutionally mediated. By rendering *allegoresis* as performance, the play suggests that our understanding of what it means to be "flesh" happens in time and through human exchange. The play's characters are themselves constructs of moral activity. The identity of Flesh (Caro) is manifest in his "brod brustun-gutte" (235), the extravagance of his tower timbered with "tapytys of tafata" (239), and in his resolution to seduce Humankind into a "lyfe . . . wyth lustys and lykynge ilent" (238). Or, as Clopper puts it: "Caro is active; he is present; he is not just an idea."[35] Physical space is also a component of moral behavior. Caro is both a character and a *locus*. As an embodied, performing character, he is not an abstraction despite the allegorical generality of his name. Vice and virtue exist in the performance of them.

The opening scenes of the *Castle* foreground the material dimensions of human existence and the temporal structures that give Humankind's world its form. Presenting penance as the primary structure that shapes Humankind's self-understanding, the play describes a process of ritualized differentialization of moral and amoral space.[36] The first scene describes a negotiation of the playing space, asking the play's audience to consider who controls it, how to understand it, and what relation it bears to the world outside. The play opens with speeches given by each of the traditional "Three Enemies of Man"—the World, the Flesh, and the Devil—and with the character World calling for the audience's attention:

Worthy wytys [persons] in al þis werd wyde,
  Be wylde wode wonys and euery weye-went,
Precyous prinse, prekyd in pride,
  Þrowe þis propyr pleyn place in pes be ʒe bent!
Buske [prepare] ʒou, bolde bachelerys, vnder my baner to abyde
  Where bryth basnetys [helmets] be bateryd and backys ar
  schent [destroyed].
Ʒe, syrys semly, all same syttyth on syde,
  For bothe be see and be londe my sondys [messengers] I
  haue sent,
    Al þe world myn name is ment.

$$(157–65)$$

World's speech directs the audience's attention to both their situated-
ness in the world as "worthy wytys" and their location within theatrical "place," asserting the inevitability of their geographic, political,
and moral subjection to World's reign. The stage plan presents one
moral structure for organizing the world, the penitential, but World
argues for another. Positioning himself as an attractive alternative to
"Goddys seruyse [service]" (593), World presents himself as a feudal
lord whose claim extends, as he has earlier declared, from Assyria and
Achaia to Rhodes and Rome (170–78). To be of the world, World suggests, is to be worldly.[37] The inevitability of Humankind's subjection
to World's reign will play a crucial part in the continual process of fall
and redemption the play explores.

World's imperious claims serve less to challenge God's authority
per se than to point to the World as the condition of human knowing.
The power of World's hegemony over the world is indicated in the
paradox of his assertion to have claimed it:

Mundus: All þese londys at myn avyse
Arn castyn to my werdly wyse.
My tresorer, Syr Coueytyse,
  Hath sesyd hem holy to me.

$$(179–82)$$

But from whom would World seize the world? When World threatens
that "whoso spekyth aʒeyn þe Werd / In a presun [prison] he schal be

sperd [confined]" (192–93), he points to the difficulty of what it would mean to defy the world you inhabit and of which you are a part. It is in the world—in all its worldliness—that Humankind first discovers himself. World's words also serve to align space with moral behavior. When he asserts that his treasurer, Sir Covetousness, has "sesyd" (taken possession of) lands for him, he uses a term from feudal contract law in wide circulation in the fifteenth century.[38] In doing so, he locates the "worldliness" and materialism lollard writers associated with the contemporary church firmly in the feudal, secular space of the World, opposing it to the virtuous space designated by the castle of perseverance.

The play describes the life of Humankind as a process of becoming, where the world is the situation in which he discovers himself. His first words convey his newborn vulnerability and innocence. Born only "þis nyth [night]" (276) and naked except for his baptismal garb, he proclaims he knows not why "I was to þis werld browth" (288) and that he is unable to "helpe myself in no doynge" (291). His Good Angel enjoins him to "serue Jhesu, heuene kynge" (332); his Bad Angel promises he "schal hym drawyn to þe Werdys seruyse" (342). Promising Humankind that he will "dwelle wyth caysere, kynge, and knyth [knight]" (343) and that "sone þou schalt be ryche" (348), the Bad Angel is more responsive to his more immediate physical and emotional concerns. As Humankind is a temporal being whose ability to understand virtue and vice depends upon his location in the world, his choice to put in "þis World . . . al my trust" (398) seems almost inevitable.

Just as the play foregrounds the material and temporal dimensions of Humankind's fall, it also presents the work of recognizing sin and coming to contrition as a process that occurs in a mind firmly located in church and community. In contrast to lollard arguments that present repentance as a primarily interior process, the play foregrounds both the difficulty and social nature of contrition. No one forces Humankind to repent, but he also does not come to contrition on his own. Still under the vices' influence when Shrift first appears, Humankind shoos him off, telling him to come back on Good Friday (1346–54). In doing so, he acts out modes of resistance to Lenten obligations against which late medieval pastoral manuals specifically admonished.[39] Shrift persists in enjoining him to confess, but he only forsakes his sins when Penance pierces him with her "poynt" (1377). Humankind's contrition, if abrupt, is not arbitrary: it is a simultaneously external and internal process in which his knowledge of himself as sinner is predicated on his location in a landscape in which virtue and vice and penitential reconciliation are the defining—and, indeed, inescapable—features. His dependence upon his Good Angel, Shrift, and Penance to come to contrition demonstrates that repentance is both an interior *and* a social process. The play includes an extended staging of Humankind's confession, underscoring the critical role of the institutional church as the agent of his salvation and foregrounding areas of penitential practice criticized by lollard writers. Shrift explicitly invokes the power of the keys. He speaks on the authority of "Petyr and Powle, apostoly, / To whom God ʒafe powere to lese and bynde" (1496–97) and unambiguously claims the power to absolve Humankind of sin, reiterating his power to do so three times in the course of the confessional scene (1500, 1507, 1520).

Humankind's self-understanding changes as he moves through the set's penitential terrain. Critics, including Richard Emmerson, Lawrence Clopper, and Sarah Beckwith, have rightly challenged the critical commonplace that the characters of the morality play simply designate abstractions.[40] The meaning of "humankind" develops in and through his negotiation of physical space and his experiences of sin and redemption. At the beginning of the play, the newly born Humankind identifies himself according to his lack of knowledge:

> I am nakyd of lym and lende [loin]
>> As Mankynde is schapyn and schorn [fashioned].
> I not wedyr to gon ne to lende [come]
>> To helpe myself mydday nyn morn.
>
> (279–82)

As World's retainer, his self-understanding changes as he becomes adept at negotiating the world. Under the direction of Covetousness, he learns to engage in simony, extortion, and false assize; to help others when it serves his self-interest; to withhold his servants' wages; to betray his neighbors; to avoid paying tithes; to be deaf to the cries of beggars; and to buy and sell using false weights (841–53). In short, he learns to fulfill the World's definition of what it means to be a man:

> . . . Goddys seruyse þou must forsake
> And holy to þe Werld þe take
> And þanne a man I schal þe make
>   Þat non schal be þi pere.
>   (593–96)

From Covetousness's scaffold, he defines himself as one enmeshed in vice:

> Mankynde I am callyd be kynde,
>   Wyth curssydnesse in costys knet [with wickedness in habits
>   knit].
> In sowre swettenesse my syth I sende,
>   Wyth seuene synnys sadde beset.
>   (1238–41)

Once confessed of his sins, he describes himself from the castle according to his struggle to persevere in virtue against vice:

> Whanne Mankynd drawyth to goode
> Beholde what enmys he schal haue!
>   (1998–99)

When he eventually leaves the castle, succumbing once again to Covetousness, Humankind gives himself over to yet another self-definition, where his negative formulation signals the insatiability of his desire and his abandonment of self to vice: "Qwenche neuere [my covetousness] no man may," he says. "Me þynkyth neuere I haue inow [enough]" (2765–66). When he finally faces death, he makes overt reference to his iconic and exemplary role, entreating the "good men" of his audience to "takythe example at me" (2995). As the representative of what it means to be human, Humankind demonstrates human susceptibility to sin and the false allures of the World: he is deserving of damnation, he recognizes, and utterly dependent upon God's grace (2997–3007). Yet as his appeal to the members of his audience to "do [provide] for ʒoureself whyl ʒe han spase [time]" (2996) suggests, humankind is also capable of change and reform.

Like the meaning of "mankind," the material spaces designating the play's *platea* and *loci* structure prove to be dynamic. As Humankind's self-understanding is shaped and reshaped though his penitential experience of temptation, fall, and recovery, that trajectory is in turn reflected in the play's set design, which gives physical form to the dominant categories and metaphors of contemporary *pastoralia*. In giving a material location to the seven deadly sins, the vices' scaffolds reflect the systematic categorization and classification of sin that provide the primary framework for contemporary penitential manuals. The castle, the most prominent feature of the play's set design, is strongly aligned with penitential practice. Shrift first conducts Humankind to the castle: as long as he stays within the protection of this "precyous place, / Ful of vertu and of grace," Shrift explains, "No synne schal hym schende [injure]" (1555–56; 1558). The castle stands as a "place of surete" (1543), a symbol of protection in which penance and virtue, in Shrift's formulation, become a fortress-like defense against sin. Yet the play sets up the castle as a fixed, material structure only in order to undermine its spatial stasis. The castle is both a static structure and a fluid place of performance. The physical space the castle designates is defined by the activity of persevering in virtue; the castle itself—the material stone edifice indicated by the play's set design—presumably only lasts the duration of the play.

The topos of the castle draws upon homiletic and devotional imagery in which the struggle to persevere against sin is metaphorically imagined as the defensive fortifications of a fortress.[41] In allegorizing a castle as a place of religious virtue, the play draws upon an established vernacular literary tradition that drew upon architectural metaphors and courtly tropes to instruct a popular audience in Christian doctrine and belief. The play's plot strongly resembles that of Grosseteste's popular allegorical poem *Le Chateau d'Amour* (ca. 1230), whose speaker, pursued by the Three Enemies and the Seven Deadly Sins, seeks refuge in the Castle of the Virgin Mary, which, fortified with Christian virtue, provides him with "solas and . . . socour."[42] The individual features of such castles were sometimes given explicitly penitential dimensions. For instance, in the Assumption Day sermon of his *Festial* (ca. 1400), Mirk compares the Virgin Mary to a castle defended by a "depe dych" filled with the water of "compassyon þat a man haþe for his owne gylt oþer for any oþer monnys deses [misfortunes]," a drawbridge of "discret obedyens" that "schall be drawen vp aȝeynys enmys, and lete downe þe frendys þat wyl kepe þys castell," an outer wall of "wedloke" and "pacience" and an inner wall of "maydenhode," and a gate of "fayþe" surmounted by a tower of charity.[43] For Mirk, such devotional images do not merely serve to illustrate the necessity of persevering against sin, but themselves foster virtue. By supplying the devout a compressed and accessible moral framework, such metaphors can provide emotional reassurance and spiritual guidance to even a small child: "for ryȝt as men and woymen and childyrn fleyn ynto a castell for drede of enmys, to haue socoure," he explains, "so all men and woymen fleon to oure lady for socoure in all hor deses, yn so moch þat þe lest chyld þat con speke, anon as he ys aferde, he cryþe: 'Lady, lady!'" (230/24–28). In Mirk's formulation, the castle's compact moral imagery conditions a devotional response in which a cry for our "lady" synecdochically stands in for an entire structure of support provided by the "socoure" of a fortress of exemplary virtue.

Lollard writers revised such structural metaphors in order to critique the established church and develop alternative forms of Christian community, as Fiona Somerset has recently demonstrated.[44] For instance, the reformist treatise the *City of Saints* describes a community of those "þat schal come to þe blisse" governed by a mayor named Charity (God) and bound by the obligation to keep the Ten Commandments.[45] Similarly, in the antifraternal lollard polemic *Dialogue between Jon and Richard*, Jon denounces false friars who leave the "cloister of soule" bounded by the "foure wallis" of the "foure cardinal vertues," and insists that, as opposed to the "clouted" [patched-together] rule of the friars, "oure rule is better," as it is the "gospel þat Iesu Crist made."[46] Such structural metaphors, Somerset suggests, allow lollard writers to "develop modes of religious life . . . that sidestep or even compete with the religious institutions that inhabit brick-and-mortar structures."[47] Insofar as it uses a building allegory to foreground a Christian self defined by virtuous practice, the *Castle* resembles these reformist texts. However, in marked contrast to such texts, the play's "Castel of Vertu and of Goodnesse" (2019) is both dependent upon and produced by—rather than imagined as an alternative to—mainstream ecclesiastical institutions and practices.

The *Castle* emphasizes that with penance comes the continued obligation to pursue a life of virtue. Inside the castle, the virtue Humility instructs Humankind to "stonde hereinne as stylle as ston" (1697). Notably, Humility instructs him not to *become* a stone but to *perform* standing still as one. As Christiania Whitehead observes, in naming its most prominent iconographic and stage feature "perseverance," the play implies that "the good life requires *steadfastness* in virtue" and thus "necessitates *staying put*."[48] The castle is not a place of stasis; instead, residence in the castle requires a vigilant process of fortification. Humankind and his audience's own movements to and from the castle would have highlighted the performative nature of both inconstancy and standing still. Described here by Humankind, the castle is both a static thing, a physical edifice standing at the center of the play, and a process, something that exists only in the practices of those within it:

> Certys I schuld ben ouyrlad [defeated],
>> But þat I am in þis castel town,
>>> Wyth synnys sore and smerte.
>> Whoso wyl leuyn [live] oute of dystresse
>> And ledyn hys lyf in clennesse
>> In þis Castel of Vertu and of Goodnesse
>>> Hym muste haue hole hys hert.
>>>> (2014–20)

The castle is described as both the product of human virtue and its guardian. Once inside, the virtues prescribe penitential disciplining of the body: "For whoso wyle Slawth putte doun," instructs Business, "Wyth bedys and wyth orysoun / Or sum oneste ocupacyoun, / As boke to haue in honde" (2361–64). The castle's fortification against vice *is* the governance of those within it.

Yet, as the play's central metaphor, the castle as a defined space of virtuous living remains in tension with a more fluid and inclusive model of a church defined by penitential performance. By virtue of its very structure, the metaphor of the castle draws a firm boundary dividing the "good people" within its walls and the "bad people" outside of them, a configuration that would have been all the more evident to a fifteenth-century audience, interspersed among the vices' scaffolds and forbidden entry into the area immediately surrounding the castle.[49]

That Covetousness is the vice who instigates Humankind's fall is perhaps unsurprising given that Paul identifies it as the "root of all evils" (1 Tim. 6:10); covetousness was traditionally identified as the source of the other deadly sins. The virtue Generosity invokes this tradition when she identifies Covetousness as the "grounde" that nourishes "pride, envye, and hate" (2456–57).[50] However, Covetousness's appearance at the end of the play also serves to redirect contemporary concern about the commodification of penance by showing there are forms of covetousness experienced by people other than confessors and other members of the clergy. Humankind forsakes the castle when Covetousness exploits his physical and emotional vulnerability in old age and fear of poverty. Calling him his "frend" and offering to slake his "sorwe," Covetousness promises Humankind that he will be his "leche" (physician) and that he will guide him "to thedom [prosperity] and to þryfte [wealth]" (2472–78). By identifying himself as Humankind's doctor, Covetousness inverts reformist critiques of contemporary penitential practices: this avaricious physician provides Humankind with material goods instead of vice versa. In doing so, penance is reestablished as the antidote to covetousness rather than imagined as its victim.

In a play that emphasizes the material as the condition of human knowledge, it is also fitting that Covetousness is the play's chief vice, as it is the sin most directly concerned with the right relation to the material world. The virtues and vices are persuasive insofar as they are responsive to Humankind's physical and emotional needs. As Humankind ages, he becomes increasingly helpless and dependent, as his painful inventory of the markers of his growing fragility and physical decline witnesses (2482–87). Covetousness preys upon Humankind's physical, financial, and emotional vulnerability, and his ability to convince him to abandon the castle rests in part upon the friendship he extends. When Humankind protests he does not want to forsake the "ladys" who have been his "best frendys" (2514–17), Covetousness insidiously twists the language of friendship to ratchet up his attack:

And þou schalt fynde, soth to sey,
    Þi purs schal be þi best frende.
Þou þou syt al-day and prey,
    No man schal com to þe nor sende,

But if þou haue a peny to pey,
   Men schul to þe þanne lystyn and lende [listen and pay
      attention]
      And kelyn [assuage] al þi care.

(2520–26)

"Purse" becomes "frend" as Humankind, on Covetousness's suggestion, desperately attempts to shore up the companionship and support
of those who otherwise will not visit, will not listen to, and will not
care for an old man, and Humankind allies himself with Covetousness
in an anguished attempt to retain the illusion of self-sufficiency in the
face of death.

Through the figure of Covetousness and the precarious "surete"
the physical structure of the castle of perseverance provides, the play
dramatizes both human dependence upon the material world and
the dangers of that dependence. Like the *Castle*, the early fifteenth-
century penitential treatise *Jacob's Well* identifies covetousness with
fear of poverty, but *Jacob's Well* further associates that fear with a
failure to place one's faith in *either* God *or* the world:

> Coueytise is a vyce þat rewlyth loue to wordly catell, whiche loue
> man hath of vntrust and vnsykernesse to god, for dreed of pouert,
> wenying þat god & þe world schulde faylen hym, but ȝif he
> gaderyd myche muk to hepe.[51]

Like a porcupine who "wyth hise scharpe pryckys" gathers together a
great hoard of apples "thynkynge in his kynde þat his lyiflode schulde
faylen hym," the covetous man "wyth manye scharpe sleyghtys &
sotyltees of falsnes" hoards worldly goods "wenyng ellys þat god & all
þe worlde schulde faylen hym" (117/18–24). *Jacob's Well* also relates a
story of a gardener who had been charitable all his life, but in his old
age begins to dread poverty and infirmity, "noȝt trustyng full þat god
schulde kepyn hym in his age as he dede in his ȝouthe" (125/9–11). The
gardener leaves off his alms deeds, giving himself over to covetousness
and gathering together a vast sum of money. But he gets a foot disease,
and spends all his money on doctors, who tell him he must have his leg
amputated at the knee. The night before the procedure, he cries out:

whyle I gaf almes, I was heyl in alle my lymes, to getyn my lyiflode, & now, in my coueytise, I am lame, and to-morwyn my rotyn foot schal be smyten of. my monye is spent þer-aboute, I am a beggere. Allas, þat euer gadryd I monye on hepe, to trustyn þere-vpon, & lefte myn almesdede! (125/17–22)

Notably, in this last example the gardener describes his "fall" into covetousness both in terms of how he understands his worldly possessions and how he understands his relation to God, as the transference of his love and trust in God to a distrust manifest in the accumulation of goods, a distrust that (the narrative implies) results in a literal loss of physical limb. Both the *Castle* and *Jacob's Well* foreground the sin of covetousness in order to dramatize how human vulnerability can cause one to place false trust in material things while, at the same time, adamantly insisting upon the necessity of the tangible and institutional dimensions of faith.

Making a Bad Death Good

The other Macro plays and *Everyman* culminate in an epiphanic moment in which the plays' central characters realize their sins and, through penance, return to a state of grace. In contrast, the *Castle* does not end after its central character's experience of penance. Instead it presents a particularly bleak assessment of the state of the human soul, dramatizing rather than just acknowledging the human propensity to fall back into sin. Although Humankind is able to affect his own actions through perseverance, the effects of penance endure only as long as he pursues a life of virtue in the castle, and his single attempt to do so proves only fleeting. Dying in the grip of Covetousness, he realizes that World has arranged for all his goods to go to a young upstart, and is tormented by the thought that "I Wot Neuere Who" will be his only heir (2993–94). He only cries out for God's mercy with his dying breath (3007). A priest is conspicuously absent. Shrift and Penance literally have a role to play the first time Humankind repents, but they make no deathbed reappearance. As the play draws to a close and the Bad Angel leads him off to hell, Humankind appears headed for damnation. In the terminology of the *ars moriendi*, the late medieval manuals on the art of dying well, he has made a "bad death": he has not received the last rites to ensure he dies in a state of grace.[52] The debate between the Four Daughters of God that ensues turns upon whether Humankind's deathbed cry was sufficient for his salvation. As the debate is resolved in Humankind's favor, the play retreats from its earlier emphasis on the priest's role in the binding and loosing of sin. In his closing speech, God effectively relegates the role of priests to mere informant, saying that he "schal inquire of my flok and of here pasture [pastors]" whether the members of the estates have lived virtuously (3624–25).

By having Humankind die without receiving last rites, the *Castle* avoids making his ultimate salvation appear to be a contractual agreement between penitent and priest. Although emphasizing the institutional structures that shape Humankind, the play suggests that the importance of penance has little to do with priests' power to, in the words of the *Twelve Conclusions*, "byndin and unbyndin at here owne wil."[53] Shrift's warning that he must stay in the castle in order to reach heaven does not hold. Instead, by showing church, world, and penitential practice to be mutually productive, the play suggests that the importance of penance inheres in its ability to shape the life of Humankind by establishing the very terrain through which he recognizes his own sinfulness and divine mercy. By staging penance as a drama in which good and bad angels, virtue and vice vie for the soul of Humankind, the play illustrates the dramatic nature of penitential ritual—and the redemptive potential of drama—to show forth divine mercy.

The conclusion of the *Castle* might concede something to lollard views about the priest's role in penance, but it has already reframed the entire discussion in penitential terms. Through the interplay of its ritual and theatrical framing of human experience, the play demonstrates the centrality of penance as a church-mediated public ritual in the structure of Christian life. The play's pessimism about the obduracy of human sinfulness is balanced by a resilient optimism that virtue can be found in the material and worldly and that divine mercy is available to even the most inveterate sinner. Rather than a "dead sign," penitential ritual in the *Castle* becomes the overarching structure that organizes the experience of humankind and allows God's mercy to be known.

The debate of the Four Daughters of God at the conclusion of the play reframes questions about the individual fate of those who die un-houseled and unconfessed within the larger context of salvation history. The *Castle* is unusual in setting this common topos of medieval literature at the time of the judgment of an individual soul immediately after death. More typically, the Four Daughters' debate occurs as part of the narratives of the Incarnation and Annunciation — or in the case of *Piers Plowman* after the crucifixion. Christ's sacrifice is offered as the solution to the apparent impasse between the demands of God's justice and mercy after the Fall.[54] The Daughters kiss in reconciliation, satisfying David's prophesy: "Mercy and truth have met each other; justice and peace have kissed" (Ps. 84:11). Transferring the debate from the Annunciation to the moment of judgment after the death of Humankind, the *Castle* debate reframes Humankind's particular fate in terms of salvation history and God's ultimate act of mercy, Christ's redemption. In downplaying the role of auricular confession in the final scenes, the play risks suggesting that the performance of penance itself will take the place of the priest, where performance, rather than sacerdotal absolution, becomes the medium through which Humankind will be saved. The role of the church, like the role of the Four Daughters' debate itself, becomes both testament and witness to the drama of human redemption:

> Whanne man crieth mercy, and wyl not ses,
> Mercy schal be hys waschynge-well:
> Wytnesse of Holy Kyrke.
> (3144–46)

If mankind will be saved from sin, as Mercy here suggests, it will be through such performances.

The picture of humankind in the *Castle* is of a Humankind that sins more than he repents and repents only to sin again. Yet it will be the very undeniability of his guilt and the relative insufficiency of his contrition that allows God's mercy to become most fully manifest. In the *Castle*, the sanctity of holy places resides not in their apotropaic powers: Humankind returns to a life of sin despite his residence in the castle of perseverance. "Þe place," as the *Lanterne* author would say, "myȝt not holde him." Instead, such places are not static but sacred as material sites defined through communal actions. They are sacred as sites that, through the very performances that define them, are revelatory of divine grace. What finally makes Humankind's bad death "good" is literally an act of theater. It is not a theater that is reducible to so many acts of necromancy (to echo lollard polemic once again) but that, like the church, bears witness to divine mercy. The play demonstrates that the theatrical aspects of orthodox practice do not amount to so many "iapes feyned of prestis" but instead shows performance to be a distinctively efficacious force. Divine grace is made manifest and discovered in the performance of forgiveness. As, in the world of the play, the meaning of "humankind" depends upon Humankind's apprehension of that grace (and thus his participation in penitential performances), language of the self and the language of performance are inextricably intertwined.

Humankind is saved through the ability of ritual and theatrical performances to model the world and to mold and define "mankind" according to a penitential schema ultimately revelatory of divine mercy. The play pins its hopes for the soul's reformation on theater itself. At the very end of the *Castle*, the actor playing God steps out of his role, and delivers a memento mori that can also be read as a defense of playing:

> Þus endyth oure gamys.
> To saue ȝou fro synnynge
> Evyr at þe begynnynge
> Thynke on ȝoure last endynge!
> Te Deum laudamus!
> (3645–49)

If Humankind's obdurate sinfulness raises the question of how to promote the life of virtue, the actor playing God suggests the power of the "gamys" of allegorical theater to help save Humankind from sinning through its particular form of witness.

CHAPTER TWO

A Theater of the Soul's Interior

Contemplative Literature and Penitential Education in *Wisdom*

The Augustinian monk Walter Hilton, in his late fourteenth-century guide to the contemplative life, *The Scale of Perfection*, describes the inner transformations wrought by the sacrament of penance as by definition unfelt and unseen:

> But he that is reformed in his soule bi the sacrament of penaunce to the image of God, he feeleth noo chaungynge in himsilf, neithir in his bodili kynde withoutin, ne in the privé substaunce of his soule withinne, othir than he dide. For he is as he was unto his feelynge, and he feelith the same stirynges of synne and the same corrupcioun of his fleisch in passions and worldli desires risynge in his herte as he dide biforn. And yit neverthelees schal he trowe that he is thorugh grace reformed to the likenesse of God, though he neithir feele it ne see it. (2.8)

For Hilton, penitential restoration of the soul from a state of sin to a state of grace, critical to salvation, remains imperceptible even to the penitent. Nor will the penitent detect a change in his or her disposition toward virtue or vice, but will be subject to the same sinful desires that were present prior to penitential cleansing. The changes enacted by penance are thus invisible, and knowledge of penitential absolution is an act of faith.

Yet, as Hilton's description suggests, penitential changes, though invisible as effects, nevertheless maintain a kind of presence as a ritual process experienced in time. Penitential changes are simultaneously visible as rites, and invisible but present as changes in a sinner's self-knowledge: the penitent shall nonetheless "trowe [trust] that he is thorugh grace reformed to the likenesse of God, though he neithir feele it ne see it." Notably, in Hilton's formulation, the soul's self-knowledge depends not upon knowing something with certainty but upon an intentional act of acknowledgment. Whereas Eucharistic ritual puts particular emphasis on the visibility of the elements, on the moment of consecration when the priest elevates the Host for adoration, penance is traditionally understood as a series of acts done by penitent and priest: contrition, confession, and satisfaction. Yet like the Eucharist, penance is a miracle only seen with the eyes of faith. Indeed, it could not be otherwise, as Roger Dymmok points out in his 1395 treatise against the lollards, for the sensible elements of the sacraments point to a reality far beyond anything the senses can represent.[1] Like the other sacraments, penance consists in tension between the visible and invisible, between what is external and set before the senses and what is internal and hidden. As Hilton indicates, from within that tension penance educates its participants in the most profound and intimate demands of Christian faith.[2]

As the large number of surviving manuscripts attest, Hilton's *Scale* was one of the most popular devotional works in late medieval England, and the author of the late fifteenth-century East Anglian morality *Wisdom* turned to the *Scale*, and a host of other devotional texts, to craft the dialogue of his play.[3] However, even as the author of *Wisdom* drew on Hilton's ideas, he also significantly modified them. For the play's author notably makes visible precisely what for Hilton must remain invisible. In *Wisdom*, the changes wrought upon the soul by the experiences of sin and penance are anything but hidden. Whereas *The Castle of Perseverance* allegorically merges physical space and moral action in order to demonstrate their interdependence, *Wisdom* reimagines contemplative instructional models in order to show how the performance of penitential ritual activates the soul's self-knowledge.

Wisdom personifies the human soul as the female, complaisant, naïve, and remarkably protean Anima. In the first scenes, she is depicted as the *sponsa* of bridal mysticism and student of divine Wisdom. When she is drawn by Lucifer into a life of sin, the play conceptualizes her fall in terms of the doctrine of the *imago Dei* and the trajectory through which the soul is corrupted by sin and then restored through divine grace to its original state in God's image. Through a series of costume changes, the play visually charts Anima's progression from her initial state of purity tainted by original sin through her fall into sin and her return to grace after she confesses. Initially, Anima appears clothed in a white robe and black mantle, but she loses that costume, becoming horribly disfigured under the influence of Lucifer. Her eventual return to grace is indicated by a corresponding return to the white robe and black mantle. The changes wrought by penance are thus signified through reference to another sacrament, as Anima's costume changes reverse the liturgical clothing of a newly baptized infant in a white chrismal robe.[4] More strikingly still, in this highly material depiction of the soul, female Anima is recast in the middle of the drama as her three male "mights," Mind, Will, and Understanding.[5] As in the Augustinian contemplative tradition from which the play draws, the inner faculties of the soul are a trinity with functions parallel to the divine Trinity. In that tradition, the soul gains self-knowledge by entering into itself through meditation, thereby coming to spiritual knowledge of God. However, in *Wisdom* the inner faculties of the soul are radically exteriorized: Anima's mights appear as three new actors and replace her for much of the remainder of the drama. Portraying the soul's faculties as they move through the stages of sin and penance, the play thus presents a particularly energetic late medieval account of the relationship between exterior experiences and institutions and the interior motion of the soul.

By appropriating the contemplative discourse of the soul's self-knowledge, *Wisdom* suggests that the sensible, material signs of orthodox liturgical practice are the very matter through which humans gain knowledge of, as Anima puts it, the "Godehede incomprehensyble" (94). A personification allegory that stages the processes through which its protagonist learns the meaning of her own name, the play investigates how the initiate learns the meanings of words that are central to the formation of the Christian subject. Early on, Anima states:

> O soueren Auctoure most credyble,
> Yowr lessun I attende, as I owe,

I þat represent here þe sowll of man.
    Wat ys a sowll, wyll ȝe declare?
                    (99–102)

Anima reveals that the label "soul" at present means nothing to her. Her inability to read the allegory of which she is a part is caused by (and indeed equivalent to) her lack of self-knowledge. Her catechetical questions at the beginning of the play point to her lack of the forms of self-recognition that would inform even a rudimentary Christian understanding of what a "soul" is. She will only gain that knowledge through being initiated into the forms of human life shared by the church, and through penitential ritual in particular. *Wisdom* depicts the formation of the Christian soul through a process that moves both inward to identify the soul's inner faculties and outward to describe those faculties' experience of sin and repentance in the world.[6] Presenting her initial innocence not as sinlessness but as a lack of self-knowledge, Anima will only recognize herself as a sinner and creature through the penitential experiences of sin, repentance, and forgiveness.

By foregrounding the experiential nature of self-knowledge, the play indicates the importance of social and material performance and ritual practice to learning a language, including a language to describe the self. Such an emphasis on the social practice of language can usefully be understood in Wittgensteinian terms. For Wittgenstein, language is more than the mere attachment of labels to things; rather, "the *speaking* of language is part of an activity, or of a form of life."[7] Anima's bewilderment suggests that a person does not learn what a "soul" is simply by being told that she is one. Nor does one learn what a soul is, as the play will show, by being given a schematic description of its faculties. Rather, the play demonstrates that one only comes to that knowledge through sensible and communal processes of generating meaning. Learning a language is bound up with one's specific, discernible experiences and interactions in the world. The play suggests that the answer to Anima's question lies not in merely knowing the word for "soul" but in knowing what it is *to be* a soul. For it is one thing to believe in the forgiveness of sin and another to know what it is to be forgiven. That distinction is helpfully elucidated by Stanley Cavell, here explaining Wittgenstein's vision of language:

In "learning language" you learn not merely what the names of things are, but what a name is; not merely what the form of expression is for expressing a wish, but what expressing a wish is. . . . In learning language, you do not merely learn the pronunciation of sounds, and their grammatical orders, but the "forms of life" which make those sounds the words they are, do what they do. . . . Instead, then, of saying either that we *tell* beginners what words mean, or that we *teach* them what objects are, I will say: We initiate them, into the relevant forms of life held in language and gathered around the objects and persons of our world.[8]

Anima is introduced to the forms of Christian life through her experiences of sin and reconciliation through penitential ritual. Penance acts as a form of instruction that literally shapes the human soul, as Anima and her mights participate in the divine activity of penitential cleansing and are reformed in God's image in one and the same movement.

Although *Wisdom*, like the *Castle*, makes no explicit reference to the lollard movement, *Wisdom*'s valuation of visual signs and ritual experience stands in stark contrast to two of the most threatening lollard views: their challenge to the centrality of the sacraments and condemnation of the use of images in orthodox devotional practice. By the time that *Wisdom* was written, most likely in the late 1460s, lollard activity had largely been driven underground, but contemporary trial records indicate the persistence of Wycliffite ideas in East Anglia throughout the fifteenth century.[9] Moreover, its specter can be seen in a renewed interest in orthodox artistic productions of the sacraments in East Anglia during this period, including dramatic works such as the Croxton Play of the Sacrament and the morality plays themselves.[10] Significantly, in *Wisdom* the pedagogical value of penance is not restricted to Lenten homiletic or catechetical instruction, nor does the spiritual education prescribed by the play depend upon lay access to and study of scripture, as Wycliffite pedagogical models required. Instead, the ritual experience of penance is itself the locus of the sinner's education. The play thus functions as a complex response to lollard views about the sacraments: *Wisdom* shows that penance is not simply a vehicle for the communication of church doctrine and authority, but a ritual that constructs meanings and values (such as what a soul is) that are central to Christian faith.

Contrition, Confession, and Satisfaction: The Matter of Penance

In depicting the inner faculties of the soul as they experience penitential ritual, *Wisdom* enters into a particularly fraught area of medieval theology. Of all the sacraments, penance was most problematic because of the relationship between the inner and outer actions involved in it. Medieval penance required penitents to feel sorrow for their sins, confess their sins to a priest, and perform acts of restitution to God, church, and neighbor. It thus entailed both inner acts of contrition and outer acts of confession and satisfaction, whose relationship to one another and role in sacramental efficacy was subject to controversy, as seen in the Scholastic debates that surrounded the sacrament during the twelfth and thirteenth centuries.[11] Those who followed in the tradition of the twelfth-century theologians Peter Abelard and Peter Lombard stressed the importance of the penitent's sorrow, holding the priest's role to be merely declarative. However, such "declarative" theories of absolution risked making the priest superfluous to the forgiveness of sin. In contrast, the "indicative" theories that became prominent in the thirteenth century gave the priest much more power. For Thomas Aquinas, only the dual action of the contrition of the penitent and action of the priest produced grace. Justification came from the "work worked" (*opere operato*): the power of the sacramental sign. Duns Scotus emphasized the role of the priest even more, distinguishing between the fully contrite and the merely attrite. As most sinners fell into the latter category, they required sacerdotal absolution to make up for the deficiencies of their sorrow. According to Scotist doctrine, the priest's act of absolution—not contrition, confession, and satisfaction—is the very essence of the sacrament. Although the *Omnis utriusque sexus* decree made annual auricular confession mandatory, the different theories of forgiveness remained in tension with one another. As Thomas Tentler has shown, no one Scholastic doctrine of forgiveness prevailed in the *summas* and manuals for confession and pastoral care that came out of twelfth- and thirteenth-century developments in theology and ecclesiastical legislation.[12]

Wisdom's staging of the soul's inner faculties can be read as a similar attempt to reconcile the inner and outer acts demanded by penance, because the play progressively charts the changes wrought upon the soul's interior as it falls into sin, becomes contrite, and subsequently confesses. Notably, even though the play's visual iconography makes clear the absolute necessity of both contrition and confession, Anima's confession takes place offstage. In sharp contrast to the Scotist emphasis on sacerdotal absolution, any mention of a priest and his speech acts are absent.

Questions about the relative roles and necessity of contrition, confession, and satisfaction were not just the province of Scholastic debate. In elaborating the relation between the inner and outer acts required by penance, *Wisdom* also takes up a set of well-defined pastoral concerns. The tension between the different components of penance is felt acutely in orthodox penitential manuals, and perhaps most vividly in the early fifteenth-century treatise *Jacob's Well*, a work that explicitly inveighs against the "fals techyng" (164/34) of the lollards. The exempla of *Jacob's Well* repeatedly underscore that the forgiveness of sins depends equally upon the penitent's inner sorrow and the outer ritual actions performed by penitent and priest. On the one hand, *Jacob's Well* cautions that the emotional requirements of contrition are rigorous: a penitent's sorrow must be "depe in sorwe downward, to helle-warde, thynkyng how þou for þi synne art boundyn to þe pytt of helle for euere, 3if þou deye wyth-oute sorwe" (170/11–13). Contrition must also have the correct motivation: in one exemplum, a man is damned despite his deathbed confession to a priest, because his sorrow for his sins "was more for dreed of helle þan for sorwe of wretthyng my god" (177/1–2). Yet, in danger of emphasizing the importance of contrition at the expense of confession and satisfaction, the author of *Jacob's Well* simultaneously stresses that contrition alone is insufficient for cleansing the soul from sin:

> And 3if þi sorwe be neuere so grete, & þou wylt no3t be schreuyn, & do penaunce, ne make amendys, þe synne is stylle in þi soule, for þi sowre þanne castyth it no3t out. (174/16–18)

Inward states must manifest themselves in outward acts: contrition must be accompanied by a willingness to confess and perform acts of satisfaction. A sick man who is in "full sorwe" (66/10) and confesses to his priest nonetheless goes to hell because he refuses to restore the goods he has wrongfully obtained for fear of leaving his wife and children in poverty. In yet another exemplum, a woman sleeps with her son, becomes pregnant by him, and kills her infant. Her sorrow for her sins is profound, she submits herself to severe acts of penance, yet she does not confess. Indeed, it is the very depth of her contrition that erroneously prevents her from confessing: "In here herte, sche was sory, & alwey preyed god of mercy, & dede scharpe dedys of penaunce, & made restitucyoun of here wrongys, saaf sche durste noȝt be schreuyn of here cursyd synne, for schame" (67/2–5). When a fiend disguised as a clerk publicly accuses the woman of her crimes, she finally confesses. Her completion of penance renders a transformation so complete that she is no longer even recognizable to the fiend: "It is noȝt þis womman þat I haue accusyd; þis womman is holy, & marie kepith here" (67/25–26). Illustrating the dangers of omitting any one part of the penitential process, *Jacob's Well*'s narratives by their very profusion attest to the necessity of imagining the parts of the sacrament as an integrated whole and the difficulty with which that integration might be achieved. Stressing the importance of one aspect of penance runs the risk of devaluing others.

Like *Jacob's Well*, *Wisdom* assiduously illustrates the steps a penitent must take to cleanse the soul from sin. The play leaves no doubt of the necessity of both the interior act of contrition and the exterior act of confession, showing the effects each of those steps has upon the soul and its faculties. However, the play's "showing forth" of the soul's inner faculties and valuation of penance as a church-mediated ritual form also must be seen in the context of lollard challenges to the church's authority over the sacrament's administration and to the sacramental system as a whole. Lollard writers gave new urgency to the old problem of defining the relationship between the inner and outer acts of penance. As Katherine Little argues, lollard writers frequently underscored the ways in which traditional confessional discourses and practices, and the power relations inherent in them, served to obstruct rather than facilitate the expression of a penitent's interior experience, thereby suggesting their inadequacy as a means of representing the interior.[13] Moreover, as Little shows, lollard arguments about the difficulties inherent in speaking about the interior had a profound impact on orthodox and heterodox writers, shaking their confidence in the traditional languages of self-definition.[14] In contrast to lollard dismissals of contemporary confessional practices, *Wisdom* insists that such exterior acts have profound interior effects.

Wisdom's demonstration of how penance shapes the soul's inner faculties can be seen as a response to Wycliffite critiques of contemporary penitential practices. By avoiding staging the content of Anima's confession and the words of her confessor, the play downplays speech acts upon which lollard writers had put considerable pressure.[15] Indeed, when Anima goes to confess, no mention is made of a priest or his words of absolution whatsoever; the emphasis is instead upon the church as an institution. Wisdom sends Anima to be reconciled with "yowr modyr, Holy Chyrche" (982), and, upon returning from her confession, Anima states that it is Holy Church that has given her grace (1078). Shifting the emphasis away from the more controversial aspects of penance, the play instead concentrates on the role of contrition and confession in the acquisition of self-knowledge. Moreover, if, as Little contends, lollard writers suggested that traditional confessional language was an inadequate means of representing the interior, *Wisdom* takes an entirely different perspective. The play demonstrates the role of penitential ritual in shaping that very interior and the impossibility of splitting the interior from the exterior practices that define it.

The play's arresting visual imagery can also be read as a tacit riposte to lollard views on images. Wyclif and his early followers were only critical of devotional images insofar as their veneration was potentially idolatrous, but some later lollards rejected the traditional role of images as "the books of the unlearned."[16] William Thorpe, for instance, wrote: "it sufficiþ . . . to alle men þoruȝ heerynge and knowinge of Goddis worde . . . to bileuen into God þouȝ þei seeȝen neuere ymage maad wiþ mannes honde" (59/1150–53). Such trust in "dede ymagis," another Lollard writer argues, comes at the expense of loving God through keeping his commandments and practicing the works of mercy to one's poor neighbors, who are Christ's true image.[17] For those Wycliffites, the "sensible signes" of orthodox devotion are inferior to instruction through the direct study of scripture and, moreover, distract the faithful from more meaningful forms of worship.[18]

In sharp contrast to the antisacramentalism and iconoclasm expressed in lollard trial records, *Wisdom* mounts its defense of the sacrament of penance through a series of dramatic visual spectacles. Although, most readily, the play demonstrates the absolute necessity of confession to a priest, the play's rejoinder to lollard ideas presses far

beyond a simple, dogmatic visual assertion of the necessity of sacerdotal confession. Whereas lollard writers raised concerns about
whether mandatory confession could be considered a voluntary action
of the will, *Wisdom* puts Anima's "Will" on stage, demonstrating the
primary role played by both visual spectacle and sacramental ritual in
realigning the soul's will to God's. The play suggests that confession is
not merely an outward marker of a penitent's inward sorrow, but is—
as one of the human acts that make up the "matter" of penance—a
ritual act that is instrumental in the formation of Christian subjects.
Because the spectacles *Wisdom* employs to describe penitential action
derive primarily from the language of contemplation, I next examine
the play's appropriation of that tradition.

Inward Contemplation and Outward Performance

Critics have long noted *Wisdom*'s debt to contemplative literature.[19]
Whereas the Middle English cycle plays draw from Franciscan forms
of devotion, with their encouragement of affective identification with
Christ in his humanity, *Wisdom* is unique among the English moralities in its heavy reliance on contemplative texts for both its dialogue
and the conceptualization of its characters. As emerges from Walter K.
Smart's 1912 source study, much of its dialogue has been patched together from passages taken from a variety of devotional texts in English
and Latin. Wisdom and Anima's amorous opening exchange is drawn
from the English version of the *Orologium Sapientiae*, known as "The
Seven Poyntes of Trewe Wisdom," a translation of the German contemplative Henry Suso's fourteenth-century Latin text. When Anima
and Wisdom's flirtation gives way to a discussion of the nature and
structure of the human soul, that discussion is largely taken from
book 2 of Hilton's *Scale*.[20] When Wisdom tells Anima she will have
knowledge of God through "knowynge of yowrsylff" (95), his words
follow the pseudo-Bernardian *Meditationes Piissimae de Cognitione
Humanae Conditionis*, as do the sections of the play in which Anima's
three mights first appear and explain their theological significance and
attributes. The character Will's description of the nature of the human
will and Anima's account of God's benefits to humanity appear to be
elaborated through reference to another work once ascribed to Ber-

nard, the *Tractatus de Interiori Domo*, and Bonaventura's *Soliloquium de Quatuor Mentalibus Exercitiis*, respectively. In crafting his temptation of Anima's mights, Lucifer takes his arguments from Hilton's *On the Mixed Life*, twisting Hilton's advocacy of the "mixed life" — a life that balances the demands of a public, active life and the worldly renunciation necessitated by a life of contemplation — into an argument designed to persuade Anima's mights to abandon contemplation altogether. Once the fallen Anima has undergone penance, the play adapts distinctions made by Hilton in the *Scale* between the soul's reformation in faith (available to all Christians through confession) and the soul's reformation in feeling (achieved through contemplation and with great effort over a long period of time) to its description of the reformation undergone by Anima.[21] When Anima goes to confess, Wisdom outlines the "nine points" pleasing to God as described in the *Novem Virtutes*, a text once attributed to Richard Rolle, while Anima is offstage. In addition, the play's dialogue incorporates a number of Latin biblical verses and other short English texts.

Contemporary critical accounts of *Wisdom* have done much to identify the play's sources and unpack its theological influences, but they have not examined what is at stake in bringing such an array of devotional material to the morality play's penitential trajectory of innocence, fall, and repentance.[22] *Wisdom* is usually read as a straightforward, if somewhat confused, dramatization of the metaphors of contemplative and other devotional material, as a play that "derives its theatrical form from the visualizing of metaphor, from the concretizing of homiletic and scriptural proposition."[23] Such a dramatization has struck some critics as highly suspect, for the medium of theater seems particularly ill suited to "contemplative," let alone "mystical," experiences.[24] We are used to thinking of contemplation as an inward psychological state inimical to the temporal and public nature of theater, and the inherently interior and ineffable goals of contemplation would seem to stand in direct opposition to the inherent exteriority and corporeality of theater. Perhaps in part a response to such assumptions, a number of critics have highlighted the ways in which *Wisdom*'s theatrical form adds to — or subtracts from — the contemplative metaphors and propositions it adopts. For instance, Eugene D. Hill observes that the lines that introduce the mights' successive entrance "hammer home the idea of three-hood," thereby reflecting Augustine's distinction between the Trinity, which is "co-eternal, incorporeal, and ineffably unchangeable and inseparable," and the human soul, which is "subject to time and change."[25] More recently, Ruth Nisse shows that through its visualization of contemplative metaphors, the play reveals the spiritual dangers inherent in allegory and theater's particular susceptibility to carnal misreading.[26]

Yet *Wisdom*'s theatricalization of contemplative metaphors does more than underscore the distance between the human world and the divine and expound the dangers of misunderstanding contemplative directives. Rather, it co-opts contemplative metaphors in order to demonstrate the pedagogical value of the social and ritual practices that ground contemplative language. The contemplative tradition provides the play with an instructional model whereby the soul gains spiritual knowledge through self-knowledge. However, that model is transformed by the play's theatrical medium. Wisdom's presentation of the soul's inner faculties will not introduce a contemplative retreat away from the world, but it instead propels the soul into a very carnal world where sex is cheap, crime brings easy profits, and juries can be bribed. By bringing Anima's experience of sin and penance to the contemplative discourse of self-knowledge, the play relocates the site of instruction from the practice of contemplative inwardness to penitential ritual, making the language of contemplation inseparable from outward social and religious performance and practice. By bringing the discourse of self-knowledge to Anima's experience of penance, contemplative literature provides the play with a language for articulating the interior motions of the soul as it moves through the stages of initial innocence, fall, and repentance. In doing so, the play suggests the degree to which penance, like contemplation, engages the soul's self-knowledge of itself as sinner and creature and therefore its knowledge of God.

In *Wisdom*'s sources in the contemplative tradition, the soul comes to knowledge of God through meditating upon the soul's ability to remember, behold, and desire him, a practice that ultimately derives from Augustine's suggestion in *On the Trinity* that since humans are created in God's image, humans can gain knowledge of God through examining the human soul. In the course of their first conversation, Anima asks Wisdom how she may have knowledge of God, and Wisdom suggests that she will gain that knowledge through self-knowledge:

By knowynge of yowrsylff ȝe may haue felynge
Wat Gode ys in yowr sowle sensyble.
(95–96)

Notably, Wisdom suggests that such self-knowledge will produce a
"felynge" of God in her "sensyble" soul, suggesting that God's presence is learned and known in the arena of the sensible. Wisdom later
elaborates a route to such self-knowledge, prompting the entrance of
Anima's three mights:

> *Wysdam*: Thre myghtys euery Cresten sowll has,
>   Wyche bethe applyede to þe Trinyte.
> *Mynde*: All thre here, lo, byfor yowr face!
>   Mynde.
>   *Wyll*: Wyll.
>   *Wndyrstondynge*: Ande Vndyrstondynge, we thre.
>   (177–80)

By looking within the mind, says Mind, the soul sees the "benefyttys
of Gode and hys worthynes" (186). When we have good will, Will continues, "Gode ys in ws knett" (231). Understanding explains that "by
wndyrstondyng I beholde wat Gode ys" (246). As Smart has shown,
these passages sometimes loosely follow and sometimes quote directly
from the pseudo-Bernardian *Meditationes*. Like *Wisdom*, the *Meditationes* describe knowledge of the inner faculties of the soul as a route
to knowledge of God:

> *Per cognitionem mei valeam pervenire ad cognitionem Dei. Quanto
> namque in cognitione mei proficio, tanto ad cognitionem Dei
> accedo. Secundum interiorem hominem tria in mente mea invenio,
> per quae Deum recolo, conspicio, et concupisco. Sunt autem haec
> tria, memoria, intelligentia, voluntas sive amor. Per memoriam
> reminiscor; per intelligentiam intueor; per voluntatem amplector.
> Cum Dei reminiscor, in memoria mea eum invenio, et in ea de eo
> et in eo delector.*[27]

Wynkyn de Worde's 1496 translation of this passage reads:

By knowlege of myself, I maye ascende and come to the knowlege of God. For the more I prouffyte in knowlege of myself, the more nygh I drawe to the knowlege of God. In the inward mannys behalf I fynde thre thynges in my soule wherby I remembre, behold, and desire my lord God. The whiche ben the mynde, the understondynge, and wyll or love. By the mynde I remembre him. By the understondynge I beholde him ghostly. And by wyll or love: I love and desyre hym. Whan I remembre God I fynde in hym in my mynde. And fele therin in him swetnesse and playsur of hym.[28]

Wisdom thus adopts a contemplative instructional model that identifies self-knowledge (whereby one looks to the powers of the soul through which one remembers, beholds, and desires God) as a route to knowledge of God. However, the contemplative "inward beholding" that leads to self-recognition is realized through a markedly outward *showing*. Visually dramatizing the soul's fall and recovery, the play demonstrates that the route to self-knowledge is a manifestly and materially penitential one. The pseudo-Bernardian *Meditationes* appear to be the direct source of the passage in which the mights first appear; however, in dramatizing the soul's recognition of its disfigurement by sin, *Wisdom* also roughly follows the contemplative trajectory Hilton describes in book 1 of the *Scale*. For Hilton, the soul's *recognition* of its fallen state is crucial to cultivating its desire to reform. The task of contemplation rests upon the soul's discovery that the original perfection of the *imago Dei* has been lost through sin. By turning inward, the soul will both see its original nature and desire to recover it:

In this inward biholdinge thou schalt mow see the worschipe and the dignité whiche it hadde bi kynde of the firste makynge, and thou schalt see also the wrecchidnesse and the myschief of synne whiche thou art fallen in. And of this sight schal come grete desire with longynge in thyn herte for to receyve agen that clennesse and that worschipe whiche thou hast lost. (1.42)

In *Wisdom*, Hilton's contemplative recognition of the soul's sin and subsequent desire to reform becomes highly ritualized. Anima's mights, having revealed their "wrecchidnesse" by abandoning contemplative pursuits for worldly ones, "bihold" their own sin and defilement when

Wisdom visually demonstrates the effects of sin upon Anima. They then desire to be reformed to their divine likenesses, a reform that takes place through their ritual performance of penance.

Despite the play's paralleling of contemplative and external forms of recognition, *Wisdom*'s invocation of the faculties of the soul might come off as odd to a modern reader: today we are used to thinking of contemplation as a wholly interior exercise. Notably, Anima's three mights derive from a contemplative tradition that has been understood to privilege intellectual union with the Godhead that takes no sensory or symbolic form.[29] Anima's acquisition of self-knowledge via her rambunctious three mights looks very peculiar when contrasted with the ultimate source of that tradition: Augustine's *On the Trinity*. In that work, Augustine suggests that because the mind is not a sensible thing, when the soul inquires into itself, it must withdraw from those sensible images that the mind has added to itself in order to see itself alone.[30] The mind must withdraw itself both from desire of the corporeal and any traces—footprints, to use Augustine's term—of the corporeal in the mind.[31] Having done so, the mind will gain knowledge of itself by making its own self-presence the object of its scrutiny: it must inspect its own powers of knowing. On that basis, Augustine singles out the trinity of *memoria*, *intelligentia*, and *voluntas* to show how the image of God can be found in them. Augustine's focus on inwardness and ascent gets taken up by later contemplative writers, including Hilton, whose *Scale* is another possible source of Anima's three mights.[32] Hilton follows Augustine in encouraging his reader to "entre into thyn owen soule bi meditacion, for to knowe what it is, and bi the knowynge therof for to come to the goostli knowynge of God" (1.40). He also follows Augustine in invoking the inner faculties or "myghtes"—"mynde, resoun and wille" (1.43)—as part of a contemplative progression in which the soul gains knowledge of itself as it withdraws from the senses and sensory images within the mind:

hanne schalt thou drawe into thisilf thi thought from thi bodili wittes, that thou take noo kepe what thou heerest or seest or felist, so that the poynt of thyn herte be not ficchid in hem. Aftir this drawe inner thi thought from al ymaginynge, yif thou mai, of ony bodili thyng, and from alle thoughtis of thi bodili dedis bifore doon, or of othere mennys dedys. (1.52)

Significantly, in this tradition the mind must know itself so that it may live according to its own nature in God, but is led into forgetfulness of itself when it becomes fixed upon external things. Indeed, when the mind connects itself too intimately with the images of the corporeal world, Augustine explains, it begins to think of itself as a corporeal thing.[33] Anima and her mights would seem to be an instance of that error par excellence.

The materiality of Anima's inward turn thus may seem to be an extraordinary misapplication of the contemplative text, especially given contemplative writers' repeated warnings against taking spiritual language literally.[34] In contrast to Augustine's and Hilton's emphasis on the gradual attenuation of the mind's attachment to sensory experience in the highest forms of contemplation, in *Wisdom* the interior of the soul is vigorously material. However, the apparent differences between contemplative and theatrical text belie the extent to which both Augustine and late medieval contemplative writers reflexively engage the interplay between the failure and necessity of using human signs to represent an unknowable God.[35] Tellingly, in *On the Trinity*, when Augustine states that the mind must inspect its own powers of knowing in order to locate the image of God within, he notably does so by directing his reader to concentrate upon a linguistic sign: "But when it is said to the mind, Know thyself; then it knows itself by that very act by which it understands *the word* 'thyself'; and this for no other reason than that it is present to itself."[36] The self is known through attending to one's acts of intention that are themselves produced and represented through the "sensible signs" of linguistic experience.

Moreover, whereas it might seem paradoxical from a modern perspective to show forth the faculties of the soul, that paradox is perhaps only due to the modern critical focus on interiority and inwardness, which depends upon the distinction between "inner" and "outer." For what is ultimately at stake for Augustine and the contemplative writers who followed him is *not* the assertion of a self with an "interior" in opposition to the sensible world. In Augustinian terms, the formation of the Christian subject is only comprehensibly understood in its reformation to its divine image. For Augustine, the self is only made complete through its participation in the love and beauty of the divine Trinity.[37] Such participation can only be achieved doxologically, through Christ's dual nature. In other words, such participation can only take place through the liturgical and other acts of devotion that *Wisdom* so carefully stages. In both Augustine and *Wisdom*, the soul's interior reform is inseparable from its exterior participation in acts of worship. Indeed, *Wisdom*'s theatrical portrayal of penitential self-knowledge inherently resists the notion of autonomous selfhood by showing that self to be a series of relations and positioning that self in front of an audience.

At issue for Augustine in his "retreat" from the sensible is not the discovery of an interior but the question of where one directs one's love. A focus on the self for the self's sake misses Augustine's point entirely, as becomes clear in Augustine's discussion of the earthly and heavenly cities in the *City of God*: "We see . . . that the two cities were created by two kinds of love: the earthly city was created by self-love reaching the point of contempt for God, the Heavenly City by the love of God carried as far as contempt of self. In fact, the earthly city glories in itself, the Heavenly City glories in the Lord."[38] For Augustine, the self only exists insofar as it participates in divine reality. Similarly, in *Wisdom*, the faculties come into being through their participation in the Trinity:

> *Wysdom*: By Mynde feythe in þe Father haue we,
>   Hoppe in owr Lorde Jhesu by Wndyrstondynge,
>   Ande be Wyll in þe Holy Gost charyte.
>   (285–87)

Here the soul is realized in and through a temporally and materially situated posture of devotion as it engages in the virtues of faith, hope, and charity. The play also suggests through its costuming that the soul only exists in its reformation to its divine image: Anima herself is constituted by her likeness to divine Wisdom, becoming disjointed and disfigured—and indeed invisible offstage—as she and her three mights fall into sin.

THE EDUCATION OF ANIMA

If *Wisdom*'s contemplative sources stress the acquisition of self-knowledge, Anima's most striking feature at the beginning of the play is her utter lack of it. She parrots the language of affective devotion but lacks the forms of self-recognition necessary to understand the nature of her relationship to Wisdom and thus the meaning of her words. She will only recognize what it is to be a soul (and thus her relation to Wisdom) through the "sensyble" penitential experiences of fall and redemption. In Wittgensteinian terms, she has not yet been initiated into the Christian "forms of life" that would give her words the point and shape they have in Christian lives.[39] The contemplative language of self-knowledge thus is shown to be deeply inadequate in the absence of the soul's self-recognition of its true relation to God, a recognition that can only take place through the soul's participation in Christian ritual and practice. In thus transferring the site of instruction from contemplation to the soul's experience of fall and redemption, the play presents a pedagogy in which performances—and especially the performance of the sacrament of penance—literally take center stage.

In transferring the site of instruction from "interior" contemplation to "exterior" material and temporal experiences, *Wisdom* does not in fact stray at all far from medieval contemplative practices as they were traditionally understood. The use of the senses to bring knowledge of the divine is of course the central strategy of positive forms of contemplation that, like the sacraments, focus upon the senses' capacity to direct souls to God. The first scenes of the play are rooted firmly in the positive tradition. Wisdom and Anima's opening exchange, based on Suso's *Orologium*, draws upon positive and affective traditions derived from Bernard of Clairvaux's *Sermons on the Song of Songs*. When Anima identifies herself as the spouse and lover of Wisdom (17–20), her words draw on the Bernardine tradition of allegorizing the erotic imagery of the Song of Songs to describe the relationship between the human soul and Christ.

From her first encounter with Wisdom, however, it is clear that her role as the *sponsa* of bridal mysticism is compromised by her inability to connect carnal meanings to their spiritual significance. As writers in affective tradition were well aware, a possible danger in that mode of devotion lay in a reader's inability to move beyond literal, carnal meanings.[40] In the first scenes of the play, Anima's adoration of her beloved resembles a schoolgirl crush. Wisdom brags at length about his brightness, power, and goodness: "How louely I am, how amyable, / To be halsyde and kyssyde of mankynde" (43–44). Meanwhile, Anima gushes:

"A, soueren Wysdom, yff yowur benygnyte, / Wolde speke of loue, þat wer a game" (39–40). Wisdom's words may appear to make him culpable, but the point here is not that the Son of God is a Casanova, but that a soul without self-knowledge could not tell the difference between the Son and a Lothario. Without a certain kind of self-knowledge (a kind of self-knowledge that would help Anima avoid the seductions of Lucifer), the play suggests, the human position in relationship to the figure of Christ is naïve, even bordering on the sycophantic. The play thus reflects the danger in affective piety in mistaking the medium for the message. Anima's counterpart in the English *Orologium* displays a similar lack of spiritual understanding. When the disciple longs for Wisdom's "speciale love amounge alle oþere," the *Orologium* Wisdom corrects him for understanding his love carnally: "þi love, þowh hit be feruent, neuerlese hit semeþ sumwhat blendete, in as miche as þou felest of goddelye and heuenlye þinges in manere of erþlye þinges."[41] Anima makes a similar error: like the *Orologium* disciple, she has a limited understanding of her relationship to the human Christ. However, Anima is not guilty of only reading the *sensus literalis*; after all, she understands herself not to be just a lover but also a soul. She is simply unsure what a soul is.

Love of Christ—the engagement of the *affectus*—without the forms of self-recognition necessary to understand one's true relationship to Christ proves to be a deeply insufficient mode of devotion.[42] Put into the mouth of the naïve Anima, her catechetical questions betray her ignorance of the doctrine of redemption and dramatize the limits of her understanding that she as "soul" is lover of Wisdom. Indeed, her very mode of questioning, in that it seems to seek doctrinal answers, signals her lack of self-knowledge at this point in the play. Told that she is "dysvyguryde be hys [Adam's] synne, / Ande dammyde to derknes from Godys syghte" (117–18), she asks, "How dothe grace þan ageyn begynne? / Wat reformythe þe sowll to hys fyrste lyght?" (119–20). Yet her questions reveal that even if her adoration of Wisdom is naïve, such adoration allows her to anticipate God's grace. She thus exhibits the beginnings of Christian self-knowledge (she understands herself to love and be loved by God and desires further knowledge of him), yet fails to recognize that knowledge as a form of self-knowledge.

Specifically, Anima lacks the forms of self-recognition that would ground her knowledge of the doctrines Wisdom has taught her. A speech given shortly before Lucifer's arrival illustrates the nature of the limitations of her understanding:

> Soueren Lorde, I am bownde to the!
> Wan I was nought þou made me thus gloryus;
> Wan I perysschede thorow synne þou sauyde me;
> Wen I was in grett perell, þou kept me, Cristus;
> Wen I erryde þou reducyde me, Jhesus;
> Wen I was ignorant þou tawt me truthe;
> Wen I synnyde þou corecte me thus;
> Wen I was hewy þou comfortede me by ruthe.
>   (309–16)

Ignorant of the doctrine of redemption at the beginning of the play, Anima now proclaims an understanding of it. However, her understanding of her debt to Christ is couched in the language of experience; as the audience has witnessed, she has had little access to the forms of life about which she speaks. Until she is initiated into those forms of life, her words remain empty.[43] Even though she can now give an account of her debt to Christ, she does not yet have the deeper understanding of that debt the experiences she describes would afford her. From what the audience has seen, the ingenuous Anima has not in fact been disabled by sin, found refuge in Christ when she was in peril, or possessed a heart weighed by sorrow. Terms such as "sin," "peril," "refuge," "comfort," and "grace" will only have any purchase once she has undergone the experiences of sin and penance and, through them, begun to grasp grace and recognize herself as a sinner and creature. Until then, her understanding of the doctrines Wisdom has taught her remains tenuous and artificial, leaving her vulnerable to Lucifer's machinations.

Anima and her mights' fall depends upon their failure to recognize Lucifer, who disguises himself during their encounter. Their failure to recognize him is finally a failure of self-recognition, for his temptation succeeds only insofar as they fail to recognize themselves and their true relation to God. Lucifer's costuming, a distorted version of Anima's layered "foul and fair" attire, suggests the degree to which his temptation presents a false *imago Dei*.[44] The stage directions specify that he enters "in a dewyllys aray wythowt and wythin as a prowde galonte" (324sd). Accordingly, the actor playing Lucifer must take off his devil's costume in order to appear as a gallant in front of Anima's mights. Tony Davenport has pointed out the irony that as the character of Lucifer "puts on" the costume of a gallant, the actor playing him sheds one.[45] Muddying any easy distinction between outer appearance and inner reality, Lucifer's costume strives to make any act of "recognition" incomprehensible: his "true" identity—which can only be discovered somewhere "underneath" his external appearance—is paradoxically the façade. He is, in other words, at heart a deceiver.

Through his attempts to pervert the mights' understanding of the temporal world, Lucifer attempts to alienate Anima's mights from God and their divine origin. Contemporary contemplative manuals warned that anything that causes the contemplative to withdraw from worship of God or the pursuit of virtue is a sure sign of the devil's influence.[46] Lucifer's temptation is an attempt to get the mights to do exactly that. He misquotes Hilton's reminders in *On the Mixed Life* that a man who wishes to pursue a life of contemplation must not neglect his worldly responsibilities, because others depend upon him for their well-being (405–11).[47] Similarly, the Augustinian doctrine that because God created the world, there is no evil inherent in it becomes in Lucifer's hands an argument for hedonism:

> What synne ys in met, in ale, in wyn?
> Wat synne ys in ryches, in clothynge fyne?
> (473–74)

An audience easily recognizes Lucifer's words as the talk of the devil; the mights' failure to do so indicates their failure to recognize the world's and their own proper relation to God. In contrast, the mights' eventual reform is presented as an act of recovered self-recognition. Faced with the visual evidence of Anima's disfigurement via her own sartorial transformation, the three mights are brought to horrified recognition of their disfigurement and thus "remembyr" (873) themselves.

Anima will only gain the forms of self-recognition she lacks through her initiation into the forms of Christian life. That initiation begins with Wisdom's verbal instruction; however, it is only completed through Anima and her mights' participation in a series of performances. Notably, although the play shows forth the soul's cognitive faculties, Wisdom himself puts particular emphasis on the role the faculties of sensation and cognition play in learning about God (135–60). The play places the sacraments — and penance in particular — at the center of that initiation. When Anima inquires how the soul can be re-formed to its original likeness, Wisdom sets out to describe all seven sacraments but stops short after only describing baptism, deferring discussion of the other sacraments, including penance (121–32). Because Anima is liturgically innocent at this point in the play, it is only appropriate that she is only taken as yet through the sacrament of baptism, the sacrament that signifies a soul's entry into Christian community. And, because it must be done on the infant's behalf, baptism also signifies the soul's creaturely dependence upon Christian community.

A staged performance makes *Wisdom*'s visual emphasis on the role of ritual, performance, and pageantry in shaping the human soul unmistakable. The stage directions include four processionals, and much of the action in the scenes of the mights' fall is taken up with the dances of the mights and their liveried retainers. Riggio's comments on the 1984 Trinity College production of *Wisdom* give a sense of the importance of ritual to the play's structure and form:

> The play begins with a long expository dialogue between Wisdom and Anima, followed by a liturgical procession of Anima's five virgin "wits," expository speeches of Anima's three faculties or "Mights," and a chanted recessional. But *Wisdom* also operates on a principle of dramatic opposition. Lucifer's world of sin opposes and inverts Christ's state of grace in a way that polarizes piety and sin. Structurally, the play sets liturgical processions in opposition to masque dances. The result is a courtly play which ironically attacks the value of courtly entertainment and redefines courtly pageantry in liturgical terms.[48]

In accordance with the play's experiential, participatory, and active vision of the soul's interior, vice principally appears as social wrongs: when the mights succumb to Lucifer's arguments, they quickly become involved in contemporary abuses of power and manipulations of the law associated with the practice of maintenance, including blackmail, false arrest, bribery of juries, and unjust forfeiture. The soul's reformation also will be defined according to its activities in the social world: at the close of the play, in a passage that implicitly endorses the active life, Wisdom describes the life of virtue as a life defined by acts of charity and right relations with one's neighbor in a passage modeled on the *Novem Virtutes* (997–1064).[49] Through such experiences, Anima and her mights' understanding of Wisdom will expand and contract. As their ability to recognize Wisdom as the Son of God changes, the word "wisdom" is redefined: in Anima's fallen state, her might Understanding insidiously will proclaim: "To be fals, men report yt game; / Yt ys clepyde wysdom" (603–4). Similarly, the meaning of words such as "clene," "grace," and "hales" vary according to Anima's and her mights' spiritual states.[50]

In its emphasis on the formative role of ritual and other forms of sensory experience, the play does not imagine the Christian faith as primarily a set of beliefs or doctrines. Rather, it presents Christianity as, in Wittgensteinian terms, an activity, a set of practices and performances that shape the human soul. Explicitly rejecting the learning of the "schools," the play reimagines intellectual inquiry in a different mode. In contrast to the lay biblical exegesis and religious questioning so crucial to Wycliffite pedagogies, Wisdom reflects the orthodox view that learned disputation should be reserved for the clergy. When Anima requests that Wisdom teach her the "scolys of yowr dyvynyte" (86), he admonishes her to avoid schoolbook knowledge and encourages her instead to practice "heelfull dyscyplyne" (89) through which she must rid herself of the "wedys of synne" (91), fear God, and cultivate "swete wertuus herbys" (92). This passage departs from its source in the English *Orologium* in which worldly schools are rejected for the "scole (of) soþfaste diuinyte" (327).[51] In *Wisdom*, by contrast, learned disputation is rejected in favor of a kind of knowledge that can only be gained through "heelfull dyscyplyne," that is, the performance of virtue and other acts of devotion.

ANATOMY OF A SACRAMENT

By showing the transformation undergone by the soul and its inner faculties as they fall into sin and then progress through the stages of penance, *Wisdom* suggests the impact of exterior experiences and institutions—for better or worse—upon the soul's interior. In doing so, it uses its theatrical form to reaffirm the role of the church in the forgiveness of sins by elaborating a deep relation between exterior acts—

and especially the exterior acts entailed by penance—and the soul's interior processes. In opposition to lollard polemic, the play's staging of Anima's performance of penance demonstrates the necessity of both confession to a priest and contrition. Yet more importantly, its depiction of the soul's trajectory through sin and penance seeks to redress lollard critiques of the sacraments by showing that Anima's reformation takes place through a set of materially and temporally situated performances and ritual practices that serve to shape her innermost faculties, at once reforming them to God's image and providing Anima with the forms of self-recognition she initially lacks. *Wisdom* thus presents penance as a performance that is instrumental to the very formation of Christian subjects, for in the same moment penance reforms the soul to God's image, the soul learns what a soul is.

Anima's epiphanic moment of inward self-understanding occurs through a visual, highly ritualized, and exteriorized demonstration. As the play progresses, interior and exterior experiences become increasingly indistinguishable. Anima's mights' externally realized transgressions are revealed to have markedly inward effects. Wisdom shows the mights the disastrous consequences of their sins by bringing Anima, now disfigured, back on stage. In *Wisdom*, the wages of sin must be visually demonstrated before they can be felt: the *sight* of Anima's disfiguration alone serves as the catalyst of the mights' spiritual reform.[52] As I will describe in chapter 3, the protagonist of *Mankind* is tortured at the hands of the vices until he cries out for Mercy. In contrast, Anima does not realize the implications of sin through emotional and physical suffering.[53] Rather, the play shows that the mights will only "see themselves" through being *shown* and not just *told* something. When Wisdom reappears at the end of the play, he attempts to arouse their contrition using words alone: "O thou Mynde," he begs, "remembyr the!" (873), but they fail to respond. In a moment that emphatically affirms the didactic and transformative power of visual signs, the mights finally realize the implications of their sins only when Anima reappears, "in þe most horrybull wyse, fowlere þan a fende" (902sd) and Wisdom directs them to "loke veryly in mynde" (902). Reinvoking the Trinitarian and baptismal imagery of the first scenes of the play, Wisdom admonishes the mights for defouling their natural likeness to God (905–6). He directs their attention to the seven deadly sins—dramatized by seven small boys dressed as devils who run out from under Anima's cloak and back in again—who now inhabit the soul (912sd).[54]

As if to answer any uncertainty about whether contrition or confession was the crucial factor in the forgiveness of sins, Anima's performance of penance is carefully choreographed to show the necessity of *both* contrition and confession. The sacramental effect of penance is shown iconographically as a two-stage process that recalls the contemporary liturgical practice in which the devil is exorcised outside the church before an infant is taken inside to be baptized.[55] Similarly, in *Wisdom*, the devil first must be routed out by Anima's sorrow for her sins before she goes to confess to a priest. The play leaves no doubt that it is Anima's *contrition* that drives the devil out. The mights quickly discover that simply recognizing that they have sinned is not enough to bring about a change in Anima's state (925–62). It is only when Anima, prompted by Wisdom, expresses sorrow for her sins that a virtual exorcism takes place: the same seven boys dressed as devils run out from under her mantle (979sd), leaving the stage, as Wisdom declares, "Lo, how contrycyon avoydyth þe deullys blake! / Dedly synne ys non yow wythin" (979–80). In the second part of her reform, Anima must confess in order to be absolved of sin—actions that take place offstage—before she can shed the costume of her disfigurement and resume her original finery (981–96; 1064sd). Her lines after she has confessed imply that the essential action of the sacrament—the work of God forgiving sin—has taken place during her time offstage (1071–72). Anima's offstage confession is on the one hand pragmatic—it provides the actor playing her with an opportunity to make the necessary costume change; on the other, it serves to establish contrition as the most visually dramatic moment of the soul's restoration. It thus marks the importance of penitential sorrow for one's sins in an altogether different way than penitential manuals with their emphasis on the examination of conscience, yet simultaneously underscores the necessity of confession and the crucial role played by the established church in the justification of sin. And, by having Anima's confession take place offstage, the play is able to elide the juridical role of the priest in penance, one of the most objectionable elements of the ritual, according to lollard critiques. Finally, in sending Anima offstage to confess, it avoids the dangerous suggestion that sacerdotal confession and absolution are mere theater.

Yet it is not only the necessity of both contrition and confession that is at issue here. By putting the faculties of the soul onstage to go through the rite of penance, the play demonstrates that the sacramental action of penance brings together the intentional ritual subject in relation to prescribed ritual action. Reorganizing the three mights according to their role in the penitential process, Wisdom suggests a deep relationship between outer and inner actions:

> By wndyrstondynge haue very contrycyon,
>   Wyth mynde of your synne confessyon make,
>   Wyth wyll yeldynge du satysfaccyon.
>
> (973–75)

As Wisdom reorganizes the mights according to their role in the penitential process, contrition becomes not an exclusively inward act but one that is finally inextricable from outward participation in penitential ritual. Whereas in theological and pastoral accounts of the sacrament inner contrition and outer ritual form are only joined with difficulty, in the play inner and outer become one. Wisdom's words insist that confession is an activity of the mind as well as the mouth, and that satisfaction is an activity of the will as well as the body. In that formulation, as sorrow binds the soul to confession and satisfaction, outer ritual acts are deeply tied to the inner subjective state of the penitent.

By so deeply embedding inner and outer actions, the play underscores the importance of contrition while heading off any suggestion that an inner act of the will outside of any ritual action is sufficient for the forgiveness of sin. More importantly, Anima and her mights' dramatic transformation suggests the critical role played by penitential performances in reshaping the soul to God's image. When Anima leaves the stage to confess, she is accompanied by Mind, Will, and Understanding. Anima and her mights, who have become increasingly disjointed and conflictive as the play has progressed, are now coordinated in procession and song. Anima proclaims:

> Wyth Mynde, Vndyrstondynge, and Wyll ryght,
>   Wyche of my Sowll þe partyes be,

To þe domys of þe Chyrche we xall vs dyght,
    Wyth veray contricyon thus compleynnyng we.
                                            (993–96)

Accompanied by her mights, Anima exits singing verses from the Holy
Thursday liturgy (996sd). When they return, Anima is preceded by
her Fyve Wyttys, flanked by Mind and Understanding, and followed
by Will, who together sing the verses of thanksgiving from Psalm 115
that are traditionally spoken by the celebrant of the Mass (1064sd).[56]
Ritual is instrumental in organizing Anima and her mights into a uni-
fied posture of piety. Anima's and the mights' inner coordination as
"we" is inextricable from their outer coordination in ritual action,
where the liturgical use of the second-person plural serves to bring together multiple speakers, as Paul Connerton has observed, indicating
that "they are acting collectively, as if they were only one speaker, a
kind of corporate personality."[57] Whereas the mights' earlier behavior
dramatized the contrast between the immutable divine Trinity and its
image within the human soul, the mights' reformation in God's image
is both demonstrated and achieved through performances that bring
them into a single body.

Looking to the "interior" focus of contemplative practices, the
play elaborates the complex reforming of the human soul that takes
place in and through orthodoxy's central rituals. Through its adaptation of the contemplative tradition's detailed discussion of properties
of the human soul, the play insists upon the intentionality of ritual action in the face of accusations that sacramental rituals are but empty
forms; through its appropriation of the contemplative language of self-
knowledge, Wisdom shows that such language is itself inadequate, and
indeed incomprehensible, without the forms of self-recognition only
available through Christian ritual practice. In other words, Wisdom's
showing forth of the faculties of the human soul as they move through
the stages of penance is less an attempt to demonstrate that the soul
is defiled through sin and purified through penitential ritual than an
attempt to reveal how the formation of the Christian soul takes place
though the visible ritual practices that seek to acknowledge (rather
than represent) a divine reality that will finally always remain invisible.

For, as in Hilton's description of the inner transformations wrought
by penance in the Scale, in Wisdom the changes enacted in the soul by
penitential ritual are finally invisible. In contrast to her earlier speeches

in which she praised Wisdom's beauty, Anima's words at the end of the play are grounded in her knowledge of herself as a sinner and of Christ's mercy. Returning to the language of bridal mysticism that character-ized the first scenes of the play, Anima's words are now informed by an acknowledgment of her debt. Through a language itself a marriage of opposites—action and thought, human and divine, death and resur-rection, carnal and spiritual—her words testify to her knowledge of divine mystery and love:

> O Jhesu, þe sune of Vyrgyne Marye,
>   Full of mercy and compassyon!
>   My soule ys waschede be thy passyon
>   Fro þe synnys cummynge by sensualyte.
>   A, be the I haue a new resurreccyon.
>   The lyght of grace I fele in me.
> (1067–72)

Sin, as Anima acknowledges, comes "by sensualyte," but the play has also demonstrated that the same realm of the senses and experience is central to generating knowledge about virtue. Anima's words speak to a knowledge, acquired through her experience of sin and other sensible experiences, that now informs her devotion to Wisdom, for here the play situates her penitential reconciliation within the ultimate sym-bolism of penance: Christ's death and resurrection as a reconciliation of humans with God. The elaborate spectacle of Anima and her inner faculties' penitential cleansing is finally a visible sign of the invisible grace of human redemption. For it is, *Wisdom* insists, through the elaborate spectacles of orthodox practice, the sensible signs through which the divine is not studied but recognized, that such grace is known.

CHAPTER THREE

Speaking for Mankind

What is required in confronting another person is . . . your being willing, from whatever cause, to take his or her position into account, and bear the consequences. If the moralist is the human being who best grasps the human position, teaches us what our human position is, better than we know, in ways we cannot escape but through distraction and muddle, then our first task in subjecting ourselves to judgment is to tell the moralist from the moralizer. When Auden heard "the preacher's loose, immodest tone," he heard the tone of one speaking in the name of a position one does not occupy, confronting others in positions of which one will not imagine the acknowledgement.
— Stanley Cavell, *The Claim of Reason*

Prechyng is þo best, if hit be wil done.
— Wycliffite treatise "On the Seven Deadly Sins"

The East Anglian Shrovetide play *Mankind* commences with an address that is delivered, as has often been observed, in highly aureate language: "The very fownder and begynner of owr fyrst creacyon," grandly commences a character who will soon identify himself as Mercy, "amonge ws synfull wrechys he oweth to be magnyfyede" (1–2). Likely dressed as a priest or a friar, Mercy continues in this vein, admonishing his audience that their "obsequyouse seruyce to hym xulde be aplyede" (5) and beseeching them their "condycyons to rectyfye" (13).[1] Such prefatory homilizing—often delivered by God himself—is not unusual in late medieval drama. But when the vice Mischief enters, he specifically takes Mercy to task for the dullness, pomposity, and Latinity of his opening speech: "Yowr wytt ys lytyll, yowr hede ys mekyll [large], ȝe are full of predycacyon" (47). Mischief and three new vices, New Guise, Nowadays, and Nought, proceed to ridicule Mercy ruthlessly for his "Englysch Laten" (124) and "clerycall manere" (134). In short, they accuse him of alienating his audience, that is, of moralizing.

The act of moralizing—one form of speaking *to* people—is inextricable from *Mankind*'s concern to speak *for* all mankind. Though the play implicitly claims, in its choice of title character, to speak for mankind, it finally only authorizes that claim through exploring the question of how to speak *to* mankind. How to address lay audiences was of great concern to fifteenth-century preachers. In highlighting Mercy's Latinity, *Mankind* enters into much larger fifteenth-century debates about the authority of the clergy, the quality and purposes of preaching, and the most effective means of educating the laity on the principles of Christian faith. The Wycliffite emphasis on the direct preaching of God's word and condemnation of superfluous stylistic ornamentation, including extrascriptural stories, poems, and fables (and presumably moral allegories like *Mankind*), is well known.[2] Mercy's aureate language appears to reflect the actual practice of orthodox preachers. In her comprehensive survey of late medieval English sermons, H. Leith Spencer notes that "there seems to be some justice in the view that ambitious preachers throughout the period, but especially towards the second half of the fifteenth century, had a taste for long words."[3] Both *artes praedicandi* and orthodox sermons of the period advise preachers to be attentive to the needs and capacities of their audience, including when making stylistic choices. Some stress the need for eloquence: "What does not please is easily despised," observes one fifteenth-century preacher.[4] Others warn against excessive rhetorical decoration and vain self-display: "He who teaches what cannot be understood by his audience seeks not their benefit but his own ostentation."[5] Jeannette Dillon accordingly reads *Mankind* as a "plea for a middle way" between the excesses of Latinity that characterized fifteenth-century preaching and a Wycliffite emphasis on plain English.[6]

Yet the play's first scenes suggest that more is at stake between Mercy and the vices than questions of homiletic style. As the vices vie to take control of the stage action, they also attempt to control and determine the definition of "mankind." Mercy puts forward one version of the "human condition," to adopt Cavell's phrase, defining "mankind" primarily according to his obligation to God.[7] Mischief and his fellow vices seek to disrupt Mercy's pious pronouncements, styling his words as empty "predycacyon" and "dalyacyon" (47; 46) and implicitly redefining "mankind" according to self-interest and pleasure. In doing so, they threaten to steal the show entirely. When New Guise, Nowadays, and Nought enter, they declare themselves "mynstrellys" (72): they "leppe about lyuely" (76), volunteer to break their own necks for "sporte" (78), and try to goad Mercy into dancing with them. Mercy attempts to regain control of the play: "Do wey, do wey þis reull [revel], sers! do wey!" (82). Nowadays counters by telling him their antics are none of his business:

Do wey, goode Adam? do wey?
Thys ys no parte of þi pley.
(83–84)

Whereas Mercy has sought to confer a degree of sermonic solemnity to the events transpiring on stage, the vices proclaim they have substituted Mercy's "pley" with one of their own.[8] They mark their attempted overthrow with more metatheatrical humor. Nought orders Mercy to make a costume change, directing him to dress in a way more suitable to dancing: "of wyth yowr clothes, yf ȝe wyll play!" (88). Having himself "tracyed sumwhat to fell" [danced too violently], Nought complains that the space is too "narow" (96–97) for dancing. If the audience has grown bored with Mercy's sermonizing, the vices' shenanigans relieve the tedium. However, their antics also constitute a pointed assertion of their authority to control the play itself, as they seek to replace Mercy's somber exhortations with their own "mery chere" (81), to cast aspersions on Mercy's meanings, and to attempt to redefine the parameters of the playing space to accommodate their revelry: "How may yt be excusyde befor þe Justyce of all / When for euery ydyll worde we must ȝelde a reson?" (172–73), Mercy warns once the vices leave the stage, invoking the gospel admonition in Matthew 12 that we will have to give an account of our words on Judgment Day.[9]

It is only out of this contested theatrical space that Mankind, the play's representative of what it means to be human, first appears. At the opening of the play, Mercy invokes Mankind's name twice in relation to the narrative of Christian redemption (9, 39), but Mankind himself appears only after Mercy's authority to control the stage action, and thus define "mankind," has been called into question. In riling Mercy for his excessively Latinate diction, the vices demonstrate the ways in which Mercy's opening speech has failed to take the position of Mankind and his audience into account. Modern critics, reading the play according to Romantic understandings of allegory, often understand Mercy as the spokesperson of the play's "message," where Mercy carries the weight of a static, reductive allegory about the necessity of avoiding vice and remaining steadfast in virtue. In this view, Mercy's self-described "talkyng delectable" (65)—his opening allegorical message—is disrupted by the vices' attempts to undermine his words through their infectious but ultimately insidious "ydyll language" (147).[10] Instead, the vices' challenge to Mercy's authority is central to the play's developing allegorical definition of "mankind." Contrary to prevailing understandings of allegory, the meaning of "mankind" and the other social and moral terms central to the play's allegory are not a given, didactically asserted in Mercy's sermons, but instead emerge through the interactions of the play's characters, including the interactions of Mercy and Mankind with the play's vices. By looking at the play in this way, we can see how what is usually seen as inimical to the allegorical work of the play is actually necessary: the vices are not in opposition to the play's allegory but essential to it.

When the author of the Wycliffite treatise "On the Seven Deadly Sins" insists that "prechyng is þo best," he means that a priest's highest calling is the preaching of God's word. When he qualifies that statement, saying "if hit be wil done," he acknowledges that the preacher's words need to be both well said and well received by his audience.[11] *Mankind* resists the idea, as another Wycliffite treatise stresses, that "al[l]" the priest's "wark be in preching, and in doctrin."[12] *Mankind*'s action demonstrates that such a formulation forgets that the social and moral concepts upon which the preacher's words rely themselves emerge out of human interactions, and in particular the interactions structured by the sacrament of penance as the rite that manifests God's mercy through sacerdotal absolution. Through its use of personification allegory, the play demonstrates the limitations of preaching and other forms of pious exhortation as pedagogic modes. Perhaps more than any of the other Macro plays, *Mankind* demonstrates that moral selfhood takes place in time and through conversation. Through its dramatic mode, the morality play suggests that the meaning of "mankind" is not solely determined through preached doctrine (or private introspection for that matter) but instead develops through social and dramatic performances and in particular through the experience of penitential ritual. In this way, the play interrogates the basis of its own moral authority, for it suggests that it can only speak for "mankind" to the degree that it is responsive to the human position as represented by Mankind and as embodied in the members of the play's audience. The definition of "mankind" emerges through an exploration of the nature of mercy, a process that must itself be characterized by mercy and must be responsive to the human condition as represented by Mankind. The play's authority to speak for "mankind" therefore rests with its responsiveness to Mankind's varied experiences in the world— including the experiences of pleasure, pain, and redemption—because one's understanding of what it means to be human grows out of such experiences.

Never Merry, Always Sorry? Preaching and Pleasure

Preaching as a means of providing instruction in the rudiments of the faith had long been recognized as an essential part of mainstream pastoral care, but lollard writers gave the clerical obligation to preach the gospel particular emphasis. Wyclif had held that the best means of realizing God's love is through the careful study of his law, and his followers often stress that preaching is a priest's most important duty.[13] For example, the author of the lollard tract *De Officio Pastorali* declares that the "riȝt preching of goddis word is þe mooste worþy dede þat prestis don heere among men."[14] Preaching should be held in such esteem, the writer asserts, because Christ himself commanded it: Christ preached when he was on earth and bade his apostles to do the same. He did so because good preaching is *the* most effective way to nurture love of God: the goodness of a work is measured by its "fruyt," he contends, and "more fruyt comeþ of good preching þan of ony oþer werk" (441). Building upon Paul's reproductive metaphor in 1 Corinthians 4, the writer goes on to explain that, by preaching God's word, a priest "getiþ goddis children & makiþ hem to come to heuene."[15] Such preaching, he stresses, is an even more vital office than consecrating the Eucharist, for "crist preisiþ more preching of þe gospel þat gendriþ þis chirche þan gendering of his oune body." Through preaching, the priest plants God in man's soul "bi [the] seed þat is goddis word" (441).

The first scenes of *Mankind* might be read as a study in the perils that such a reliance on preaching might entail. Through his homilizing, Mercy seeks to nurture in his audience a love of God, but the first thing that his words "gendriþ" is Mischief personified.[16] As critics often note, by the time Mischief arrives, the play's audience is likely to have grown weary of Mercy's "predycacyon," making them complicit in the arrival of vice onto the stage. If *Mankind* dramatizes the perils of sententious preaching, the object of the Wycliffite *Dialogue between a Wise Man and a Fool* is to demonstrate what "riȝt preching" and its "fruyt" look like in practice.[17] Whereas *Mankind* seems to admit to the inadequacy of Mercy's speeches (delivered in the Latinate "high style" associated with the established church) as a didactic mode, the Wise Man (who favors the dense quotation of scripture and heavy use of interpolation characteristic of Wycliffite sermons and treatises) will meet his pedagogical goals through preaching alone.[18] However, like *Mankind*, the *Dialogue* gives particular attention to the human desire for pleasure, and specifically the desire for the pleasures in an "idel ymaginacioun" (135/169), presenting that desire as a standing threat to moral and biblical instruction. In *Mankind*, the pleasures and follies of an "idel ymaginacioun" are demonstrated through the vices' love of "pley." In the *Dialogue*, they are associated with stories and poems and other "fals lesyngis" (false lies) (135/169–70).

Like *Mankind*'s Mercy, the *Dialogue*'s Wise Man invokes the prohibitions against idle words in Matthew 12 and seeks to persuade his interlocutor, in the case of the *Dialogue* a Fool, to repent his "veyn spechis" and follow Christ (130/12). And, like *Mankind*'s vices, the Fool seeks to replace his interlocutor's sober exhortations with his own "mery chere." Taking the biblical commandment that "thou shalt not kill" as his starting point, the Wise Man denounces the forms of "goostly slauʒtur" that take place through the telling of "talis of pride, glotony and lecherie and of alle manere synnes" (130/3–4; 130/6). The Fool's primary objection to the Wise Man's argument is that he is not enjoying listening to it. Having listened for some time to trials faced by the "blessed lollers" (131/41), who speak God's word and live according to his law, the Fool pleads to hear a romance instead: "I preie þee, leeue þees spechis, and telle me a mery tale of Giy of Wariwyk, Beufiʒ of Hamton, eiþer of Sire Labewʒ [or] Robyn Hod" (134/162–63). The Wise Man nonetheless persists in his scriptural exposition, calling "devil's children" those who love such "fantasyes, fablis and lesyngis" more than "þe gospel, þat is verey trouþe" (136/218–19). The Fool once again emphasizes that such pursuits are not pleasurable: "What? What þanne be þi tale? We schulden neuere be merie but euer sory? For it semeþ þou woldist haue alle men to speken of Goddis lawe, and to þenke on peynes þat ben ordeyned for synners, and also of here eendynge, and þis wolde make hem die for sorowe" (136/230–33). However, despite the Fool's objections, the Wise Man doggedly pursues his goal, unwavering in his rhetorical strategy.

The *Dialogue* will ultimately endorse the Wise Man's instructional mode. Holding the Fool's objections but a testament to his folly, the Wise Man argues the Fool must redirect his will and reorient his desires. "Delite ʒou in þe lawe of oure Lord," he advises, drawing on Psalm 1; "ioie [rejoice] ʒe in ʒoure tribulaciouns, for þei ben nouʒt in comparison to ʒou in þe world to-comynge" (137/238–39; 137/254–55). In response to the Fool's bored exasperation, the Wise Man enjoins him to obey the Ten Commandments, fear the pains of hell, follow God, and abandon his ignorant retorts and idle words. The Wise Man will finally only ensure the Fool's conversion by glossing a scriptural citation (Luke 10:2) that endorses his own instructional activity:

Þe kynge of alle criatures seiþ þat "þere is myche repe [ripe] corne, but þere ben ful fewe werkmen. Praie ʒe þerfore [to] þe lord of þis ripe corne þat he wole sende good werkmen into his ripe corne." Bi þe ripe corne, þis vnderstonde, þoo [those] peple þat gladly wolden lyve wi[sl]e ʒif þei westen in what manere [knew how]; bi þe werkmen ben vnderstonden prestes þat schulden wit good wordis ket [cut] away synnes fro mennes soules, and so make hem able to be caried to þe hyʒe kynges berne, þat is, þe ryche blisse of heuene. (140–41/371–77)

In the Wise Man's harvest metaphor, biblical instruction takes on a sacrament-like function: the Wise Man's "good wordis" attain their end when they describe the very thing they would perform. By saying *that* the good preaching of the workmen-priests will cut away the sins from the "ripe corne" of men's souls and ensure their place in heaven, the Wise Man effects the Fool's transformation: the Fool acknowledges Christ as Lord and asks for God's mercy.

In *Mankind*, by contrast, Mercy's words prove less efficacious. Unsurprisingly, the vices remain unpersuaded by Mercy's pious pronouncements, but Mankind himself will struggle to adhere to Mercy's teaching and eventually succumbs to the vices. At the end of the play, Mercy will scold Mankind for having been too easily "obliuyows" (forgetful) of his "doctrine monytorye" (879). Yet, in suggesting the limitations of preaching as a pedagogic mode, the play makes room for an allegorical investigation of the meaning of "mankind," presenting an alternative pedagogy in which Mankind will learn the meaning of God's mercy through a process that acknowledges—rather than rejects—the human need for pleasure.

The Moralizer and the Moralist

"Moralizing," Mark Eccles concedes in his introduction to the EETS edition of *The Macro Plays*, "must be expected in a moral play."[19] The morality plays' unhappy reputation for moralizing and didacticism must be laid at least in part at the feet of its use of the allegorical mode, where allegory is considered, as Larry Scanlon has put it, "the stable signifier par excellence."[20] According to post-Romantic models of allegory, the morality play authorizes its definition of "mankind" by invoking an inflexible framework of orthodox doctrine and received commonplaces already familiar to its audience. The character of Mankind gives expression to—or in Goethe's terms is "bounded in" or contained by—an unambiguous, semantically stable conception of "mankind" that is based on such givens.[21] According to this view, by restricting the definition of "mankind" to the version it presents, the play excludes all but one way of defining what it means to be human. In this way, *Mankind*—and the medieval morality play as a genre— seemingly seeks to preempt the prerogative of its audience members to accept or reject its definitions. It does not take our "position into account," to borrow Cavell's phrase, but seeks to impose its meanings upon us.[22] If, in the words of Paul de Man, personification "deals with the giving and taking of faces, with face and deface, *figure*, figuration and disfiguration," the medium of theater would seem to intensify the dangers inherent in the figure, for here the body of a living human being, an actor, does not signify a human character but a concept masquerading as one.[23]

Even as they take notice of *Mankind*'s didactic content, modern commentators often have also remarked upon the ways in which the play resists its own "ostensible moral purpose."[24] As the spokesperson for the play's official ideology, the character Mercy and his "Englysch Laten," in the words of one critic, is "remote, pretentious and ineffectual"; the vices' exuberant antics easily upstage him.[25] According to this view, the play's theatricality works in opposition to the allegorical content of the play. Anthony Gash notes that "the vices' strategy is to open up every form of equivocation which the closed formal discourse of Mercy seeks to seal off."[26] "Performance," Gash contends, works to "undermine allegory."[27] In this view, Mercy's stage presence as a sanctimonious churchman threatens to eclipse his allegorical significance as the representative of divine mercy. The magnetism, entertaining immediacy, and infectious vitality of the vice characters distract from the play's allegorical narrative about the struggle between good and evil. The vices are usually seen either duly to fulfill their allegorical role by illustrating the dangers of "ydyll language," or, subversively, to undermine the allegorical content of the play through their festive inversions and pointed social critique.[28] Yet rather than either simply illustrating or subverting the play's allegorical meanings (which are assumed to be static, ahistorical, and predetermined), the vices dynamically participate in the moral and allegorical content of the play. Personification allegory itself emerges as a vehicle for moralism (in Cavell's sense of the term) and as a pedagogical strategy in opposition to the forms of moralizing evinced in Mercy's initial speech.

The question of who has the authority to interpret and speak for human experience is explicitly raised in the play's first scenes. At the beginning of the play, Mercy identifies himself as divine mercy, God's compassion that forebears punishing Mankind for his sins even when God's justice demands it (17–18). Repeatedly referred to as "Father,"

Mercy also represents clerical authority as the earthly mediator of salvation. Having established his allegorical identity, Mercy proceeds to
give a lesson on how to read figuratively. When he asserts his prerogative to "certyfye" (33) the meaning of the heads and bodies of the audience, Mercy introduces a set of questions about interpretive authority
that will preoccupy the play:

> O ȝe souerens þat sytt and ȝe brothern þat stonde ryght wppe,
>   Pryke not yowr felycytes in thyngys transytorye.
> Beholde not þe erth, but lyfte yowr ey wppe.
>   Se how þe hede þe members dayly do magnyfye.
>   Who ys þe hede forsoth I xall yow certyfye:
>   I mene Owr Sauyowr.
>
>   (29–34)

Mercy's lesson in figurative reading consists of a series of bodily, social,
and spiritual hierarchies—between sovereigns and brethren, sitting and
standing, permanence and impermanence, heaven and earth, head and
body, Christ and church—which finally all point to the hierarchy between God and man.

When Mercy promises he will "certyfye" the meaning of his audience's heads and bodies, he seems to be allegorizing in the post-
Romantic sense of the word. To paraphrase Coleridge, he is translating
"abstract notions" into a "picture language" and in doing so refusing to
partake "of the reality that it renders intelligible."[29] He is seeking, in de
Man's words, to submit "the outside world entirely to [his] own purposes."[30] For in demanding that his audience "beholde not þe erth," as
Paula Neuss observes, Mercy "is virtually telling them not to look at
the play."[31] Yet, despite his command, Mercy does not in fact dismiss
the material. Insofar as he tells his audience to behold not the earth,
he asks them to look at their own heads and bodies according to their
spiritual significance. Just as the sitting and standing positions of the
audience reveal the social hierarchy, Mercy suggests, the hierarchical
relationship between their heads and bodies reveals the relationship
between Christ and the body of the church. That understanding is
achieved through reference to yet another hierarchy, that of corporeal
sight and spiritual insight, or as Mercy puts it, a demand that the audience in some sense both behold and not behold the earth in front of

them. In doing so, he demands that his audience see their heads and bodies as he sees them, yet his Latinate diction and complacent certainties may well make that sight difficult to see. At this point, he embodies the position of Cavell's moralizer rather than moralist. Mercy appears to be interested in the heads and bodies of his audience only as far as they serve as illustrations of the larger spiritual truths he wishes to expound. However, his engagement of the material reality of his audience prepares him to emerge as a moralist by the end of the play.

It is upon Mercy's complacent certainties, and the version of moral discourse they represent, that the vices put pressure. The battle *Mankind* stages between Mercy and the vices calls into question who has authority to interpret human experience and where that authority comes from. For Mercy, food, corn, and chaff point to God's nourishing, salvatory power, and his impending judgment of mankind:

> Ther ys non such foode, be water nor by londe,
>> So precyouse, so gloryouse, so nedefull to owr entent,
> For yt hath dyssoluyde mankynde from þe bytter bonde
> Of þe mortall enmye, þat vemynousse serpente,
> From þe wyche Gode preserue yow all at þe last jugement!
>> For sekyrly þer xall be a streyt examynacyon,
>> The corn xall be sauyde, þe chaffe xall be brente.
>>> (37–43)

The vices joyously seek to empty Mercy's words of their spiritual content. Mischief asks Mercy to clarify the meaning of his rhyme, thereby putting Mercy's entire hermeneutic schema into question:

> Mysse-masche, dryff-draff,
> Sume was corn and sume was chaffe,
> My dame seyde my name was Raffe;
>> Onschett yowr lokke and take an halpenye.
>>> (49–52)

Through his sing-song rhyming, Mischief privileges the sound of words over their sense in an attempt to subvert the meaning Mercy gives them. Mischief's purpose is to relish the pleasures of words that have no sense and imply that what Mercy says is utter nonsense.

Mischief's nonsense presents an alternative way to "make sense" of human experience and thus to define "mankind." In his parody of biblical exegesis, the letter of the text is no longer a means of understanding the spiritual, but indicates the practical needs of a worldly existence. For Mercy, corn and chaff signify the Last Judgment; by contrast, as Kellie Robertson observes, Mischief's ridicule is directed at "the distance between biblical metaphors of work as glossed by preachers or friars and the reality of the laboring life."[32] Suggesting that Mercy and his preaching are not responsive to the particularity and materiality of Mankind's experience, the vices seek to return Mercy's words to the particular and the material. In the fifteenth century, relations between the abbey at Bury St. Edmunds and its tenants were particularly fraught, and the corn harvest was a focal point of conflict between agricultural laborers and landowners. Mischief tells Mercy he has hired a "wynter corn-threscher" (54) who can disprove Mercy's "dalyacyon" (46):

> Ande ȝe sayde þe corn xulde be sauyde and þe chaff xulde be feryde,
>> Ande he prouyth nay, as yt schewth be þis werse:
>> "Corn seruit bredibus, chaffe horsibus, straw fyrybusque."
> Thys ys as moche to say, to yowr leude wndyrstondynge,
> As þe corn xall serue to brede at þe nexte bakynge.
>> "Chaff horsybus et reliqua,"
> The chaff to horse xall be goode provente,
> When a man ys forcolde þe straw may be brent,
>> And so forth, et cetera.

(55–63)

By giving social body to Mercy's "spiritual labor" through the figure of the corn-thresher, Robertson notes, Mischief "points out the literal physical labor that makes ecclesiastical discourse on allegorical labor possible."[33] If Mercy's Latinate speech has alienated the audience, Mischief makes Latin entertaining and accessible. In Mischief's economy, corn and chaff are valued according to their practical use in the world rather than according to their moral significance. Corn and chaff no longer signify the saved and the damned but the means of making bread to eat, feeding one's horses, and keeping warm.

Through punning, parody, and social critique, the vices breathe new "life" into Mercy's words. Whereas Wittgenstein suggests that the life of a sign is in its use, in the *Poetria Nova*, Geoffrey of Vinsauf provides yet another formulation of what gives a sign "life," one that serves as a valuable gloss on the role of *Mankind*'s vices and a complement to Wittgenstein's remarks about how linguistic signs take on meaning.[34] For Geoffrey, all figurative language is a nascent form of personification. Dividing words into an inside and an outside, he distinguishes between the *minds* of words, their interior signification, and their *faces*, their exterior sound. In doing so, he might appear to embrace the kind of mentalist picture of language Wittgenstein resists. However, in equipping words with minds and faces, Geoffrey also gives them feet. Only by exploring a word as it moves through different contexts, he suggests, can we both realize and appreciate the full richness of its meaning:

> In order that meaning may wear a precious garment, if a word is old, be its physician and give to the old a new vigour. Do not let the word invariably reside on its native soil—such residence dishonours it. Let it avoid its natural location, travel about elsewhere, and take up a pleasant abode on the estate of another. There let it stay as a novel guest, and give pleasure by its very strangeness. If you provide this remedy, you will give to the word's face a new youth. (43)

Words only used in their habitual contexts are subject to stagnation. Bringing a word into a new context—exploring its *uses*, in Wittgensteinian terms—revives both the word and the contexts within which it is spoken. Likewise, the vices give Mercy's words new life by bringing them to new locales, exploring the meanings of "mankind" and concepts associated with it as they arise in different contexts and are spoken by different characters.

The vices exploit the polyvalency of words—their inability to be "contained"—in order to disrupt the hierarchies of meaning Mercy has sought to establish. The vices are masters at capitalizing on the potential of words to get away from the intentions of their speakers, as the entrance of a second set of vices—New Guise, Nowadays, and Nought—adeptly dramatizes. The manuscript leaf in which the three vices first enter is missing; however, the extant text strongly suggests that they have appeared in response to Mercy's invocation of their names in his sermonizing: "I trow of ws thre I herde yow speke" (98), says Nought shortly after his arrival on stage. If, for Geoffrey, personification is the "poetic license [to] confer a tongue" (32), Mercy's words, given their own tongues, have literally gotten away from him. They talk back and have minds of their own. In fact, Mercy's words have gone so far afield of his intentions that when Nought explains his identity by explaining that "I harde yow call 'New Gyse, Nowadays, Nought,' all þes thre togethere," Mercy still does not recognize them: "Say me yowr namys, I know yow not" (111, 114). And with this inadvertent pun that simultaneously proclaims he knows Nought and knows him not, Mercy's words slip away from him once again.

Similarly, if the "native soil" of ecclesiastical Latin is the church, the vices gleefully allow Latin to "travel about" elsewhere. Nowadays shows that Latin can literally signify shit. He asks Mercy to render "I haue etun a dyschfull of curdys, / Ande I haue schetun yowr mowth full of turdys" in a "clerycall manere" (131–32; 134). To drive the point home, the vice demonstrates that Latin can be used equally for the sacred and profane. He tells Mercy: "Go and do þat longyth to þin offyce: / Osculare fundamentum!" (141–42), an imperative that, if accompanied by the appropriate gesture, would have indicated to even non-Latinate members of the audience his meaning. By telling him to go "kiss my ass," Nowadays voices his distain for Mercy and the ecclesiastical authority that underwrites Mercy's own. By suggesting in Latin that such ass kissing is Mercy's true "offyce," he suggests that the office of the priesthood amounts to obfuscated obscenities.

When Mankind enters, the vices thus have already called Mercy's moral and interpretive authority into question. The vices show Mercy ironically fails to be merciful insofar as he fails to be responsive to the more immediate and pressing cares and concerns of Mankind. The vices' challenge to Mercy, and the Latinate ecclesiastical authority he represents, is responsive to Mankind's own situation as a poor laborer, and the vices' lively antics also recognize the needs of an audience that may have well grown weary of Mercy's pedantry. In other words, the vices promise Mankind and his audience a form of mercy—

where mercy is understood as a kind of responsiveness to Mankind's condition—seemingly missing in his initial exchange with Mercy. However, what at first appears to be merciful proves to be another form of temptation: the play describes Mankind's efforts to follow the injunctions of Mercy to eschew idleness and resist the machinations of the vices, who, predictably, seek to lead Mankind into a life of crime and debauchery.

The "mercy" first offered by the vices foregrounds the church's indifference to Mankind's material well-being, continuing the critique of ecclesiastical authority they mounted prior to Mankind's arrival on stage. No matter how Mankind's crop fares, Nought observes, any profit he makes will go to pay church tithes:

He ys a goode starke laburrer, he wolde fayn do well.
He hath mett wyth þe goode man Mercy in a schroude sell.
For all þis he may haue many a hungry mele.

(368–70)

Mankind acknowledges that the vices' arguments prove to be "summe-what to nere" (402). They are seductive to Mankind insofar as they re-spond to aspects of his situation that have so far gone unacknowledged by Mercy. And, apparently, *Mankind*'s playwright could assume that the vices were more responsive to the needs of the play's contemporary audience: as critics often note, the vices cultivate audience anticipation of the play's most spectacular devil, Titivillus, informing the play's spectators that they must give them "rede reyallys" (gold coins) if they wish to see his "abhomynabull presens" (465). By literally making them pay to see the devil, the vices make the audience complicit in the seduction of Mankind that follows.

Just as the vices exploit the polyvalency of words, "mankind" also proves to be a polyvalent term. When he first identifies himself, Man-kind announces inconstancy as his defining trait, describing himself according to the mutability of his will: "I am onstedfast in lywynge; my name ys Mankynde" (214). Mercy responds to Mankind's self-definition by substituting one of his own. "The temptacyon of þe flesch," he says, "ȝe must resyst lyke a man" (226). As Richard Em-merson notes, in the morality play, the actor as sign always signifies in relation to other signs; as he moves through different syntactic con-texts, the actor activates different potential signifieds.[35] Accordingly, in the presence of Mercy, Mankind is primarily defined according to his obligations to God:

> Thynke well in yowr hert, yowr name ys Mankynde;
>   Be not wnkynde to Gode, I prey yow be hys seruante.
>   (279–80)

In the initial interaction between Mercy and Mankind, Mankind is thus primarily defined by both his innate mutability and the imperative to be "stedefast in condycyon" (281). As long as Mercy is on stage, Mankind is able to follow his prescription to "thynke on my doctryne" (258). In his absence, Mankind tries to follow Mercy's mandates by copying the Ash Wednesday verse, "*Memento, homo, quod cinis es et in cinerem reuerteris*" (Remember, man, that you are dust and to dust you will return) (321), and pinning it to his breast.[36] By doing so, he hopes to have "remos [remorse] and memory of mysylff" (319) and to follow Mercy's admonition to "be not varyant" (281). Despite Mankind's efforts to restrict through writing the definition of "mankind" to the one endorsed by Mercy, however, the plot bears out Nowadays' contention: "*Cum sancto sanctus eris et cum peruerso peruerteris*" (With the holy thou wilt be holy, and with the perverse thou wilt be perverted) (324).[37] When the vices enter the stage, they are easily able to "peruerte" Mankind's "condycyons" (386). Nowadays provides his own definition of Mankind, saying of Mercy, "Men haue lytyll deynte of yowr pley / Because ꝫe make no sporte" (267–68). For the vices, Mercy's sermonizing is but a game, another form of "pley," and not a particularly entertaining one.

Under the vices' influence, Mankind is now defined by his rejection of both Mercy's form of playing and the kind of play Mercy would have *Mankind* be. He is no longer defined according his ability to "resyst" the "temptacyon of þe flesch" but by his impatience with Mercy's teachings. Mankind initially has understood his labor according to its spiritual significance: he works "to eschew ydullnes" (329). The vices work to undermine that understanding by revaluing Mankind's labor in economic rather than spiritual terms. Nowadays asks:

> Xall all þis corn grow here
> Þat ꝫe xall haue þe nexte ꝫer?

Yf yt be so, corn hade nede be dere,
Ellys ȝe xall haue a pore lyffe.
(352–55)

In the mouths of the vices, Mankind's spiritual labor becomes a heavy, tiring exercise in futility. Mankind tries to drive the vices off by buffeting them with his spade, and Titivillus, seeking revenge, steals his grain and places a board where he is trying to dig. Mankind eventually accepts the vices' literalization of his labor:

Thys londe ys so harde yt makyth wnlusty and yrke.
I xall sow my corn at wynter and lett Gode werke.
Alasse, my corn ys lost! here ys a foull werke!
I se well by tyllynge lytyll xall I wyn.
(545–48)

The hardness of land he tills is itself comically signified by the hardness of the floor of the playing space: Mankind has indeed fallen prey to the vices' valuation of the "letter." He has replaced his understanding of his tilling and sowing as spiritual exercises that direct him toward God with an appreciation of only their ultimate economic worth. Rather than identifying himself with God's creation, he sees God's "werke" as an alternative source of labor to his own.

Mankind's fall takes place in the context of a solitary prayer made in a field and outside the communal protection of the church. As Mankind gives up on his labor, he hears evensong and prays but does not go to church. Instead, staying in his field, he asserts: "Here in my kerke I knell on my kneys" (553). Gash points out that in the 1457 trial of William and Richard Sparke of Somersham, Huntingdonshire, for lollardy, the brothers were charged with stating that "a prayer made in a field or other unconsecrated place is just as efficacious as if it were made in a church."[38] In having Mankind echo such sentiments during the scene of his temptation, the play implicitly critiques those sentiments by showing that its central character becomes vulnerable to the vices precisely at the moment he willfully turns away from the ritual life of the church. As Mankind prays in the field, Titivillus whispers in his ear, assuring him that "a schorte preyere thyrlyth [pierces] hewyn" (558), and ushers him off the stage: "Aryse and avent þe! nature compellys" (560). As Mankind exits to relieve himself, his actions confirm his earlier statements about human mutability and realize the vices' earlier prediction that he shall be holy with the holy and perverted with the perverse. Yet the circumstances of Mankind's fall speak as much to the importance of human communities and corporate ritual in the maintenance of virtue as to the inevitability of human sinfulness.

PENANCE AND THE OFFICE OF PRIESTHOOD

I have been arguing that, through the vices' critique of Mercy's Latinate preaching, the play articulates and then disrupts the very forms of moralizing many critics today are still wont to saddle the morality play with as a genre. Rather than offering a distraction from the play's orthodox message, the vices' magnetism is imperative to the play's representation of Mankind's learning process. In order to speak *for* mankind, the play suggests, one must first learn to speak *to* — and *with* — him. The play develops a definition of "mankind" that must be coherent with and responsive to Mankind's experience in the world, as it grows out of those very experiences. The meaning of "mankind" is not simply established through the recitation of church doctrine or learned exposition of scriptural truths, but it arises through Mankind's developing understanding of the meaning of God's mercy. One learns what it means to be mankind only by first understanding the nature of mercy, an understanding that is only possible through experiencing the need of it. Here the ideological work of the personification allegory — which represents Mercy as a preacher or a priest, that is, a word as a person and a familiar figure as a word — comes into view. For rather than insisting upon a rigid equation of the two, the play gradually reveals the office of the priesthood as that which, through the sacrament of penance, manifests divine mercy. Importantly, in *Mankind*, the meaning of mankind and the work of God's mercy do not primarily emerge through preaching (or scriptural instruction or prayer, for that matter) but through penance. In doing so, the play suggests that preaching is a necessary, though limited, means of educating the faithful.

The meaning of "mercy" changes in the course of the play as the term is variously used and embodied by different characters, but the play never doubts Mankind's ultimate need for mercy. When the vices' antics take a more sinister turn, the play foregrounds the presence and absence of mercy in the characters' interactions and its striking tenacity as a concept that defines the relationships between them. If the vices have offered Mankind a form of mercy earlier in the play, that mercy disappears as the play progresses. Mischief returns to the stage sporting broken fetters, bragging that he has murdered his jailer and (he implies) raped the jailer's wife (643–46). New Guise, Nowadays, and Nought, still suffering from Mankind's attempts to ward them off with his shovel, approach Mischief, who, in a travesty of mercy, promises to clear Nowadays of the pain Mankind's blow has done to his head by chopping it off. The vices gain full authority over Mankind when they convince him that Mercy has been hanged.[39] It is in this context that Mankind paradoxically must beg the vices for mercy for the "sorrow" he has caused them:

> I drempt Mercy was hange, þis was my vysyon,
> Ande þat to yow thre I xulde haue recors and remocyon.
> Now I prey yow hertyly of yowr goode wyll.
> I crye yow mercy of all þat I dyde amysse.
>
> (655–58)

The vices' refusal to honor Mankind's plea signifies mercy's absence; however, the fact of the plea itself signifies mercy's obstinate presence as part of the language Mankind and the vices use to define their relationships with one another.

In the trial scene that follows, the vices attempt to cast Mercy in the role of a landowner seeking a fugitive laborer (779–81), but it is clearly now the vices, and not Mercy, who perform the role of the oppressor.[40] In a scene that parodies the procedures of a manorial court, Nowadays, assuming the role of a beadle, summons Mankind to be tried before the "cort of Myschyff," declaring him "on of owr men" (668–69). Continuing the play's earlier social critique, the vices begin procedures by noting Mankind's "syde gown may be [s]olde" (671), and, in the course of the trial, progressively shorten Mankind's long winter cloak in order to sell off the material until he is left with only a ridiculous, sawed-off (and, according to contemporary sumptuary laws, forbidden) "fresch jakett after þe new gyse" (676).[41] Gash notes the trial scene serves as a "Shrove Tuesday debunking of an oppressive institution" in which "the offender against Church law was paraded to public gaze in vest and hose, or clad in a short shirt or vesture."[42] Building on Gash's account, Robertson reads the scene in the context of the reissuance of labor statutes in the midcentury: "On the allegorical level," she observes, we are asked "to see Mankind's innocence despoiled by the devil; what we actually see on stage is a half-dressed agricultural worker who has just renounced his work standing in front of a manorial tribune." The scene's "fake Latin" and "mock oaths," Robertson contends, *show up the coercive force implicit (but usually invisible) in the 'ordinary' language of a familiar juridical situation.*"[43] Not content merely to humiliate him, the vices force Mankind to swear he will go "robbe, stell, and kyll" (708); forbear all corporate forms of worship, that is, "masse and matens, owres, and prime"; and spend Sundays at the alehouse with them instead (711–12). They imagine for him a life of base and violent crime where Mankind will act as a highway robber awaiting "trew men" to "ryde be þe wey," so he can "take þer monay, kytt [cut] þer throtys [throats], thus ouerface [overcome] þem" (715–16). The vices push Mankind to the brink of suicidal despair: when Mankind learns of Mercy's return, he cries out for a rope with which to hang himself, proclaiming his unworthiness (800). The vices have rendered him unable to receive the mercy Mercy offers.

Initially, the vices were easily able to style Mercy as a moralizer. The sheer ruthlessness of the vices' treatment of Mankind at this point in the play opens up a space for Mercy to reemerge as something other than the mouthpiece of an abstract doctrine, and Mercy now assumes the position of the moralist. When he comes back on stage, Mercy is just as long-winded and as full of "Englysch Laten," and, as before, begs Mankind to "fle" the "felyschyppe" of the vices (726). But the nature of his confrontation with Mankind has changed: he says his mind is distracted, his body "trymmelyth as þe aspen leffe" [trembles as the aspen leaf] (734). He tells the audience: "The terys xuld trekyll down by my chekys, were not yowr reuerrence" (735). Mercy himself has not changed, but Mankind's recognition—and through him the audience's recognition—of him has.[44] His words now directly address Mankind's present situation: Mankind now is clearly in need of mercy.

Mankind will only truly understand his relation to Mercy—and thus the meaning of what mercy is—by experiencing his need for mercy at the hands of the vices. In *Mankind*, knowledge of divine mercy is shown to emerge from one's experiences, including one's experience of suffering. In *Culture and Value*, Wittgenstein remarks: "Life can educate one to a belief in God. And *experiences* too are what bring this about; but I don't mean visions and other forms of sense experience which show us the 'existence of this being,' but, e.g., sufferings of various sorts. . . . Experiences, thoughts, — life can force this concept on us."[45] When Mercy first introduces himself, Mankind only understands mercy as an abstract doctrine, a part of a set of catechetical formulations: he has "herde tell of ryght worschyppfull clerkys" that Mercy is "aproxymatt to Gode" (222–23). Mankind only recognizes the true meaning of mercy when, terrorized by the vices and brought to the point of despair, he cries out for it. Encouraged by Mercy in the penitential language of confession to call on God's mercy, Mankind voices his need for mercy first as an exclamation, then as a question, and only then as a proclamation:

> Þan mercy, good Mercy! What ys a man wythowte mercy?
> Lytyll ys our parte of paradyse were mercy ne were.
>
> (835–36)

Beckwith observes that Mankind's earlier invocation of Mercy is in the idiom of "nerdy recall" rather than "genuine recognition."[46] By contrast, when at the end of the play he cries out for Mercy, Mankind "acknowledges at one and the same time his specific relation to the character Mercy (that he is direly in need of him), to himself (that *he* is in need) and to God (this is what it means to be one of his creatures, mankind)" where "the recognition of Mercy is not so much a naming *of* him as a call *to* him."[47] Mankind's recognition of God's mercy and his own self is simultaneous. Mankind shows that human knowledge is not predicated upon unchanging realities that Mankind must simply accept. Instead, human interactions are the ground of our knowledge. When Mankind declares that "to aske mercy and to hawe, þis ys a lyberall possescion" (859), he begins to understand mercy through experiences that, in showing him his need of it, illustrate its donative nature.

In a play so concerned with how one learns the meaning of a word, it is notable that when Mankind first introduces himself, he writes himself into his own miniature personification allegory. Invoking a

common homiletic theme, he describes himself as composed "of a body
and of a soull," which, he explains, are "of condycyon contrarye" (195):
"He þat xulde be subjecte," he laments, "now he hath þe victory" (197).
The flesh governs the soul and, he continues, "wher þe goodewyff ys
master, þe goodeman may be sory" (200). It is important not to read
such statements as a proto-Cartesian moment. In personifying his own
body and soul, Mankind reinvests his soul with a body and, presumably, his body with a soul. In showing our understanding of the
meaning of "mercy" and "mankind" to be discovered in and through
human relationships, *Mankind* demonstrates an understanding of a self
that is only discovered through human activity and exchange. In this
way, the play anticipates a Wittgensteinian version of the self in which
"I discover myself, not in some pre-linguistic inner space of self-
presence," as Fergus Kerr explains, "but in the network of multifarious
social and historical relationships in which I am willy-nilly involved."[48]
The version of selfhood in *Mankind* is most coherently understood as
one whose embodied presence is necessary for the full realization of
that self in penitential ritual and other acts of devotion that acknowledge and reveal the donative nature of God's mercy. In *Mankind*, as in
Augustine, the self becomes fully constituted through the acknowledgment of divine gift.[49]

Critics who read Mercy as the spokesperson for the play's allegorical message align the play's use of personification allegory with
Mercy's didacticism and sermonizing. I have suggested that, in contrast, personification allegory functions in *Mankind* in precisely the
opposite way. Instead of using personification allegory to *illustrate*
the words of the preacher, the play uses it to both demonstrate the limitations of preaching as a pedagogic mode and as a vehicle to elaborate
a process of meaning-making that must be responsive to the lived experience of those they address. In *Mankind*, personification allegory
emerges as a vehicle for moralism (in Cavell's sense of the term) and as
a pedagogic strategy in opposition to the forms of moralizing evinced
in Mercy's initial speech.

CHAPTER FOUR

Everyman and Community

Where is now the helpe of my frendes? where ben now the
good byhestes of our kynnes-men?

—Henry Suso, *Learn to Die*

In *Everyman* (ca. 1500–10), the character Death makes his portentous
entrance on stage only to be met with utter misrecognition and incomprehension. When Death explains that he is here to take Everyman on
a "longe iourney" (103) to make his "rekenynge . . . before God" (106–
7), Everyman's incomprehension is humorous even as it reveals him
to be deeply unready for Death's summons: he asks Death, "Sholde
I not come agayne shortly?" (149). Everyman's inability to recognize
the permanence of Death's "journey" raises the question for the audience of what might constitute such a recognition. Depicting death as
a presence initially inscrutable to its central character, *Everyman* asks
what it means to make our own mortality present to us, to recognize
our finitude, and to remember that we must die. The play's circuitous
answer to those questions takes place through a sustained investigation of how one learns the meaning of a word where, as in the plays
we have discussed in previous chapters, individual understandings of
words, concepts, and mortality emerge through the interpersonal relations and communal rituals that reveal and guarantee their meanings. Everyman will discover that to recognize death is to understand
oneself as a sinner and a creature, an understanding that develops out

of and through human interactions established by penitential ritual. Written on the eve of the Protestant Reformation, *Everyman* thus suggests the persistence of late medieval understandings about the performative dimensions of penance and selfhood into the early years of the sixteenth century. Whereas the previous three chapters read the plays of the Macro manuscript as responses to lollard critiques of penance, in this chapter I show how *Everyman* engages the *ars moriendi* tradition and tensions within that tradition between communitarian and individualistic forms of devotion. Although *Everyman* is typically read as a play that demonstrates the solitary nature of death, in focusing on the interrelational dimensions of penance, *Everyman* puts particular emphasis on the impact of community on the formation of Everyman's self-understanding. Everyman learns to recognize his separation from others, and thus the individual self, only by affirming his relation and responsibility to the corporate body, the collective whole of which "everyman" is a part. Rather than simply foregrounding his isolation, Everyman's dramatic encounter with death unsettles the distinction between the individual self and community, proving that distinction to be surprisingly superficial and misguided.

As a personified figure, Everyman is both a representative of a collective whole to which the members of his audience belong and, as James Paxson has pointed out, "ontologically identical" to any single member of that audience.[1] His symbolic representation itself interrogates the very distinction between the collective and the individual and between an actor and audience. The play seeks to portray the plight of a character named Everyman; yet, if we are its audience, then it also seeks to shatter the illusion that we can avoid death and that the Everyman who dies in front of us on stage has no relation to us. Death's entrance introduces the question of Everyman's right relationship to the world in which he lives, and the play's prologue and God's opening words correspondingly introduce the claims that the play's Christian morality makes upon its audience. The play's investigation of the relationship between the general and the particular is evident in God's opening words:

Euery man lyueth so after his owne pleasure,
And yet of theyr lyfe they be nothynge sure.
. . . .

Therfore I wyll, in all the haste,
Haue a reckenynge of euery mannes persone.
(40–41; 45–46)

Although God speaks about every man generally, his speech vacillates between singular and plural pronouns.[2] Referred to here in the abstract, every man will shortly appear as a particular man named Everyman. *Everyman* begins by locating the general and abstract in the particular and concrete. Members of the play's audience are asked to understand their individual participation in the collective "we" the play addresses. We are called, the messenger who delivers the prologue tells us, to "a morall play" named *"The Somonynge of Eueryman"* (3–4). The play is, quite literally, a story about another, a man played by an actor, but we are also to understand it as a story about ourselves, "that of our lyues and endynge shewes" (5). An observation in the abstract, "every man must come to terms with death," is made concrete, as Everyman, an actor, is seen by Death at a distance: "Loo, yonder I se Eueryman walkynge" (80). We are asked to see the abstract "every man" of God's sermon as a particular man, as the play seeks to demonstrate the substance of God's words by literally giving them a body. If every man (in general) is prone to evade his particular accountability, the play resists such evasions through the self-consciousness of its particularization of the abstract.

The play will ultimately seek to demonstrate its audience's individual accountability to the words God states in his opening speech, but it also elaborates upon the all-too-human refusal to be accountable. Everyman's friend Fellowship will profess twice that his loyalty toward Everyman extends even to death:

If ony haue you wronged, ye shall reuenged be,
Thoughe I on the grounde be slayne for the.
. . . .
For, in fayth, and thou go to hell
I wyll not forsake the by the waye.
(218–19; 232–33)

When his promises are safely in the abstract, Fellowship promises Everyman the world and his departure from it on Everyman's behalf.

Upon learning that Everyman actually wants him to make good on his promises, Fellowship's tune changes. Pronouncing the social contracts his performatives engender—"Promyse is duty" (248)—Fellowship quickly reneges. By refusing to give his words substance, Fellowship makes Everyman a nonpresence. By denying his responsibility and relationship to him, he turns both Everyman and himself back into abstractions. *Everyman*'s allegorical theater is a drama of responsibility that seeks to correct the facility with which we make ourselves absent to our words and thus to one another.

As in the earlier moralities, in its personification of words such as "fellowship," "goods," and "good deeds," *Everyman* repeatedly demonstrates that our knowledge of social and moral concepts comes out of the familiar interactions of everyday life. In *Everyman*, those interactions are tested by the appearance of Death, whose presence radically changes how Everyman and the other characters interact and how they understand their relationships to one another. At a crucial moment of the play, Everyman discovers that, in the presence of the personification of his own mortality, he has misunderstood the significance of most aspects of his daily existence. When Death informs him that he must bring before God an account of his good and bad deeds, Everyman, terrified, turns to his earthly friends, begging them to accompany him. Fellowship, Kindred, Cousin, and Goods each reject him in turn with unflinching cruelty. Cousin, for instance, offers the excuse of having a cramp in her toe (356). Everyman's overwhelming desire to have others accompany him to the grave only accentuates his isolation; he finds that his friendships with Fellowship, Kindred, Cousin, and Goods have limits that were not apparent before Death's presence. Correspondingly, in the presence of Death, the concepts that those characters manifest take on new meanings. As his friends refuse him, Everyman's understanding of his relationship to the members of his community is brutally altered; he can no longer take them for granted but must relearn his relationship to them.

The play emphasizes the transformation of his social relationships in order to underscore the importance of penance: the one familiar interaction whose true worth and reliability will be magnified rather than diminished by the presence of death. In the course of the play, the ritual practice of penance will shape instrumentally Everyman's understanding of his relationships to the other characters, and thus of the concepts they signify. In order to recognize death, he must recognize the extent to which he is separate (and separable) from the world in which he lives; penance emerges as the rite that holds individuals both responsible to their community and accountable for their actions before God. Penance prepares an individual for death and God's judgment, but also—importantly—penance is itself presented as a practice that binds the individual to his community. Paradoxically, it is only when his community is made so frighteningly separate from Everyman that it can be made fully present. Everyman's theatrical performance of penance and his final, deathbed drama are the avenues through which he at last recognizes his true relationship to the world: he is truly separate from all but Good Deeds, the emblem of his responsibility to others. In this play, to recognize death fully is to recognize that one is a part of one's community and therefore responsible to it, yet also separate from that community and therefore alone accountable for one's actions. By defining the relationship between the individual and his or her community, penance enables both the individual's and the community's transformation.

THE CRAFT OF DYING

Everyman's focus on the communal practices established by penitential ritual reflects the degree to which, in the late Middle Ages, both sin and penance were public matters.[3] As an annual obligation traditionally fulfilled before a churchgoer received the Eucharist at Easter, Lenten confession was conducted in full view of other parishioners. It was therefore a highly public ritual performed corporately and openly as part of the liturgical year. Notably, late medieval penitential and pastoral manuals present sin as simultaneously an offense against God, neighbor, and church, stressing both the importance of confession and the necessity of making amends with the members of one's community.[4] Communal reconciliation was necessary both to worthy reception of the Eucharist at Easter and to making a "good death." For instance, John Mirk's *Instructions to Parish Priests* includes among the "Seven Questions" to be asked of one who is near death several questions designed to confirm that the dying person has forgiven those who have harmed him, asked forgiveness of those he has offended, and restored that which he owes.[5]

Nor were one's deathbed preparations a private affair. The bedroom of the dying in the Middle Ages was full of people from the community. Because the last moments of life were considered critical to the soul's salvation or damnation, relatives, friends, and priests surrounded the deathbed to look after the spiritual condition of the dying. Visitation of the sick was one of the seven works of mercy necessary to salvation; the laity were expected to attend and participate in the deathbed rituals. As Amy Appleford has recently shown, beginning in the late fourteenth century, laypersons were increasingly encouraged to adopt duties toward the dying that had traditionally been the preserve of the clergy. The widely circulated deathbed manual known as the "E" version of *The Visitation of the Sick* (ca. 1380), written as a vernacular supplement to the Latin liturgical visitation rite, gave lay lords and householders a more active role in the counseling of the dying and providing them with spiritual guidance.[6] In wide circulation in the late fifteenth and early sixteenth centuries, *The Book of the Craft of Dying* (ca. 1430) similarly presents preparing an individual for death as a collective effort, exhorting both clergy and laity to help the dying struggle against the temptations of the devil by urging them to remember their faith in Christ and to receive the last sacraments.[7] The *Craft* punctuates the urgency of that duty, advising that the whole city should come together to assist a person who is dying:

> But lett no man wondre ne þinke þat it is inconuenient þat so grette charge & diligence & wise disposicion & prouidence & besy exortacion shuld be had & mynystred to hem þat bene in poynt [brink] of deþe & in her last ende. . . . for þei be in such perill & so grete nede at þat tyme þat, & it were possible, all a cite [city] schuld com to-geder with all the haste [in all haste] to a man þat is in dyinge. . . . þerfor it is redde [advised] þat religiouse people [the religious], & women, for þe honeste of hir astate [estate] schall not ren [run], but [except] to a man þat is a-dyinge, [&] for fere [in case of fire].[8]

The deathbed was surrounded by immortal and mortal helpers. The shorter, illustrated block-book version of the *Craft* presents death as a bedside drama in which the divine Trinity and a legion of angels and saints crowd around the deathbed in a struggle with Satan and an army of demons for the soul of the dying. In the communal vision of the *ars moriendi*, as Eamon Duffy describes it, "every individual is surrounded by a host of helpers and opposers, every lonely step in the drama of dying in reality a participation in a communal effort, in which living friends and relatives and dead patrons and intercessors join hands to assist."[9]

Late medieval penitential practices associated with purgatory were likewise communitarian in emphasis, binding the living and the dead in networks of mutual obligation and exchange.[10] Whereas the dead depended on the prayers, masses, and good works of the living to shorten their time in purgatory, the living profited from the good works of the dead in the form of benefactions for services and objects of worship. As Duffy observes, late medieval funerals were "intensely concerned with the notion of community, a community in which living and dead were not separated, in which the bonds of affection, duty, and blood continued to bind."[11] Duffy dramatically depicts the strength of that community in late medieval culture and portrays the violence of its rupture with Reformation attempts to curtail practices associated with purgatory. With the reformed Edwardian prayer book of 1552, the priest no longer addressed the corpse to commend its soul to God; rather, he turned away from the corpse to address the living congregation. Duffy describes this as a moment of intense loss: "In the world of the 1552 book the dead were no longer with us. . . . Here the dead person is spoken not to, but about, as one no longer here, but precisely as departed: the boundaries of human community have been redrawn."[12] Duffy's account is admittedly nostalgic, especially in light of contemporary concerns about the financially driven nature of such exchanges, as most famously voiced by Chaucer's Parson, in the *General Prologue* to the *Canterbury Tales*, who condemns the material motivations of priests who abandon their parishes to run "to Londoun unto Seinte Poules" to pursue more lucrative positions as chantry priests (1.509). Nonetheless, even the economic significance of such exchanges attests to the importance of the bonds of responsibility they created.

In contrast to the communitarian emphasis of the deathbed practices and literature I just described, Appleford identifies an opposing tradition of medieval death literature based on eremitic ascetic models that "work[s] as much to isolate individuals imaginatively from community as they do to affirm their solidarity with their 'even-cristen.'"[13] For instance, in the "Learn to Die" section of Henry Suso's *Orologium Sapientiae*, for the "faire ȝonge man" (358/29) who finds himself suddenly confronted with death, the pain and anguish of dying is profoundly isolating. Yet the young man's suffering is shown to be ultimately instructive, for, as Wisdom assures his disciple, "þat þe drede of god is begynnynge of wisdam" (364/33–35). Appleford contends that such moments construct "the spiritual pain of sin, with other forms of suffering, as *productive*: as aids to sharpen one's perception of the relationship between divine and human and to encourage disengagement with the world."[14] The *Craft of Dying*, she argues, combines these two traditions, drawing heavily upon the isolationist rhetoric of ascetic death literature and on communitarian religiosity of the *Visitation E*. Exhorting the dying to reflect on how often and in how many ways they have sinned, the *Craft* advises that no man can be saved "but yf he knowe himself" where "the drede of God" is "the begynnynge of wisdom" and the "helthe of mannes soule."[15] For Appleford, the *Craft of Dying* pushes its readers "away from . . . reliance on the sacraments."[16] "Downplaying the role of external elements such as the sacraments and priestly absolution," she argues, the *Craft* "invests its hope in readers' salvation in its ability to teach them how to form a sufficient and saving attitude of repentance."[17] In Appleford's reading, the *Craft* fosters a spirituality that is cultivated primarily through internal rather than external processes.

Like *ars moriendi* literature, *Everyman* emphasizes the role of the community in preparing an individual for death and the obligations of the dying to acknowledge his or her community through acts of charity and restitution. And, in ways that echo the ascetic literature Appleford describes, the play also suggests that its central character's anguished and profoundly isolating encounter with death has a salutary and productive function, producing profound changes in his understanding of death, God, and his relationship to the world of others. However, unlike the texts described by Appleford, *Everyman* underscores the sacraments and other external practices as the *mechanism* of inward spiritual change. Both the formation of the Christian community that surrounds Everyman as he approaches death and his developing self-understanding are shown to rely upon, rather than replace, sacramental ritual.

COMMUNITY AND THE INDIVIDUAL

Up through the 1980s, *Everyman* and the morality-play tradition more broadly were regularly considered in relation to their role in the history of the rise of the individual. Despite its Dutch origins, *Everyman* is the most frequently anthologized of the medieval English moralities, and the play has often been seen as prototypical of the allegorical didacticism of a genre that, as Bernard Spivack puts it, "embraced the universal drama of mankind . . . comprehending the entire human race within a single spiritual formula."[18] Citing the morality play's predominance as a popular dramatic form during the early Tudor era, critics identified it as the medieval genre that had the greatest influence on early modern drama. For that reason, criticism dwelt on the degree to which *Everyman* does, or does not, anticipate the psychologically complex, individualized characters of Shakespeare.[19] The sine qua non of this new characterization was the expression of "interiority" in the soliloquy. Catherine Belsey, for instance, observes: "As the literal drama discards allegory, and morality personifications give way to social types, concrete individuals, the moral conflicts externalized in the moralities are internalized in the soliloquy and thus understood to be confined *within* the *mind* of the protagonist. The struggle between good and evil shifts its centre from the macrocosm to the microcosm."[20]

Even as *Everyman* was seen as *the* exemplary moral allegory, it nonetheless was also noted for its atypicality within the English tradition. Unlike the other plays of its genre, *Everyman* does not depict a battle between virtue and vice; rather, it concentrates wholly on Everyman's increasing isolation and abandonment as he moves toward death. Accordingly, critics often invoked Everyman's isolation as an early instance of the recovery of the individuated character: V. A. Kolve discerns in Everyman's abandonment the "movement-into-aloneness generic to tragedy."[21] Phoebe S. Spinrad similarly sees in *Everyman* "the beginnings of the great themes of isolation and self-knowledge treated in *King Lear* and *Hamlet*."[22] A similar focus on the individual has also been prevalent in social histories of death and the afterlife. Most notably, in his seminal study *The Hour of Our Death*, Philippe Ariès suggests that the emergence of the individual corresponds to the "new image of the pathetic and personal death of individual judgment" as opposed to an earlier emphasis on collective resurrection and eternal salvation for all Christians.[23] Because of its emphasis on the solitary nature of death, *Everyman* would appear to be easily assimilable into Ariès's history. Indeed, Ariès locates this new emphasis on the individual in two traditions commonly associated with *Everyman*: the *danse macabre*, with its images of the confrontation of the individual with the figure of Death, and *ars moriendi*, handbooks on the art of dying.[24]

Yet even as the appearance of Death in *Everyman* foregrounds his isolation, Everyman's desperate pleas to his friends to accompany him suggest equally that, in the face of death, our ties to the members of our community are most urgently felt. Critical preoccupation with the individual subject minimizes the extent to which morality drama conceives of the individual always in relation to community. As a result, criticism has largely overlooked *Everyman*'s exploration of the ways in which different forms of interpersonal relation give rise not only to new understandings of words and social concepts but also, importantly, to different understandings of the self. As Everyman's self-understanding is shaped by his experience of penitential ritual, what we would now call his interiority emerges precisely *through* his recognition that he is a sinner responsible to community and to God. The version of interiority in *Everyman* does not emerge through self-revelations voiced in soliloquy; rather, it is based on external conditions and interactions.

Although more recent criticism has sought to correct historical narratives that, in tracing the emergence of the modern idea of the individual, deny the medieval subject a sense of an individual selfhood, some of the assumptions of the old narrative persist.[25] The claim that allegorical personifications gradually make progress toward individuated characters is founded upon an assumed opposition between corporate and individual identities, an opposition that, in turn, depends on the corollary assumption that individualization is superior and more highly evolved. Often, criticism of the play still relies on an understanding of "individual" and "community" as oppositional terms, thereby making the mutually defining relationship between Everyman's identities as both a particular character and a representative of humanity difficult to see. For instance, in John Watkins's 1999 assessment, Everyman's corporate identity as "everyman" conflicts with any sense in which he can be regarded as a having an individuated identity:

Precisely because Everyman's isolation subsumes the play's nominal commitment to the Church's communitarian structures, it has become the medieval play most likely to be read in schools and universities. By definition, Everyman is a corporate figure embodying the humanity that lies beyond the *integumentum* of personality. Nevertheless, the action so compromises that allegorical premise that teachers and critics steeped in the humanist cult of the individual approach him as a character.[26]

Although Watkins criticizes the humanist preconceptions of those who discern an emergent individualism in Everyman, the oppositions he assumes between Everyman's corporate and individual identities are themselves a product of a radical notion of subjectivity that denies the communal nature of the self. I submit, however, that of the morality plays *Everyman* demonstrates the compatibility between the individual and social dimensions of the subject with particular acuteness. *Everyman* shows that any sense we have of ourselves as individuals— of having a separate, inner self that is hidden to others—develops not in isolation but through human relationships, a view that theater illustrates better than perhaps any other literary medium. Human subjects have no a priori identity that exists outside of human exchange.[27] In emphasizing the degree to which the self in *Everyman* is shown to be shaped by community, I am not advocating a return to a Burckhartian picture of medieval human beings who "lay dreaming or half awake" without a sense of themselves as individuals.[28] Rather, in contrast to both Watkins's and Burckhardt's formulations, I suggest that, at the same time that Everyman's name marks him as a representative of the collective, *Everyman* also explores that collective as a set of individuals who are in relationships with each other and who cannot be accurately conceived except in relationships. Craig Muldrew has noted in a passage of particular relevance to *Everyman* and its examination of the communal dimensions of penance:

Community has come to be interpreted as something contrary or opposite to individualism, and the fact that communities were, and are, a set or state of *interpersonal relations* themselves has often been lost. In medieval language, for instance, the condition of a person with an individual conscience in a metaphysical relationship with God, and in worldly relations with their neighbours, was a central ethical concept mediating communal relations. Thus it does not immediately follow that the history of the last 500 years has been a progression away from "community" towards individualism. Rather, the period has seen changes occur in the way social relations have been interpreted, communicated and mediated between individuals all within a set of overlapping social relations.[29]

Muldrew's observations have important implications for the history of the self. Rather than looking at that history as a progression away from community and toward individualism, we might instead describe that history more productively by examining the changes in how social relations are mediated and understood. Moreover, as if anticipating Muldrew, *Everyman* points to the particular importance of penance in shaping medieval communal relations, presenting a selfhood that is at once individualistic in its stress on individual accountability and emphatically communal in its emphasis on one's obligations to others.

EVERYMAN'S COMMUNITY AND THE CONSTRUCTION OF MEANING

The subtitle of the Skot edition of *Everyman* famously announces itself as a "treatyse . . . in maner of a morall playe." Like the Macro plays, we have no records of a medieval performance, and William Poel's 1901 London revival of the play may have well been the first time *Everyman* was ever staged. However, as David Mills has pointed out, at the very least, *Everyman*'s dramatic form encourages its reader to respond to the text as a theatrical work and according to contemporary theatrical conventions.[30] The material features of medieval staging grounds (whether actual or as imagined by readers) would have advanced the play's communal understanding of the self. The play is adaptable to an indoor performance in a great hall or an outdoor performance on either a "board and barrel" platform stage or in an open area with scaffolds designating various locations mentioned in the play. Unlike the case of a darkened modern theater in which the audience is hidden, the audience members in a medieval production of *Everyman* would have been clearly visible to one another, diminishing the distinction between actors and audience. The playing space thus would have furthered the symbolic and literal continuities between character and audience. If the character Everyman is symbolic of every man sitting in the audience, he also physically acts within the same sphere as that audience.[31]

Perhaps because of its overt address to the audience, *Everyman* is often viewed as a didactic work that expounds the doctrine of the Catholic Church. For instance, Lawrence V. Ryan suggests that "the preacher-playwright of *Everyman* is interested in answering the important question: What must a man do to be saved?" Ryan concludes that "his chief problem is to reduce the complex answer to terms of simple dramatic representation without falsifying or obscuring the doctrine."[32] In this account, in order to prepare for death and God's judgment, Everyman must redirect his trust *away* from Fellowship, Kindred, Cousin, and Goods and toward God by acknowledging his sins through the sacrament of penance. He must learn that ephemeral relationships and possessions promise solace but offer none. Although *Everyman* clearly reflects the doctrine of the established church, readings such as Ryan's incorrectly reduce the play to the dramatization of abstract tenets. What is missing in such analyses is the extent to which the characters of *Everyman* are not mere abstractions but characters who actively interact with one another and, together, represent a community. Fellowship, Goods, and Good Deeds are portrayed as characters in their own right, as people who hold specific relationships with one another. Through its portrayal of those relationships, *Everyman* demonstrates that our understanding of social and moral concepts arrives not from a static orthodoxy but from human interactions, interactions that are notably transformed in the presence of Death and through Everyman's experience of penance. What Ryan and others overlook, then, is the extent to which, in *Everyman*, Catholic doctrine is conveyed not through reiterating a compressed salvific formula but by investigating the role of penance in actively forming and transforming social and moral knowledge.

A staged performance can help to illustrate the importance of human relationships to the play's meanings. The directors of the Royal Shakespeare Company's (RSC) 1997 production quickly recognized that actors and audiences alike do not learn who the play's characters are by their abstract names but through their actions and interactions.

In an interview, director Kathryn Hunter described her approach: "I felt instinctively that if you asked actors to play concepts, they just go dead. So from the very beginning we treated every scene in terms of a relationship, and invented a community so that there is always a relationship to play."[33] In their production, Hunter and her codirector Marcello Magni imagined those relationships with great specificity: Everyman is a landlord in a rural community, and Goods is a business partner who takes care of his dirty work. Five Wits, Beauty, Discretion, and Strength—Everyman's attributes who come to aid him in his final hours—make up a circus troupe. Good Deeds, a benevolent servant, relates to Everyman as would a grandmother. Death and Knowledge arrive as newcomers to the community. By embedding the characters in specific relationships, the RSC production rightly emphasizes that we learn who those characters are not through a fixed definition but rather through their interactions. The National Theatre's excellent 2015 production of Carol Ann Duffy's version of *Everyman* likewise imagined the characters in concrete relationships, reimagining, for instance, Knowledge as a transgender street person and Goods as an ensemble of gilded, stylishly dressed salespeople proffering luxury products, exclusive memberships, and ostentatious forms of philanthropy. Such decisions to portray the characters of *Everyman* as the members of a specific community has textual precedent in other plays of the genre that, as I indicate in the previous chapters, place their characters in concrete situations. In the *Castle*, World is a feudal lord and Mankind is his knight and retainer. *Wisdom*'s Mind, Will, and Understanding, dressed as gallants, engage in abuses associated with the practice of maintenance, such as blackmail, bribery, and false arrest. *Mankind* depicts its title character as a farmer hounded by the local rabble who point out the futility of his labor.

Although a modern production proves nothing, of course, about medieval performances of the play, the text of *Everyman* clearly depicts its central character as embedded in dynamic human relationships. The alterability of Everyman's friendships is exemplified by his interactions with Goods. Having learned from Death that he must make a reckoning before God, Everyman comes to Goods hoping that Goods will agree to help him to buy off God. Everyman's mistaken assumptions about the power of his goods to settle his accounts with the divine would have had particular resonance for medieval audiences familiar with contemporary abuses of the system of indulgences, and thus would have suggested the negative consequences upon the communal order of the misuse of goods. Goods, however, informs Everyman that, whereas our goods can help us settle our accounts in this world, they do not help us settle them in the next. "Money maketh all ryght that is wronge" (413), the adage upon which Everyman has come to depend, no longer holds in the presence of death. Goods refuses to help him, explaining to Everyman that he's got it all wrong:

As for a whyle I was lente the;
A season thou hast had me in prosperyte.
My condycyon is mannes soule to kyll;
If I saue one, a thousande I do spyll.
(440–43)

Everyman discovers that his goods are not *his.* His realization is both personal and communal: our goods are lent to us only at our considerable individual peril, and we are accountable for our use of them at large. Everyman has understood that he must make a "reckoning" but has mistaken the currency. He has understood the vocabulary of "accounting" within a financial idiom but must now relearn that vocabulary within a moral and communal one.

The presence of Death discloses an unfamiliar, ascendant economy.[34] That new economy begins to take shape once Everyman recognizes that his relationship to Goods is not one of ownership but of accountability to others. Faced with death, Everyman looks for charity from Goods, but Goods tells him that he should have been using his goods to perform charitable works:

For my loue is contrary to the loue euerlastynge.
But yf thou had me loued moderately durynge,
As to the poore gyue parte of me,
Than sholdest thou not in this dolour be.
(430–33)

In that higher economy, Goods play a different role entirely. It is Everyman himself who owes a debt. The pleasure that he has taken in his goods has made him blind to the risk he faces if he fails to fulfill the obligations that come with having them. Everyman will come to a full understanding of the meaning of Goods only as he acknowledges his own death through the sacrament of penance.

As Everyman's relationship with Goods changes, so too—and drastically—does his understanding of the meaning of the word "goods" in the context of death. His impending judgment before God redefines his relationship to Goods as one governed by a penitential framework. Initially believing his goods to exist for his own pleasure, he learns that his worldly goods are transient, that his obsession with worldly goods has blinded him to his creator, and that his goods are given to him to perform charitable works. And when Everyman begins to understand that his goods are not his, he begins to understand what death means. If *Everyman* is finally a play about learning to die, then it suggests that death's meaning and our means of preparation for it can be understood only through the kind of dynamic human interactions we can see realized in theater or mediated by deathbed and penitential rituals. *Everyman* suggests that it is only in and through such performances that death is made present.

PENANCE AND KNOWLEDGE

In the course of Everyman's developing understanding of death, he finally turns to his Good Deeds. Though Good Deeds wishes to help him, she cannot, as she is lying on the ground, bound by Everyman's sins.[35] Everyman's book of works and deeds, she reveals, is blank; had he nurtured her, she explains, his accounting book would be ready. Good Deeds directs Everyman to Knowledge, who will be his primary guide through the stages of penance. Doctrinally, Good Deeds's weakness demonstrates that Everyman's good works cannot merit salvation when he is guilty of unforgiven mortal sin: only the performance of penance will restore him to a state of grace, revive Good Deeds, and make Everyman ready to render an account of his life before God. Significantly, Good Deeds only regains her strength when Everyman completes acts of penitential satisfaction, scourging himself and giving half his goods to charity and using the other half for repayment of debts and other acts of restitution (696–702). Good Deeds's revival both dramatizes the remedial importance of satisfaction and reveals the inextricability of penitential reconciliation with God and penitential reconciliation with community.

The presence of the character Knowledge onstage as Everyman undergoes penance indicates the extent to which penance both requires and engenders forms of knowing.[36] *Everyman* depicts penance as a form of education that transforms Everyman's understanding of God and his relationships to others, and thus his self-understanding.[37] When Confession remarks, "I knowe your sorowe well, Eueryman. / Bycause with Knowlege ye come to me" (554–55), he signals both that Everyman is literally accompanied by a character named Knowledge and that he comes to Confession with a certain kind of knowing. That knowledge depends upon Everyman's evolving understanding of his guilt. Through the lessons of Fellowship, Kindred, Cousin, and Goods—whether wittingly or unwittingly delivered—Everyman is filled with a shame for his past that borders on despair. Although he acknowledges to Goods that "I gaue the that whiche sholde be the Lordes aboue" (458)—an acknowledgment that is immediately followed by yet another plea to Goods to come with him—Everyman's recognition of his sins is only nascent and partial. His sense of shame, despair, and self-loathing comes out of a sense of betrayal and of his folly in placing his trust in those who now report that they will only lead him to hell. His understanding that he has been wrong is compromised by his sense that he has been wronged.

The work of penance is to transform Everyman's shame into contrition. His new understanding of his fault is signified by a costume change: Knowledge gives him a "garment of sorowe" to mark Everyman's "true contrycyon" (643, 650). Significantly, Everyman adopts the garment of sorrow only *after* he performs the ritual of penance, suggesting that the act of confession itself engenders new forms of knowing. Confession is performative: it is doctrinally integral to penitential absolution and organizes one's relationship to God. Knowledge literally will direct Everyman's posture: "Lo, this is Confessyon. Knele downe & aske mercy, / For he is in good conceyte with God Almyghty" (543–44). Penance requires the knowledge that one has done wrong, but penance and the knowledge of wrongdoing together—dramatized by the presence of Knowledge and Confession together onstage—produces new forms of self-knowledge. One's posture toward God is realigned into a posture of supplication that acknowledges both one's sins and debt to Christ.

Written in an era deeply suspicious of ecclesiastical corruption and from within a culture on the eve of the Protestant Reformation, *Everyman* notably does not seek to promote the importance of penance either by emphasizing the authority of the church or the priest's role in offering absolution. Knowledge's objections to Five Wits's characterization of priests as "aboue aungelles in degree" (749) calls into question the virtues of the priesthood and their ability to carry out their pastoral role effectively. Instead, the play confirms the absolute necessity of the sacrament of penance itself and reveals the profound transformations penitential ritual enacts upon Everyman. Through penance, Everyman's understanding that he has sinned is combined with a new knowledge of both God's judgment and Christ's mercy. Confession himself equates penitential acts of satisfaction with the recognition of Christ's suffering for humanity:

> Here shall you receyue that scourge of me,
> Whiche is penaunce stronge that ye must endure,
> To remember thy Sauyour was scourged for the
> With sharpe scourges, and suffred it pacyently;
> So must thou or thou scape that paynful pylgrymage.
>
> (561–65)

Confession identifies that recognition as a kind of knowledge, saying, "Knowlege, kepe hym in this vyage" (566). As he confesses, Everyman does more than admit that he has been mistaken—he acknowledges the consequences of sin. Through acts of satisfaction, he becomes conscious of Christ's suffering and comes to recognize Christ's love. When Good Deeds rises from the ground, freed through his penance, Everyman exclaims, "Welcome, my Good Dedes! Now I here thy voyce / I wepe for very swetenes of loue" (634–35). With Good Deeds representing the good works that Everyman has done on the behalf of his community, the play identifies the communal aspect of charity with the imagination of Christ's sacrifice and Everyman's acknowledgment of his consequent debt. Everyman's penitential almsgiving and repayment of his debts serves to transform his shame into knowledge of his communal responsibility and individual accountability.

Everyman's new understanding of himself and his community is marked dramatically by a new cast of characters. Good Deeds, Knowledge, and Confession are joined by a new set of counselors— Discretion, Strength, Beauty, and Five Wits—to replace Fellowship, Cousin, Kindred, and Goods. The sense that Everyman's relationship to his community is *transformed* through his participation in penitential ritual would have been especially apparent if a small traveling troupe performing *Everyman* had its actors double their roles. An actor who played Fellowship, for example, might now play Discretion. The presence of Knowledge, Discretion, Strength, Beauty, and Five Wits onstage as human counselors articulates the interior work performed by a community organized by the sacrament of penance. Everyman's second set of companions adopts the roles of the deathbed counselors, who, as described in the *ars moriendi*, would have surrounded a dying person in the Middle Ages. The primary role of Everyman's new companions, like that of their counterparts in the *Craft of Dying*, is to give him help, comfort, and reassurance. Discretion urges him to "go with a good aduysement and delyberacyon" (691); Knowledge and Five Wits counsel him to receive the Eucharist and extreme unction (706–27). Importantly, the play presents Everyman's interior faculties in the context of external human relationships; he learns what Discretion is through his interactions with the people who surround his deathbed. The appearance of Death has profoundly changed Everyman's self-understanding, but the mechanism through which he gains self-knowledge remains constant throughout the play.

William Munson has read the appearance of Knowledge, Discretion, Strength, Beauty, and Five Wits as evidence of Everyman's increasing spirituality and inwardness: for Munson, those inner faculties and attributes mark a turn within that is "an increasingly inward and personal appropriation of acts initially more externally and formally performed."[38] However, though Everyman's counselors foster his spiritual awareness (in directing him to the sacraments, for example), Munson's reading does not account for Everyman's eventual (and, once again, traumatic) separation from Knowledge, Discretion, and the other attributes. It is precisely Everyman's reliance on his inner attributes that he must in the end give up. Good Deeds instructs him:

All erthly thynges is but vanyte:
Beaute, Strength, and Dyscrecyon do man forsake,

Folysshe frendes and kynnesmen that fayre spake—
All fleeth saue Good Dedes, and that am I.
(870–73)

The departure of this last set of friends is as painful as the first. Everyman must also recognize his separateness from this new community in order to confront death.[39] Thus, in his desire to incorporate *Everyman* into a narrative of emerging individualism, Munson denies the separateness of Discretion and the others onstage as actors, viewing them as "not external helps but personal resources, the natural physical and mental qualities of the individual himself."[40] "When the personifications resolve into a single figure," Munson posits, "Everyman becomes the completed individual, with an inwardness now perfectly focussed in an act in the world—down into the grave and upward to God at the same time."[41] Contrary to Munson's assertions, however, *Everyman* suggests no such unification. His faculties do not unite with him. They abandon him. Insofar as they are made visible as actors, they exist separately from Everyman. It is exactly the tendency to rely on individual "natural physical and mental qualities" upon which the play puts pressure.

GOOD DEEDS

The play insists upon Everyman's isolation as he approaches death, yet when he finally steps into the grave, he is *not* alone but accompanied by Good Deeds. What is the significance of his retention of this one companion? She clearly signifies Everyman's good works, his acts of charity to his neighbor and church. Now activated through his performance of penance, she is able to assist him in his reckoning before God. His accompaniment by Good Deeds into the grave is clearly meant to signal his salvation. However, Good Deeds's lone presence at Everyman's deathbed raises the specter of Pelagianism, that is, it could be read to support the heretical idea that Everyman's salvation rests upon his Good Deeds rather than God's grace. By contrast, according to the doctrine of the established church, when Everyman steps into the grave, it is God's grace and not his own actions that will save him. The character Good Deeds's actions themselves suggest that she does not represent Everyman's good works autonomously conceived but a broader conception of Christian charity, where charity is at once a description of God's redemptive action in Christ and an endowed virtue through which one participates in the divine nature. The multivalent signification of Good Deeds, both divine charity and Everyman's good works, links God's redemptive action to individual responsibility to community.

As Everyman's good works, Good Deeds foregrounds by her very presence Everyman's communal obligations and the condition of his relationships with others. Her impairment at the beginning of the play suggests Everyman's failure to treat the members of his community charitably; her revival indicates the restoration of Everyman's charitable relations with them. Indeed, the English author of *Everyman* seems to have underscored that aspect of charity in particular. When he translated *Elckerlijc*, *Everyman*'s English author changed the name of the Dutch character *Duecht* (Virtue) to the English Good Deeds, a change attributable to the translator's desire to emphasize charity in its communal aspect as a practice. It would be a mistake, however, to interpret the signification of Good Deeds as simply Everyman's good works: the action of the play does not support a Pelagian reading. If Everyman's accounting book looks distressingly blank before he undergoes penance, we never see it reassuringly full. Although we see Everyman settle his accounts and give to the poor after his confession, his individual good deeds are never cataloged. Additionally, as Ryan has pointed out, the play expressly cautions against a Pelagian understanding of salvation, as it stresses the necessity of sacramental confession to a priest and underscores that Everyman's faculties, which abandon him in the end, are not the instruments of salvation.[42]

Good Deeds therefore signifies more than Everyman's good works; the full signification of that character becomes apparent only through Everyman's accrued experiences with her. Significantly, Good Deeds finally assumes a role that parallels the divine intercessors of the other English moralities. Whereas *Mankind* personifies divine Mercy and *Wisdom* explicitly identifies its eponymous character with Christ, Good Deeds's name and conduct suggest the action of divine charity. Her relationship to Everyman is characterized throughout the play by a kindness and compassion that serve to direct Everyman to God. She acts as a comforter to Everyman when he has been abandoned and urges him toward penitential reconciliation with God, directing him to Knowledge and Confession and thereby instigating the sacramental action within the play. Good Deeds furthermore signifies the action of God's grace as she is revived at the moment when Everyman's will is redirected toward God through penance. Indeed, several of *Everyman's* analogues explicitly identify their Good Deeds figure with charity or Christ. In a treatise on dying printed in 1507 by Wynkyn de Worde, which closely parallels *Everyman* in theme and structure, Faith, Hope, and Charity stand in the place of Good Deeds.[43] Similarly, in Caxton's translation of the thirteenth-century *Legenda Aurea*, a dying man is abandoned by all but a "faithful friend" who is identified as faith, hope, and charity, and the other good works the dying man has done.[44] In the *Gesta Romanorum* "faithful friend" tales, the Good Deeds figure is often identified as Charity, and, in two of the tales, identified as Christ himself.[45]

As a figure whose actions recall those of divine charity, Good Deeds's character points to God's love for humanity and the presence of divine charity, or Christ, in Everyman. Good Deeds both performs the function of the divine intercessor of the other moralities and is understood as something Everyman possesses. Even though her own deeds point to the action of the divine, she is clearly presented as Everyman's good deeds: they are *his*. The play depicts Good Deeds as a figure both internal and external to Everyman, suggesting that charity comprises God's love of humanity and humanity's love of God. Moreover, it suggests a deep association between the acknowledgment of Christ with acknowledgment of community. Casting Good Deeds as both divine intercessor and a figure of human virtue, it depicts Everyman's love of God as an act of grace inextricable from God's love of him and Everyman's love of neighbor. The play thus emphasizes the interdependency of the inward turning to the divine and outward acts of charity. In this regard, its vision of virtue is particularly Johannine insofar as it suggests through the figure of Good Deeds that charity dwells mutually in God and Everyman, and that Everyman's charity to his neighbor finds its source in God's love for humanity.[46] When Everyman steps into the grave, he takes Good Deeds—divine love as it is reflected in him—with him.

Good Deeds therefore most compactly illustrates the corporate nature of a self that exists in and through its participation in community and the divine. Such an understanding of charity—as uniting individual and community or individual and God—is a frequent theme of medieval religious writing. For Thomas Aquinas, charity does not originate in an individual but must be endowed by God: the same love that originates in God is the love that directs one to him.[47] We see a similar understanding in a critical moment in Langland's *Piers Plowman*, in which Will realizes, in his search for charity,

> Clerkes kenne me þat crist is in alle places
> Ac I seiȝ hym neuere sooþly but as myself in a Mirour:
> [*Hic*] *in enigmate, tunc facie ad faciem.*

> ---

> [Clerks proclaim to me that Christ is in all places,
> But I never saw him surely except as myself in a mirror.
> *Here darkly, then face to face.*][48]

Will's reformulation of 1 Corinthians 13:12 becomes a moment of self-recognition in which the self is identified with the image of Christ in each human. In a passage that echoes 1 John 4:20, Mirk's Quinquagesima sermon asserts that one's love of God must manifest itself in one's love of neighbor, which in turn must have its origin and motive in the divine nature:

> Wherfor, þagh a man wenyth [if a man who believes] he loueþe his God and loue not hys euen-cristen [fellow Christians], he ys dysceyuet [deceived]; for he loueþe his God, þat loueþe all þat God loueþe.[49]

Such an identification of love of Christ with love of neighbor is also a recurrent theme of Corpus Christi Last Judgment plays.[50] In these retellings of Christ's account of the Last Judgment in Matthew 25, Christ equates human acts of mercy to the poor and unfortunate with acts of mercy to himself during his time on earth. The Last Judgment plays share with *Everyman* a vision of charity in which the human understanding of that virtue has its origin in divine love, and in which believers recognize God's love and sacrifice for humanity through acts of kindness that recognize Christ in each human.

I HAVE ARGUED THAT Everyman's self-recognition (that he is separate) is simultaneous with his recognition of the presence of others, his relationship and responsibility to them. That simultaneity is embedded in

Everyman's very name, which engages the relationship between the general and the particular, and also in the play's attention to the structure of penance, as Everyman's recognition of his ultimate separation from others (death) brings with it the recognition that he will be judged before God. The status of Everyman's identity as simultaneously separate and corporate is equally embedded in the phenomenology of *Everyman*'s allegorical theater, and its exploitation of theater's unique capacity among literary genres to engage the question of what it is to make another human being present.

In his landmark essay, "The Avoidance of Love," Stanley Cavell observes that in Shakespearean theater we are not in the characters' *presence* (we do not imagine, for instance, that we can prevent Desdemona's death); however, theater demands that we be in the characters' *present*, that is, that we acknowledge them by making their present our own. To do so, we must acknowledge our own relationship to the play's characters:

> If the suggestion is right that the "completion of acknowledgment" [of another] requires self-revelation, then making the characters present must be a form of, or require, self-revelation. Then what is revealed? Not something about me personally. . . . What I reveal is what I share with everyone else present with me at what is happening . . . that I am I, and here.[51]

Cavell's theatergoer realizes the commonness of his shared humanity with those onstage even as he recognizes his singularity. For Cavell, acknowledging characters inside a theater (where we are hidden) shows us what it is to acknowledge others outside of the theater (where we must reveal ourselves). If we absent ourselves in various ways in our daily lives from the pain and death of others, the shrouded darkness of Cavell's redemptive theater holds out the possibility that we can stop our theatricalization of others, our fictionalization of their existence.[52]

The boundaries between actor and audience in medieval theater were far more permeable. Yet even as the play insists upon our commonality with Everyman and upon a self that is learned in time and through human interactions, the play leaves us with no doubt of his separateness. His death is his alone to suffer. Like Cavell's theatergoer, in discovering himself to be separate, Everyman does not discover something about himself *personally*. Everyman's sense of himself as separate does not derive from his perception of the uniqueness of his inner life, an inner life that, as we have seen, necessarily develops through human interaction and exchange.[53] Instead, in discovering himself to be separate, Everyman discovers that he simultaneously exists only in relationship to the intractably discrete world of others. In discovering his separateness, Everyman discovers what unites him to every man.

CHAPTER FIVE

A New Theater of the Word

The Morality Play and the English Reformation

In the Tudor morality play *Respublica* (1553), written for performance at court during the Christmas season of the first year of Queen Mary's reign, a group of vices plot to drive the play's eponymous heroine, an impoverished widow, to financial ruin. In a clear allegory of the economic abuses of the outgoing Protestant administration of Edward VI, Avarice adopts the "cloke of policie" in order to obtain a position on Respublica's council.[1] The vice Oppression follows suit by masquerading as Reformation, Insolence as Authority, and Adulation as Honesty. However, the vices prove to be bad actors whose hold on their new roles is so tenuous they have trouble remembering them. When Avarice quizzes Adulation on Oppression's new identity, he fumbles:

> *Avarice*: And what callest thowe hym here?
> *Adulation*: Dyffamacion.
> *Avarice*: I tolde the he shoulde be called Reformacion.
> *Adulation*: Veraye well.
> *Avarice*: What ys he nowe?
> *Adulation*: Deformacion.
> *Avarice*: Was ever the like asse borne in all nacions?
> *Adulation*: A pestell on hym, he comes of the Acyons.
> *Avarice*: Come on, ye shall Learne to solfe: Reformacion.
>   Sing on nowe. Re.
> *Adulation*: Re.

Avarice: Refor.
Adulation: Reformacion.
(405–11)

Adulation's malapropisms anticipate the Freudian slip and its logic of surface and depth. The joke here, one might say, is that, in the eyes of the court of the new Catholic queen, the true nature of the Edwardian Reformation, "dyffamacion" and "deformacion," surfaces in Adulation's mistaken identification. However, Freud's original word for parapraxis, *Fehlleistung*, means a "faulty act" or "misperformance." Rather than encouraging a fixed surface-depth model of knowledge, the vices' interaction encourages a performative one that defies such models. Adulation's comic confusion reminds us of the slipperiness of language, how easily "reformation" slips into "defamation" and "deformation" and back again. He thus reminds us (with Saussure) that words and concepts only make sense in performative conjunction. The vices' interaction is also suggestive of the role of performance in the formation of new identities: Avarice encourages Adulation to remember Oppression's newly adopted dramatic role through another mode of performative embodiment, song.

If the vices are meant to teach us that "reformation" is but a cover for "oppression"—and "defamation" and "deformation" to boot—those relations emerge through human performances that are always on the surface. There is nothing *private* or even hidden about the vices' disguises. They are known to the play's audience all along. If Respublica is meant to be fooled by them, the viewer never is. Adulation's misperformance thus does not reflect a model of language and the self in which the meaning of a word—such as "reformation"—exists in the solitude of the human mind (where, if we have repressed or deluded ourselves about its true meaning, our unconscious might correct us). Instead, such words are redefined through human interactions.

I have argued in previous chapters that the fifteenth-century morality play presents a version of the self that is constructed primarily through communal practices, where dramatic personification indicates a deep interconnection between exterior performances and interior processes. *Respublica*'s disguised vices are suggestive of a moral selfhood that is equally, if differently, constructed through performance. With its focus on disguise and dissimulation, corruption and false appearances, *Respublica*—and the morality plays of the sixteenth-century more generally—might seem to be easily assimilable into a narrative of incipient early modern individualism predicated on a split between inner and outer, appearance and reality, surface and depth. (Indeed, critics today regularly regard early modern selfhood as "performative" insofar as it is defined by such binaries.) However, such a narrative overlooks the degree to which, in the sixteenth-century morality plays, dramatic personification remains a mode in which both the making of linguistic meaning and the formation of the self are bound up with communal performances. The sixteenth-century plays resist mentalist pictures of the self insofar as they, like their fifteenth-century predecessors, foreground the embodied, public nature of meaning and a moral selfhood that is—even when defined by dissimulation and disguise—forged in performance.

In the course of the sixteenth century, playwrights moved away from the earlier morality plays' focus on the rite of penance. Unlike the moralities of the fifteenth century, *Respublica* does not trace the progression of a representative human figure through the stages of penitential ritual, but instead describes the decline and recovery of a republic that has become subject to an unscrupulous administration. Robert Potter argues, "A society increasingly preoccupied with the pursuit of wealth and power, and increasingly unable to agree in matters of religion, could scarcely continue to accept the microcosm of the medieval morality play as a true picture of the world."[2] As has been amply described by critics such as David Bevington, Robert Potter, and Howard Norland, during the reigns of Henry VII and Henry VIII playwrights began to reinvent the genre, adapting its trajectory of fall and redemption to more specific, secular, and topical ends that reflected the local and institutional contexts in which they were performed.[3] Henry Medwall's humanist morality play *Nature* (ca. 1495) is the first known play to make extended use of what will become the sixteenth-century morality play's signature feature: the vice disguised as virtue. Interludes such as *Youth* (ca. 1513–14) and *Hickscorner* (ca. 1514) combine moral allegory with pointed political satire. John Rastell's *The Nature of the Four Elements* (ca. 1518) and John Redford's *Wit and Science* (ca. 1531–47) feature students as their protagonists and take up academic themes. As the century progressed, political moralities performed in the vicinity of the court and focused upon the person of the monarch, such as John Skelton's *Magnificence* (ca. 1520), *Godly Queen Hester* (ca. 1530), and *Respublica*, came to dominate the genre.[4]

As playwrights begin to adapt the genre to address more specific, secular, and topical concerns, they no longer look to the rite of penance to resolve the play's meanings.[5] We can see this process at work in Skelton's *Magnificence*. Unlike the earlier moralities, *Magnificence* is not invested in showing how the performance of penitential ritual shapes its protagonist's self-understanding. However, the play continues the fifteenth-century plays' understanding of the public nature of language and performative nature of the self. The most celebrated of the early political moralities, Skelton's play satirizes the notorious excesses that characterized Henry VIII's early reign by describing the descent of a prince, Magnificence, into poverty and suicidal despair when he comes under the sway of a courtier named Fancy, disguised as Largesse, who ushers vice into the court.[6] As in the earlier moralities, *Magnificence* uses personification allegory to establish the meanings of the central social and moral concepts the play explores, most prominently the nature and value of a prince's "magnificence," or royal grandeur. The play opens with an argument between three courtiers — Felicity, Liberty, and Measure — about the respective roles of "liberty" and "measure" in maintaining the prince's "felicity" (and thus his magnificence). The vices' seduction relies on the flexibility of such terms and their susceptibility to corruption. Under the vices' influence, Magnificence comes to understand the meaning of his name as the right of a prince to immoderate "wealth at will, largesse and liberty," insisting that "Fortune to her laws cannot abandon me."[7] Predictably, the vices steal all of Magnificence's money and then desert him. Shamed by Poverty, plagued by Despair, and goaded by Mischief, Magnificence is driven to the brink of suicide.

As in earlier moralities, the same processes that bring Magnificence to despair also purge him, and the trajectory of fall and recovery traces a path toward self-knowledge. The character Adversity explicitly identifies Magnificence's fall as a failure to recognize himself: "He knew not himself, his heart was so high" (1889), he explains. As Magnificence prepares to kill himself, the vices suddenly flee, and a new figure, Good Hope, appears and enjoins him to repent. Good Hope invokes the language of repentance, yet the play's religious trajectory sits uneasily with its political commentary. Skelton's primary aim is not to show penitential progression of the human soul but to promote the Aristotelian principle of measure as a policy of good governance. *Why* Good Hope appears is not entirely clear. In the absence of an explicitly penitential focus, what *are* the forces of recovery that will reconcile the play's meanings and restore "measure" to "magnificence"? (What *would* rein in the dangerous extravagances of a young and profligate king?) Skelton appears to place his hopes in the pedagogical and redemptive power of performance itself. When Sad Circumspection addresses the audience at the end of the play, he declares the interlude we have just witnessed a "mirror encleared" in which this "life inconstant" we can "behold and see" (2520–21). By dramatically experiencing the ephemeral nature of human existence, Skelton suggests, where princes are "suddenly advanced, and suddenly subdued" (2522), both Magnificence and his audience will discover that "in this world there is no earthly trust" (2540), learn to look beyond that world, and be reformed.

In the course of the Reformation, Protestant polemicists found the morality play particularly amenable to their concerns, adapting the morality trajectory of fall into sin and recovery to reveal the corruption of the hierarchy of the Roman church and the error of traditional practices. Whereas the fifteenth-century moralities were used to defend traditional ceremonial culture, in the sixteenth century evangelical reformers used the genre to reject that culture. In particular, Protestant dramatists found that the convention of the "masquerading vice" was ideally suited to show that what the Roman church counted as virtue was nothing but vice in disguise. For A. P. Rossiter, it was "the contemporary confusion, with its atmosphere of 'propaganda' and misrepresentation" that "made the equivocator the logical symbol for the spokesmen of the other side."[8] Most prominently, that most strident dramatist of the English Reformation, John Bale, discovered in the morality play a powerful medium to deride the sacred rituals and practices of the Catholic Church by presenting them as simply a show, false illusions designed to augment the church's illicit claims to authority.[9] Yet, despite the apparent antitheater of Bale's critique, dramatic personification remains a place of communal meaning-making. In Bale, performance itself never proves to be empty.

For conservative and evangelist alike, faith can only be expressed through ceremony and other worshipful performances. I have been

discussing the ways in which sixteenth-century playwrights rein-
vented a fifteenth-century genre in order to pave the way for what
will be the focus for the rest of this chapter: the role of performance in
the construction of moral selfhood in two Protestant morality plays
that explicitly address the sacrament of penance, Bale's *King Johan*
(1538) and Lewis Wager's Calvinist morality, *The Life and Repentance
of Mary Magdalene* (ca. 1547–66). In *King Johan*, Bale stages a corrupted Roman rite of penance in order to replace it with a reformed
drama of repentance. In *Mary Magdalene*, Wager reimagines the saint
most strongly identified with penance in the Middle Ages, Mary Magdalene, as a Calvinist "true spectator" of God. I argue that, far from
suggesting that a notion of the performative nature of moral selfhood
dropped out in sixteenth-century England, the two plays participate
in the much broader reassessment during the English Reformation of
the role of ceremony and other devotional performances in the reformation of Christian souls. As Alice Hunt has recently argued, in Tudor
England, "the reformation of ceremonies is bound up with their dra-
matisation."[10] By putting rituals on stage, Hunt suggests, reformers
could explore rituals as forms of dramatic representation (rather than
as efficacious rites in themselves) equally capable of being instruments
of truth or deception. In this view, corrupt ceremonies, like bad plays,
are deceitful; legitimate rituals, like good plays, represent the truth.
The morality play relies on a structure of fall and recovery based on
penitential ritual and a literary mode, dramatic personification, that
foregrounds the role of performance in the creation of meaning. It thus
proves to be a particularly provocative site for reassessing the role of
ritual and other forms of performance in the reformation of Christian
souls and the Reformation of the English church.

  Sixteenth-century reformers amplified lollard objections to mandatory auricular confession, but the basis of their objections was different, as Michael Sargent reminds us.[11] Remember that Wyclif and
his followers started from the premise that only God can forgive sin.
Most lollards held that confession to a priest was unnecessary to salvation but acknowledged that confession to the right kind of priest
could be helpful in eliciting contrition. By contrast, sixteenth-century
reformers' objections were informed by a Lutheran theology of salvation by faith not works that was not present in lollard critiques.
Sixteenth-century reformers were also distinctly antitheatrical in their

criticism. In his highly influential *Obedience of a Christian Man* (1528), William Tyndale argues that the rite of penance has no basis in scripture and is nothing but a human invention. "Penance is a word of their own forging," he inveighs, "to deceive us withal."[12] Shrift, he declares, is "a work of Satan" (117). For Tyndale, the pope is the Antichrist, who "with the mist of his juggling hath beguiled our eyes and hath cast a superstitious fear upon the world of Christian men" and who has "taught them to dread, not God and his word, . . . but his own law and ordinances, traditions and ceremonies and disguised disciples, which he hath set everywhere to deceive the world and to expel the light of God's word" (82). The Catholic Church and its hierarchy are "monsters," Tyndale says, once again taking up the theatrical language that Bale and other evangelical playwrights will imitate, "disguised, with mitres, crosses and hats, with crosses, pillars, and poleaxes, and with three crowns" (102). He maintains forgiveness does not lie in such papist rituals and priests. Instead, true repentance consists of a lifelong "mourning and sorrow of the heart" (115) for one's failure to live according to God's law. If you repent your sins and confess your faith in God's promises, Tyndale insists, God's truth justifies you. Yet, for Tyndale, faith remains a *practice*. Knowledge of scripture is the ground of faith, but such knowledge is only the beginning and not the end. He asks: "How can we whet God's word (that is put it in practice, use and exercise) upon our children and household, when we are violently kept from it and know it not?" (16). Tyndale stresses that God's promise of forgiveness is not contingent upon auricular confession; however, the forgiveness of sins nonetheless remains a communal process:

> If he that hath offended his neighbour repent and knowledge his fault asking forgiveness, if his neighbour forgive him, God forgiveth him also, by his holy promise (Matthew 18). Likewise if he that sinneth openly, when he is openly rebuked, repent and turn, then if the congregation forgive him God forgiveth him . . . whosoever repenteth and when he is rebuked knowledgeth his fault is forgiven. (120)

Forgiveness of sins, for Tyndale, both depends upon and is known by human and public acts of repentance and forgiveness.

Radicals like Tyndale rejected auricular confession, but the English church's position on the sacrament of penance following the Henrican Act of Supremacy was the product of compromises between evangelists and conservatives. The Ten Articles of 1536 retained penance, along with baptism and communion, as a sacrament essential for salvation but also adopted the quasi-Lutheran position that the justification of sin was caused "by contrition and faith joined with charity."[13] When the tide of Henrican reform reversed, the more conservative Act of the Six Articles of 1539 declared "auricular confession" to be "expedient and necessary to be retained and continued, used and frequented in the Church of God."[14] Reversing the tide once again, the 1547 Edwardian *Book of Homilies* declared that justification was by faith alone and provided that good works were the fruits of faith. The 1549 *Book of Common Prayer* describes penance as a rite that primarily offers reassurance rather than as necessary to the forgiveness of sins. However, both the 1549 and 1552 *Book of Common Prayer* provide for the persistence of auricular confession, stressing that priests should describe private confession as an option available to only those who cannot quiet their conscience by other means. The 1549 *Book* states that private confession should be made available for those whose conscience remains troubled that they might receive "suche ghostly counsaill, advyse, and comfort, that his conscience maye be releved."[15] By contrast, the Elizabethan *Homily of Repentance* unequivocally condemns auricular confession. It allows that the priest may offer to comfort those who are troubled in conscience but stipulates that any notion that auricular confession is a *necessary* part of the processes through which sins are forgiven is an unhappy artifact of a bygone era: "It is against the true Christian liberty, that any man should be bound to the numbering of his sins, as it hath been used heretofore in the time of blindness and ignorance."[16]

The English church's changes in its position on penance were the product of factional divisions within its hierarchy, but those changes were also at least nominally responsive to a broader adjustment to the changing devotional modes through which the devout knew themselves as Christians. Cranmer is reported as having explained that the traditional ceremonies for a time should be retained "lest the people, not having yet learned Christ, should be deterred by too extensive innovations from embracing his religion."[17] Even Bale ends his morality *Three Laws* with a song praising God sung in both Latin and English, and he constructs his biblical play *God's Promises* around antiphons, as Katherine Steele Brokaw points out. Such moments suggest the ambivalence even the most ardent evangelical polemicist might have felt toward the abandonment of Catholic practices.[18]

Changes in the doctrine of forgiveness were accompanied by a broader reevaluation of the role of ceremony in the English church: without shared practices there is no community of the faithful. The Edwardian Prayer Books and Elizabethan Homilies, in their struggle to reconcile reformed beliefs with existing communal structures of worship, are suggestive of a much broader reassessment during the English Reformation of the uses of ceremony in Protestant forms of worship. Debates about the definition, legitimacy, and function of sacramental ritual persisted throughout the sixteenth century. The Elizabethan *Homily of Repentance*, in rejecting auricular confession, states that "God hath no pleasure in the outward ceremonie" but instead requires "a contrite and humble heart." Yet the homilist acknowledges that outward ceremonies have legitimate use if "we are stirred vp by them" and they "serue to the glory of God" and in so doing edify us.[19] For the Elizabethan theologian Richard Hooker, the sacraments have epistemological and performative functions. Baptism and communion do not simply teach the faithful, he stresses, but "serve as bondes of obedience to God."[20] They are testaments to our obligation to him, commemorating Christ, preserving us from sin, and securing our belief. Still more importantly, they are the "markes" whereby we know we have received God's saving grace (5.57.2). The sacraments serve a necessary epistemological function: as God "in him selfe is invisible and cannot by us be discerned workinge," he gives the faithful "some plaine and sensible token whereby to knowe what they cannot see" (5.57.3). He also emphasizes that the social aspects of worship are integral to the formation of the bonds of Christian community where "the verie meetinge of men together, and theire accompanyinge one an other to the howse of God, should make the bonde of theire love insoluble" (5.39.1). For Hooker, the communal rites and ceremonies serve both to witness and forge the bonds of Christian community.

Reformers pronounced the rites and practices of the Catholic Church to be corrupt and ineffectual, looking instead to scripture to ground their faith. In doing so, it was necessary to imagine anew the role of performance in Christian forms of worship. It is therefore not surprising that reformers looked to dramatic personification and the morality play, both rigorously verbal and inherently theatrical, as an important site to work out a new place for performance in the religion of the Word. For Bale and for Wager, performances are valuable insofar as they teach viewers to read correctly, and the meaning of a word is explored through dramas of (mis)recognition.

John Bale's Reforming Drama

Generally regarded as England's first history play, John Bale's morality *King Johan* (1538) reimagines the confrontation between the historical King John (1199–1216) and Pope Innocent II over the pope's choice of Stephen Langdon as archbishop of Canterbury. It presents the historical king as a proto-Protestant reformer whose confrontation with the papacy anticipates the English Reformation and Henry VIII's break with Rome. Refashioning Catholic penance as Lutheran repentance, *King Johan* projects the medieval morality plays' individual narrative of mankind's fall and redemption onto the larger canvas of English history. Describing an England in the grip of a Catholic Church rife with corruption and hypocrisy, *King Johan* rails against the ceremonial culture of the Catholic Church with a stridency that is perhaps unsurpassed in English drama. Bale's deeply iconoclastic theater exploits the language and mechanics of performance to expose the rituals and ceremonies that define traditional religious practice as vain spectacles, illusions that "destroye mennys sowlles with damnable supersticyon."[21] Its eponymous hero seeks to replace a corrupt church of tonsured actor-clerics, "dysgysyd shavelynges" (429), with one of "faythfull hartes and charytable doynges" (430). Yet performance itself in this play never proves to be empty. In adopting the medieval morality play's structure, *King Johan* continues its medieval predecessors' exploration of the role of performance in making linguistic meaning, where the process of *mistaking* meanings becomes integral to the process of realizing them. Bale in his play unequivocally condemns oral confession to a priest. However, as in the fifteenth-century plays, in *King Johan* the ritualized performance of sin and forgiveness provides a powerful drama of accountability in which the true meanings of words and actions are revealed and must be acknowledged.

The play describes how a group of Catholic vices led by Sedition thwart King Johan's attempts to reform the English church. After first seducing the English estates (represented by Clergy, Nobility, and Civil Order), Sedition joins forces with Dissimulation, Usurped Power, and Private Wealth, who then adopt the names of the historical figures who forced John to submit to papal authority. The vices excommunicate the king, force him to surrender the throne, and eventually stage his murder. The vices are only finally expelled from the realm after Johan's death, when two new characters, God's Verity and Imperial Majesty, appear. Verity chastises the English estates for betraying their king. The estates repent, beg Imperial Majesty's forgiveness, and swear to give their king "hys due supremyte" (2359). Clergy vows he will exile Usurped Power, Nobility promises to drive Private Wealth from the monasteries, and Civil Order pledges he will hang Dissimulation at Smithfield. Imperial Majesty sentences Sedition to be hanged, and the estates reaffirm their allegiance to their king.

King Johan was likely performed by Bale's own acting troupe under the patronage of Thomas Cromwell at the residence of the archbishop of Canterbury during the twelve days of Christmas 1538–39.[22] If so, it was performed, as Greg Walker notes, "by a company financed by one of the chief architects of the English Reformation, in the residence of another."[23] The play is clearly aligned with Cromwell's propaganda campaign to defend the royal supremacy and discredit papal authority. Paul Whitfield White has suggested that Bale may have taken his plays on tour across the realm under Cromwell's patronage as part of Henry's chief minister's campaign to shore up popular support for the supremacy.[24] *King Johan* also may have been directed at Henry himself. If played during the Christmas season of 1538–39, it would have been performed in a charged political context in which Rome threatened to excommunicate Henry and place England under interdict, and the Crown feared both immanent invasion by the Franco-Imperial alliance, together the greatest Catholic power on the continent, and dissension within the realm. Reformist leaders, including Cromwell and Cranmer, feared (rightly) that Henry was on the brink of rolling back the progress of the reformation of the English church.[25]

The play's identification of Henry first with King Johan and then Imperial Majesty thus presents him, Walker contends, "dramatically as the ardent reformer in an attempt to persuade him to adopt the role in reality."[26] The extant text, a compilation of earlier and later versions of the play, suggests that Bale revised *King Johan* for performance during Elizabeth's reign and probably during Edward's too.[27]

In adapting the traditional structure of the morality play, Bale imagines in his play a reformation that takes place institutionally and across history rather than individually and in the course of a lifetime.[28] Bale singles out penance in particular for its susceptibility to dissimulation and corruption. A series of "confessions" orchestrated by the play's vice figures reveal the ritual to be no more than a means of establishing the power of the Catholic Church and undermining King Johan's authority. Usurped Power uses confession to ensure that Dissimulation continues to practice papist ceremonies rather than preach the gospel. Sedition uses the rite to enjoin Nobility to swear that he believes as the church teaches him, will flee from the "new lernyng" (1157), and holds King Johan to be a "very wycked man" (1169) and an adversary to the church, the tyranny of which he will help to subdue.

King Johan describes the abuses to which the Catholic Church and its clergy have made England subject in explicitly theatrical terms. In the play's first scenes, the widow England laments that the pope, that "wyld bore of Rome" with his "fantasyes, dreames and lyes" and "vyle cerymonyes" (70–73), has exiled God himself from the realm; King Johan observes that the church's "Latyne howres, serymonyes and popetly playes" (415) and its "Latyne mummers" (426) have corrupted God's word and despoiled England of her land and goods. The vice Sedition proclaims that "in every estate of the clargye I playe a part" (194), explaining how he appears in turn as a monk, nun, canon, parson, bishop, friar, chantry priest, cardinal, and pope. Indeed, the play imagines the entirety of the Roman church as an elaborate conspiracy of actor-vices. As part of their plot against King Johan, Sedition disguises himself as the archbishop of Canterbury, Stephen Langdon; Private Wealth disguises himself as the papal legate, Pandulph; Usurped Power disguises himself as the pope; and Dissimulation disguises himself as Simon of Swinsett, the monk who poisons King Johan. "To present the Pope as Usurped Power in disguise is, at the most elementary polemical level, to accuse him of usurpation," Peter Womack remarks. "But it is also, secondly, to suggest that his identity as Pope is a piece of theatrical trickery."[29] Bale's use of disguise in such cases is different from, for instance, Udall's use of it in *Respublica* when Adulation dresses himself as Honesty. "When such costumes come off, the quality can be seen for what it is," as Sarah Beckwith observes. By contrast, in Bale's theater there is nothing inside the costume: "The exposure is merely *to disguise as such*; disguise is what is uncovered."[30] Or, as White puts it, "Pope and Popery do not wear the mask; they *are* the mask."[31] The Catholic Church and its hierarchy, Bale suggests, are at their core defined by dissembling and deception.

Bale's exposure of the theater of the Catholic Church is meant to vilify it as such, yet that same exposure also attests to the pedagogical power of performances to teach audiences how to read the symbols of spiritual authority correctly.[32] The probable influence of Richard Morison, Cromwell's secretary and publicist, upon Bale is widely acknowledged. In *A Discourse Touching the Reformation of the Lawes of England* (ca. 1535), Morison argues that papal authority can best be undermined by using its own instruments of social control. He emphasizes the power of plays in particular to "set forthe and declare lyvely before the peoples eies the abohomynation and wickednes of the bisshop of Rome, monkes, ffreers, nonnes, and suche like."[33] Using language that will find explicit dramatic expression in *King Johan*, Morison insists that the right kind of plays "teache and preache the usurped power of the bisshoppe of Rome." Such plays show how the followers of the pope "wente aboute to distroie this Realme" so that "the people maye abhore hym and his doyngs and not herafter be disteyned with him" (178). Here drama has both reparatory and pedagogic functions: according to Morison, plays can serve as a means of correcting "the evyll that commethe of ignoraunce" and producing "the goode that commethe of knowlage" (179). In "commen people," Morison contends, "thynges sooner enter by the eies, then by the eares" and they remember things "better that they see then that they heere" (179). White notes, "The fact that Morison's proposals were implemented across the realm indicates the extent to which the Cromwellian regime recognized drama, processions, ceremonies and other religious or quasi-religious practices as means of legitimating and internalizing its vision of a politically and religiously reformed England."[34] Although distinguishing between "good" and "bad" performances, Morison's treatise underscores the power of *all* performances—whether papist or reformed—to shape the hearts and minds of Henry's subjects.

In bringing together Morison's methods and dramatic personification, Bale does not move away from the fifteenth-century morality play's investment in the role of performance in the creation of linguistic meaning and the construction of the self. Rather, in seeking to show that deception is his papist vices' defining trait, he continues it. In a scene that looks forward to the interaction between *Respublica*'s vices, Clergy submits himself to King Johan, kneeling before him in a mock act of repentance and promising to amend his misdeeds (507–8). The falseness of Clergy's alleged reform is made evident through a slip of the tongue when he swears the "Pope" rather than his "prynce" shall be his ruler (512–14). Clergy is "only playing" his allegiance to Johan; the "truth" invariably escapes out from under the cover of Clergy's church-sponsored theatrics. Parapraxis is a "misperformance" but nonetheless remains a performance of linguistic meaning. It is also itself performative: deception is made manifest through the performing body. In Bale's play, the human body remains the best picture of the human soul. As Cavell reminds us, "the soul may be hidden not because the body essentially conceals it but because it essentially reveals it."[35] In suggesting that the pope is Usurped Power in disguise—that the pope and popery are not wearing the mask but *are* the mask, as White would have it—Bale does not suggest the "privacy" of the pope's interiority but instead suggests how closely his identity is allied with performance.

One might say that for Bale the *disguised* human body is the best picture of the *vicious* human soul. Lies, disguise, and other forms of deception easily give rise to mentalist pictures of the self. The problem of insincere promises—such as Clergy's false oath of allegiance—and the temptations they hold out is famously entertained by J. L. Austin, who challenges the common assumption that "outward utterance is a description, *true or false*, of the occurrence of the inward performance." For Austin, that assumption is encapsulated by Hippolytus's protestation that "my tongue swore to, but my heart (or mind or other backstage artiste) did not."[36] Such reliance on such "backstage artistes" to secure the legitimacy of our promises confuses the issue, according to Austin: it "provides Hippolytus with a let-out, the bigamist with an excuse for his 'I do' and the welsher with a defence for his 'I bet.'" Instead, Austin holds, "accuracy and morality alike are on the side of the plain saying that *our word is our bond.*"[37] A picture of an "inner process" does not give us an accurate idea of what a promise is. Wittgenstein likewise stresses that lying—disguising the truth—is an ordinary language occurrence. We learn what a lie is, and how to lie, through social interactions: "Are we perhaps over-hasty in our assumption that the smile of an unweaned infant is not a pretence? —And on what experience is our assumption based? (Lying is a language-game that needs to be learned like any other one.)"[38] We don't imagine that an unweaned infant is lying, Wittgenstein suggests, because that infant has not yet entered into our language games.

Lying is also itself performative. Susceptibility to mistaking meaning is also the process of realizing it. In Henry Medwall's *Nature*, the first morality play to make extensive use of the convention of the disguised vice, the disguised vice appears as a form of self-deception.[39] When Pride disguises himself as Worship (esteem, honor), he can do so because the play's protagonist, Man, has already confused the two:

Pryde: My name ys Wurshyp.
Man: Wurshyp? Now surely,
        The World told me yt was my destyny
        To come to Wurshyp or I dye.
Pryde: Truly, I am the same.[40]

In order to learn what "pride" and "worship" mean, the play suggests, one must understand the ability of one to pass itself off as the other. As Pride has earlier explained to Sensuality, Man's mistake is a common one:

Sensualyte: What ys your name?
Pryde: Pryde.
Sensualyte: Pryde?
Pryde: Ye, sykerly,
        But I am cleped Worshyp comenly

> In placys where I dwell.
> *Sensualyte*: Worshyp? Now in fayth, ye say trew:
> Ye be *radix viciorum* — rote of all vertew.
> (1.836–40)

In noting that he is called Worship "comenly," Pride indicates that his disguise makes visually manifest a "common" confusion that emerges out of social exchange. In this way, the play relies upon the common voice, including the unreliability of that voice and its susceptibility to self-deception, to define its terms. Indeed, the play implies that such infelicities are key to understanding of the nature of vice. When Sensuality translates *radix viciorum* as "the rote of all vertew," he suggests that the root of all vice is the mistranslation of vice into virtue: the "trewth" of vice can only be discerned through misrepresentation and mistranslation. Importantly, these forms of deception are shown in performance: Man learns what vice is through human interactions that demonstrate his own susceptibility to its subterfuges.

As in *Nature* and as in the moralities of the fifteenth century, the plot of *King Johan* describes a process of fall and recovery in which the characters learn the meaning of their names. Nobility is vulnerable to vice because he understands himself (falsely according to the play's logic) primarily according to his chivalric oath to defend Holy Church (361–63) and thus fails to understand his obligation to his king. At the end of the play, Verity chastises each of the estates for failing to live up to their name. "How can ye presume to be called Nobilyte," Verity demands, "Diffamynge a prynce in your malygnyte?" (2225–26). "What prayse is it to yow to be called Cyvylyte / If yow from obedyence and godly order flee?" she asks Civil Order (2277–78). Her rebuke to Clergy comes in the form of an etymological lesson. The word "clergye," she explains, comes from *cleros*, which means a "lott" or "a sortynge out," as the clergy are God's select or those who "chose hym owt" after Christ's ascension (2245–50). However, Verity fears that Clergy's name comes instead from *clerus*, the "noyfull worme" that Aristotle describes (in the *History of Animals*) as the destroyer of honeycombs. Rather than acting as God's select, she observes (and echoing lollard polemicists writing a century earlier), "poore wydowes ye robbe" (2251–54).[41]

It is not simply that, as Morison implies, "seeing is believing"; instead, theater cultivates acts of spectatorship in specific ways. The play's extensive use of doubling, a logical necessity of a small acting troupe, suggests that one's understanding of virtue relies on one's experience of vice (and vice versa). Bale's stage directions explicitly provide that England should dress for Clergy (155sd), Sedition for Civil Order (312sd), Civil Order for Dissimulation, and Private Wealth for Nobility (1062sd); other doublings are implied by the play's dialogue and action. So when King Johan accuses Clergy of holding England "in dysdayne" using explicitly theatrical terms "with yowre Latyne howres, serymonyes and popetly playes" (414–15), he marks the ill effects that such theatrics have on the realm. But he also playfully suggests, as Clergy and England are played by the same actor, the degree to which Clergy's theatrics have overtaken England's identity. At the end of the play, Clergy promises to exile Usurped Power, Nobility to drive Private Wealth from monasteries, and Civil Order to hang Dissimulation (1329–33). As Womack observes, "Reformation is expressed as the victory of each of the three actors over his bad other role."[42] Such metatheatrical moments resist the idea that, in Bale, performance *itself* is exposed to be hollow. In relying on doubling, Bale draws on a long morality play tradition in which the meaning of terms is explored theatrically. In *Mankind*, the same actor likely played both divine Mercy and the devil Titivillus, calling upon the play's audience to weigh in what sense Titivillus functions as Mercy's "double."[43] *Nature's* Reason will insist that virtue can only be known by its contrary (1094–96). In *Magnificence*, when Fancy tells Conveyance that "we lacked thee / For to speak with Liberty," the joke is that Conveyance and Liberty couldn't speak to one another because they are played by the same actor (538–39).[44] Bale himself played his chief antagonist, Infidelity, in his other extant morality, *Three Laws* (ca. 1538).

Performance is also central to the play's transformations. In *King Johan*, penitential ritual is not so much repudiated as reformed. The play disparages the Catholic rite of penance in order to replace it with a drama of Protestant repentance. When the estates beg Veritas for forgiveness, she deflects this responsibility, lest her actions look too much like an act of sacerdotal absolution. She instead assures them that she does not doubt but "the Lorde wyll condescende / To forgyve yow all"

(2315–16). Bale replaces the earlier plays' promotion of the Church's spiritual authority with the promotion of a temporal one. Imperial Majesty oversees the play's final reconciliation ritual. Indeed, in Henrican England, truth is subject to the king. When Imperial Majesty next appears, he confirms that Verity has followed *his* commands (2319). The play ends with the estates begging Imperial Majesty for forgiveness, decrying the abuses of the Catholic Church, and lauding the ability of princes to subdue the "great Antichriste" (2688) to the comfort of the nation and to the glory of God and the gospel.

In Bale's theater, moral selfhood is still forged in and through performance. Ceremonies of reconciliation, and theater itself, prove indispensable to the reformation Bale's most celebrated morality describes. The triumph of the "truth" over Catholic forms of dissimulation depends upon the dramatic appearance of Veritas where the appearance of "Gods Veryte" is itself an act of theater. In the place of a penitential theater in which characters move from ignorance to self-knowledge through their participation in Roman ritual, Bale creates a godly drama primarily defined in terms of spectatorship: both God's truth and knowledge of self emerge through the enactment of a drama of recognition and misrecognition in which the audience itself participates. Verity's grand entrance at the end of the play only allows the estates to see the "verity" of Catholic oppression that Bale has dramatically demonstrated to the play's audience all along. For Bale, plays are not merely useful, as Morison suggests, because seeing (more so than hearing) is believing. For Bale, plays—and other forms of performance—are necessary for their ability to cultivate in his audience acts of perspicuous spectatorship revelatory of God's verity.

CALVIN'S TRUE SPECTATOR AND LEWIS WAGER'S *THE LIFE AND REPENTANCE OF MARY MAGDALENE*

In *The Life and Repentance of Mary Magdalene*, Wager follows his predecessor John Bale in using the stage to depict the corruption of Catholic stagecraft. Like Bale, he exploits the propagandist potential of theater: the action of the play centers on the vices' construction of the pre-repentant Mary into the gilded, movable statues like those so adored in the Middle Ages and so reviled by evangelist iconoclasts.[45] Yet as the play unfolds Wager employs a much more sophisticated use of theater that offers a vision of reform rather than rejection of theatrical forms in evangelical forms of worship. The final scenes of the play draw heavily on passages from John Calvin's *Institutes* and the story of the unnamed sinful woman who washes Christ's feet at the home of Simon the Pharisee in Luke 7 and the accounts of the expulsion of seven devils from Mary Magdalene in Luke 8 and Mark 16. Most critics have read the play's final scenes as straightforward, if problematic, dramatizations of the Calvinist and biblical texts.[46] However, those scenes and the texts upon which they draw are intimately concerned with questions of spectatorship and the nature of devotional performances. I focus here on the theatricality of the final scenes of *Mary Magdalene* in light of one of Wager's primary influences, the writings of John Calvin. Like Calvin, Wager embraces theater's potential to forge a new relation between drama and Protestant forms of selfhood. In doing so, Wager's play participates in the much broader reassessment during the English Reformation of the uses of ceremony and place of performance in Protestant forms of worship. In the post-repentant Mary, Wager's play presents an evangelical exemplar of reformed worshipful performance and a figure of Calvinist true spectatorship of Christ.

Calvin used theatrical metaphors equally to deride the hypocrisy of the Roman church and to laud the glory of God's creation.[47] Calvin was not immune to the antitheatrical prejudices of his day and, like Bale and Wager, was deeply suspicious of the theatricality of Catholic ceremonial culture. "When the unprincipled men, who occupy the pulpits under the Papacy, speak with weeping," he railed, "though they produce not a syllable from God's Word, but add some spectacle or phantom, by producing the image of the Cross or some like thing, they touch the feelings of the vulgar and cause weeping, according to what actors do on the stage."[48] Characterizing Catholic forms of worship as dangerous and empty shows, he charges that papists "have no regard for what pleases God, nor for what he commands in his word" and see the religious and holy life as "to run about here and there; to undertake pilgrimages imposed by vows; to set up a statue; to found masses, as they call it; to fast on certain days; and to lay stress on trifles about which God has never said a single word."[49] Above all, he associated such theatricality with hypocrisy, with those who "play" at being what they are not and who "pretend to worship God by many ceremonies" while allowing themselves "to commit all kinds of cruelty, rapine, and fraud."[50]

For Calvin the antidote to such popish hypocrisy is self-examination.[51] As such, the false actor must become audience to him- or herself. To satisfy God, one must "learn seriously and inwardly to examine ourselves, lest there should be any hypocrisy lurking within us."[52] Such self-examination must take place in light of God's law. Left to their own devices, Calvin explains in book 2 of the *Institutes*, humans are "blinded and drunk with self-love."[53] God's law both shows God's demands and the impossibility of meeting those demands. In a passage drawn heavily upon by Wager in his description of Mary's conversion, Calvin compares the law to a mirror, for in the law "we contemplate our weakness, then the iniquity arising from this, and finally the curse coming from both—just as a mirror shows us the spots on our face."[54] In its capacity to humble sinners by confronting them with the consequences of their sinfulness, the law is intimately concerned with self-examination and self-knowledge: "After he is compelled to weigh his life in the scales of the law, laying aside all that presumption of fictitious righteousness, he discovers that he is a long way from holiness, and is in fact teeming with a multitude of vices."[55]

In Calvin's epistemology, such knowledge of self is intimately tied to knowledge of God. To look upon oneself is to apprehend both divine gift and the wretchedness of human sin in the face of that gift. Calvin explores these mutual forms of knowledge through images of spectatorship:

No one can look upon himself without immediately turning his thoughts to the contemplation of God, in whom he "lives and moves" [Acts 17:28]. For, quite clearly, the mighty gifts with which we are endowed are hardly from ourselves; indeed, our very being is nothing but subsistence in the one God. Then, by these benefits shed like dew from heaven upon us, we are led as by rivulets to the spring itself. Indeed, our very poverty better discloses the infinitude of benefits reposing in God. The miserable ruin, into which the rebellion of the first man cast us, especially compels us to look upward.[56]

Equally, self-knowledge can only exist in view of God: "It is certain that a man never achieves a clear knowledge of himself unless he has first looked upon God's face, and then descends from contemplating him to scrutinize himself."[57]

In so reforming false actors into true spectators, Calvin carves out a space to reimagine theater in positive terms. Whereas in *The Castle of Perseverance* the play modeled the world, for Calvin, the world is a play. "The world was no doubt made," Calvin writes in his commentary on Hebrews, "that it might be the theater of the divine glory."[58] In book 2 of the *Institutes*, he similarly describes the world as a "magnificent theater . . . crammed with innumerable miracles," shining in God's glory and replete with evidence of God's providence and kindness.[59] The faithful, irradiated by God's spirit, "see sparks of his glory . . . glittering in every created thing."[60] He warns that few are equal to that sight: "However much the glory of God shines forth, scarcely one man in a hundred is a true spectator of it!"[61] Caught up in their own vanities, most are dazzled by what they see, struck blind by their own sinfulness. In Calvin's theatrical metaphors, the faithful become the rapt audience of the spectacular drama of God's creation.

Wager's *Mary Magdalene* displays a similar concern with theater, hypocrisy, and the call for self-examination. The initial scenes imagine the pre-repentant Mary and the vices as hypocrites who take on false roles. When she first appears, Mary is cast as a highly alluring, flirtatious, and spoiled young gentlewoman who falls under the sway of the vice Infidelity and his minions, who are members of Catholic clergy and pose as virtuous counselors.[62] The vices construct Mary herself into a "puppet" of the Roman church. As the leering vices dress and adorn her body, Patricia Badir notes, she is "pointedly figured as a three-dimensional object of erotic idolatry to be decorated, worshiped, and ravished by her bedazzled popish patrons."[63] Whereas the earlier scenes describe the false theater of the Roman church, the conversion scenes refocus the audience's attention from such spectacles to the actors'—and by extension their own—acts of spectatorship.[64] By harnessing the theatrical medium to reimagine his actors as spectators, Wager maps out a new place for performance in Protestant forms of worship in which any performance must be understood as primarily an act of witnessing.

Mary's conversion literally occurs through an act of theatrical spectatorship. Wager presents her conversion in explicitly Calvinist terms, and the dialogue in this section of the play closely follows passages from book 2 of the *Institutes* in which Calvin describes how God instituted the law in order to disclose human sinfulness. Following the trajectory laid out by Calvin, Mary's conversion begins when a figure representing the Law of God appears, holding a mirror in which Mary must confront her own sinfulness. In response to Law's pronouncement that "by the Lawe commeth the knowledge of synne," a figure named Knowledge of Sin appears to witness the "horrible, lothsome, and stinkyng vilitie" of Mary's sins, and the dialogue of the play focuses upon the question of how Mary should interpret the sight of the rotten, stinking, ill-favored "pocky knaue," as Infidelity characterizes him, that stands before her.[65] In England, Mary's temptation and fall, conversion at the house of Simon the Pharisee, and subsequent life of virtue had previously received dramatic treatment in the Digby *Mary Magdalene*; in its dramatic visualization of sin, Wager's conversion scene recalls both Anima's reappearance in *Wisdom* "in þe most horrybull wyse" and the staged exorcism in the Digby *Mary Magdalene*'s recounting of the Mark 16:9 and Luke 8:2 narratives when, upon Christ's confirmation of Mary's salvation, seven devils shall "dewoyde [go out] frome þe woman" and the Bad Angel shall "enter into hell with thondyr."[66] As Coletti has shown, the relation between Mary's inwardly focused "spiritual values" and "the material signs on which sacred drama must depend to articulate these values" is also arguably a tension in the Digby *Mary Magdalene*; however, Wager's play expresses considerable ambivalence about the theatrical nature of Mary's confrontation.[67] Law locates himself "before the *conscience* sight" (1193; emphasis mine). Knowledge of Sin similarly stresses that he does not actually appear to Mary's "carnall syght" (1305). Nonetheless, metaphors of sight predominate the description of Mary's confrontation with Law and Knowledge. "I see that I am but a damned deuill in hell" (1206), says Mary. And, as Christ has yet to make an appearance in the play, she laments, "In God I see is small mercy and Iustice" (1226–27). Mary, who has up until now been the object of the vices' (and the audience's own) lascivious gaze, is now reimagined as spectator, viewing and interpreting the spectacle of her own sins first in the Law's mirror and then in Knowledge of Sin's grotesque visage.

In modeling *Mary Magdalene*'s final episode on Luke 7, Wager turns to a story that, for the Protestant commentator, raises important questions about the nature of devotional performances and the role they play in the processes through which sins are forgiven.[68] In the gospel narrative, Simon the Pharisee invites Christ to his house, where a woman of the city, a known sinner, comes and washes, kisses, and anoints Christ's feet. Sensing Simon's disapproval, Christ responds by telling a parable of a creditor and two debtors, one of which owed five hundred pence and the other fifty. As neither could pay, the creditor forgave them both. Which debtor, Christ asks, would love him most? Christ furthermore observes that whereas the woman washed his feet with her tears and wiped them with her hair, Simon has offered him no such gracious reception: "Wherefore I say unto thee, Her sins, which are many, are forgiven; for she loved much."[69] His declaration causes a stir among Simon's other guests, who wonder to themselves, "Who is this that forgiveth sins also?"[70] The story concludes with Christ sending the woman away in peace, telling her, "Thy faith has saved thee."[71]

When Calvin reads Luke 7, his burden is to refute any suggestion that the woman was saved because of any action on her part. He argues that actions did not cause the forgiveness of her sins. Rather, it was an expression of gratitude for the gift of forgiveness already received:

> *We* cannot avoid wondering . . . that the greater part of commentators have fallen into so gross a blunder as to imagine that this woman, by her *tears*, and her *anointing*, and her *kissing his feet*, deserved the pardon of her sins. The argument which Christ employs was taken, not from the cause, but from the effect; for, until a favor has been received, it cannot awaken gratitude, and the cause of reciprocal love is here declared to be a free forgiveness. In a word, Christ argues from the fruits or effects that follow it, that this woman has been reconciled to God.[72]

When Christ pronounces "thy sins are forgiven," Calvin argues, he speaks only to further "seal his mercy upon our hearts," to contribute to "confirmation of her faith."[73] The woman's actions did not earn her salvation; rather, her actions were a testament to her gratitude for a gift already given and acknowledgment of her obligation to God. Christ "looked only at her extraordinary zeal to testify her repentance, which is also held out to us by Luke as an example."[74]

Dismissing the notion that the sinful woman's actions are themselves efficacious, Calvin redirects his reader's attention to the model Luke 7 provides of true and false spectatorship of Christ. For Calvin, the sinful woman's devotional performance is not important insofar as what it *does* but insofar as what it *witnesses*. Her virtue, Calvin emphasizes, lies in "leaving no kind of duty undone to testify her gratitude, and by acknowledging, in every possible way, her vast obligations to God."[75] Calvin also stresses Simon's condemnation of the sinful woman and what it says about his understanding of Christ. For Calvin, Simon's failure to recognize Christ as a prophet is a failure of self-knowledge and failed act of spectatorship: Simon is emblematic of the "captious disposition" of those who do not see Christ correctly.[76] Simon's error lies in the fact that in condemning the sinful woman he does not perceive Christ's redemptive role: "Overlooking the grace of reconciliation, which was the main feature to be looked for in Christ, the Pharisee concluded that he was *not a prophet*."[77] Calvin attributes Simon's fault to hypocrisy:

> Let every man examine himself and his life, and then we will not wonder that others are admitted along with us, for no one will dare to place himself above others. It is hypocrisy alone that leads men to be careless about themselves, and haughtily despise others.[78]

Having failed to examine his own sins, Simon misperceives himself, the sinful woman, and Christ. The reaction of Simon's other guests to Christ's promise reveals that they, like Simon, do not examine their own sinful condition: "There is no reason to wonder that hypocrites, who slumber amidst their vices, should murmur at it as a thing new and unexpected, when Christ forgives sins."[79]

Like Calvin, Wager stages Luke 7 as primarily a scene of true and false spectatorship. Wager adds a long speech (1765–1828) to the gospel account in which Mary, acknowledging her many sins, indicates that her actions bear witness to her repentance and testify to a gift already received:

> To shew such obsequie to hym it is a small matter,
>   Which by his grace hath my synfull life amended.
>   (1803–4)

Wager's staging also emphasizes Simon and his guests' actions as failed acts of spectatorship. The stage directions suggest that Mary's acts of adoration—her washing and anointing of Christ's feet—are at least partially obscured from the audience's view, a staging decision that focuses the audience's attention on how her actions are perceived by others.[80] Infidelity styles her attentions to be those of a prostitute:

> Behold, how boldly after hym she doth procede,
>   A harlot she is truly I may tell you in counsell.
>   (1835–36)

Malicious Judgment mockingly imagines she is trying to rid the room of pests: "I pray you see, how busy about hym she is. . . . Behold, she anoynteth him to driue away flies" (1841–44). In a double act of spectatorship, he then turns his gaze to look upon Simon, who, he judges, is not pleased by what he sees (1847–48). By drawing the audience's attention on how Mary's actions are perceived by others, the play confronts the audience with their own acts of spectatorship. Theater becomes a mirror for self-contemplation.

In Wager, ceremony and worshipful performances persist as sites of self-examination where the virtue of one's performance depends upon one's ability first to see oneself as sinner and thus be a true spectator of Christ. As poor and malicious spectators, Simon and his guests are also bad actors. When Christ looks upon them, he identifies them as hypocrites and, adding significantly to the gospel narrative, contrasts their empty shows to Mary's true one:[81]

> Where as you thinke you haue done me pleasure,
>   In bidding me to eate and drinke with you here,
> Your intent was to shew your richesse and treasure,
>   And that your holynesse might to me appeare.

> But this woman hath shewed to me a little obsequie:
>   For these gestures whiche she sheweth to me,
> Procede from a true meanyng heart verily,
>   As by her humilite plainly you may see.
>   (1893–1900)

Christ then admonishes Simon and his guests to examine their own sinfulness before condemning Mary: "At this womans synne you do greatly grutche / As though your selues were iust, holy, and pure" (1921–22). Or, as Christ says of the adulterous woman in John 8, let he who is without sin cast the first stone.

What are the ramifications for theater of Wager's vision of a new place of performance in Protestant forms of worship? It is in view of *Mary Magdalene*'s last scene that I wish now to turn to the most well-known passage of Wager's play, his defense of his drama in the play's prologue. Presumably defending his play against Puritan detractors, the prologue notes that the play has been by "some . . . spitefully despised" (12) and defends its moral integrity:

> Doth not our facultie learnedly extoll vertue?
> Doth it not teache, God to be praised aboue al thing?
> What facultie doth vice more earnestly subdue?
>
> (31–33)

In defending his play's virtues, Wager draws attention to the fact that his virtuous performance requires virtuous spectators. Indeed, to view his play as anything but virtuous is to make oneself into a false actor. After providing an account of the godly playing his own theater represents, the prologue delivers a more pointed attack on its critics as hypocrites who "play" at being something they are not:

> Hipocrites that wold not haue their fautes reueled
>   Imagine slaunder our facultie to let,
> Faine wold they haue their wickednes still concealed
>   Therfore maliciously against vs they be set.
>
> (38–41)

Casting his detractors in the role that will be occupied by the vices, Wager also suggests, like Calvin, the antidote to such hypocrisy is self-examination:

> Thou shalt neither praise thyne owne industrie,
>   Nor yet the labour of other men reprehend,

The one procedeth of a proude arrogancie,
And the other from enuie, which doth discommend,
All thyngs that vertuous persons doe intend.

(17–21)

The prologue both defends its spectacle as virtuous and provides a
model of virtuous spectatorship. The right kind of spectators—those
who "take in good worth our simple diligence" (51)—will let themselves be instructed by the example of penitence, love of Christ, and
faith the post-repentant Magdalene provides. Wager insists that a reformed theater is possible where correct viewing of the play and oneself are mutual.

In Wager's reformed drama, Mary becomes a new Everyman. Like
her medieval predecessor, Mary is representative of what it means to
be human: we are meant to look at her and see ourselves. And, as in the
fifteenth-century moralities, Wager's play presents an understanding
of the usefulness of theatrical display for creating models of knowledge. Yet the play's model of performative selfhood is fundamentally
different. Unlike Everyman, Mary is not meant to be understood to be
ontologically identical to the members of her audience. Instead, Mary
is meant to be understood to be a particular individual. As she becomes
a more "rounded" character—as her singularity is foregrounded—our
allegorical identification with her flattens out. Absent is *Everyman*'s
complex interrogation of the relation between collective and individual. Indeed, we may even wonder at the privacy of Mary's inner
life. In the particularity of her iconic identity, Mary is primarily exemplary. In the medieval plays, Christian self-knowledge accrues through
the rituals of the Roman church and one's shared life with others. By
contrast, Wager presents a theater of self-examination in which one
sees oneself in Mary's sinfulness. In order to know oneself—and thus
know God—one must look at oneself and see the sinner Mary and thus
God's redemptive grace. The self has become something to be viewed
rather than performed. The audience members are no longer incorpo-
rated into the world of the play but are passive observers of the events
on stage.

WITH THEIR SWEEPING reconceptualization of Roman rite as theater,
the evangelical moralities of the mid-sixteenth century pave the way

for Christopher Marlowe's brilliant reworking of the morality play *Doctor Faustus*, in which the position of the reprobate is imagined as a necromancer captivated by his own frivolous shows. *Faustus* describes a struggle between allegorical forces of good and evil for the soul of its protagonist, and critics have long recognized Marlowe's debt to the medieval morality play's dramatic structure, devices, and themes.[82] However, whereas the medieval plays dramatize the availability of God's mercy, Faustus announces its unavailability as a willful act of defiance. "The reward of sin is death," he says, reading from Romans 6:23 and omitting the divine promise of eternal life that follows: "That's hard."[83] In dramatizing the unavailability of God's mercy, *Faustus* reverses the structure of the medieval morality play. As in the earlier plays, Marlowe's drama demonstrates the power of performances to shape the self, but the transformations those performances produce run in the opposite direction, cutting Faustus off from, rather than leading him toward, the life of the spirit. The fifteenth- and sixteenth-century morality plays confirm the potential of (the right kind of) performance to connect their audiences to linguistic processes and reveal divine truths. In contrast, in *Faustus* performance has become a site of willful self-deception rather than self-knowledge, where Faustus himself allegorizes an audience member more engaged in looking than in acting. As the play's audience, we are asked to contemplate the power of shows to distract and to transform.

It will be theater's seductive illusions—both the devil's and Faustus's own—that time and time again prevent Faustus from repenting.[84] In an open bid to distract Faustus from his doubts about selling his soul to Lucifer, Mephistopheles conjures a lively band of devils who dance before Faustus and adorn him with riches. "What means this show?" Faustus inquires. "Nothing, Faustus, but to delight thy mind withal," replies Mephistopheles (2.1.84–85). When Lucifer parades the Seven Deadly Sins before him, the Sins, who deny having any parents, appear to bear no relation to Faustus. They are not *his* sins: their theatricality underscores their exteriority to him. They are simply another diversion. Touring sights of Europe in a dragon-drawn chariot, Faustus uses his magic to create yet more trivial shows. Invisible, he snatches food from the pope, panders to the whims of the emperor by making Alexander the Great and his paramour appear before him, obtains grapes to satisfy the cravings of a pregnant duchess, and plays cruel and silly pranks on those who challenge or annoy him.[85] When Old Man begs Faustus to cry for God's mercy, Mephistopheles distracts him with yet another show, the promise that the "heavenly" Helen of Troy will be his paramour whose "sweet embracings may extinguish clean / These thoughts that do dissuade me from my vow," Faustus says (5.1.84–87). He will keep his oath to Lucifer: "Her lips," he declares, "sucks forth my soul" (93).

In *Faustus*, knowledge has a new role. The medieval plays dramatized the forms of self-knowledge that, in acknowledging oneself as creature, draw the soul to its maker. By contrast, *Faustus* shows that self-knowledge can be destroyed by the humanistic quest for other forms of knowing. When Descartes declares, "I think therefore I am," he defines the boundaries of knowledge according to the limits of human mind, rather than according to the limitless acts of recognition through which one participates in divine beauty and love, where "in that which he handles and sees he may recognize of what nature that is which he received and does not see."[86] In the play's first scene, Faustus summarily rejects philosophy, law and medicine, and theology as woefully inadequate: they are "odious and obscure," "for petty wits," "unpleasant, harsh, contemptible, and vile" (1.1.108–10). He turns to magic and its promise to "the studious artisan" a "world of profit and delight / Of power, of honour, of omnipotence" (1.1.55–57). In doing so, he dramatizes the temptation inherent in a humanistic education to exceed the human: "A sound magician is a mighty god" (64), Faustus triumphantly proclaims.

Yet, however vain and harmful Faustus's spectacles prove to be, they remain a powerful site of self-shaping. Marlowe's play testifies to the enduring power of performances to shape the self even as history moves ineluctably toward Cartesian dualism and its radical distrust of appearances. Faustus's illusions, though specious, once again do not finally prove to be empty. Performances, as actions, are necessarily performative: they *do* things, however ill or unintended their effects. Faustus first conjures Mephistopheles using an elaborate popish rite that involves a Latin incantation, the sprinkling of holy water, and making the sign of the cross, declaring himself the "conjurer laureate" who "canst command great Mephistopheles" (1.3.15–33). However, the devil immediately deflates his balloon, explaining Faustus's incantation was only the cause of his coming "*per accidens*":

For when we hear one rack the name of God,
Abjure the Scriptures and his Savior Christ,
We fly in hope to get his glorious soul.

(46–48)

Mephistopheles undermines the pretensions of Faustus's incantation, but Faustus's ritual nonetheless still effects, just not in the way he had so vaingloriously assumed. Likewise, the ceremony through which Faustus hands his soul over to the devil will indeed lead to his damnation, but not because his pact with the devil is actually binding: the continued pleas of the Good Angel and Old Man strongly suggest it is still possible for Faustus to repent. In *Faustus*, performances still *effect*. However, they distract from and thus conceal, rather than reveal, divine mercy.

Conclusion

Morality Drama Inside Out

Teachers of allegory everywhere applauded the release of Pixar Animation Studio's ingenious and delightful 2015 film *Inside Out*. Directed by Pete Docter, *Inside Out* personifies the interior life of an eleven-year-old girl named Riley as she adjusts to her family's move from Minnesota to San Francisco. Most of the film takes place inside Riley's brain, whose Headquarters are controlled by five emotions: Joy, Sadness, Disgust, Fear, and Anger. Her lead emotion, Joy, literally aglow in yellow, is an irrepressibly sunny micromanager; Sadness is a blue, frumpy, sluggish melancholic; Disgust is a green, snooty cool girl; Fear is a purple, jittery paranoiac; and Anger, whose head is prone to burst into flames, is a literal hothead. *Inside Out* provides ample evidence that personification allegory and the morality play are still vibrant cultural forms. As in the medieval plays, the film both depicts the mind's inner landscape and traces a redemptive narrative of fall and recovery in which its protagonist will discover the true meaning of a word, here "sadness," as its meaning is unfolded and revealed through characters' interactions with one another. In doing so, the film presents a decidedly non-Cartesian and performative picture of the self: despite its title, it works less to turn its protagonist's mind "inside out" than to collapse the boundary between inside and outside. The film, like the medieval plays, shows it is impossible to split the interior self from the exterior experiences that define it. *Inside Out* thus marks a return to the medieval plays' faith in the redemptive and self-defining potential of performances. The film's postmodern moment and use of new cognitive science attests to the endurance of a pre-Cartesian (rather than poststructuralist) model of performative selfhood that, as Wittgenstein's philosophy of language bears witness, we have never fully left behind.[1]

In personifying Riley's emotional life, the film displays the classic hallmarks of a morality play insofar as it is a *psychomachia* taking place within the internal architecture of the mind. Riley's emotions perform an analogous role to the virtues of the morality plays and are endangered not by vice per se but by good intentions. In the post-Freudian psychology of the film, it will be Riley's attempts to repress her sadness that will cause her bad behavior. As Riley struggles to adjust to a new home and school, her parents just want her to stay their happy girl. "Your dad's under a lot of pressure," her mom confides at bedtime. "But if you and I can keep smiling, it would be a big help. We can do that for him, right?" Meanwhile, inside Headquarters, Joy tries to prevent Sadness (without much success) from touching and transforming Riley's "core memories," the glowing golden orbs that power her Islands of Personality, theme park–like structures representing defining parts of her identity. Joy, who sees it as her job to keep Riley happy all day long, draws a chalk circle around Sadness and gives her the "super-important" task of staying inside it. When Joy's repressive tactics backfire, Joy, Sadness, and Riley's core memories are suddenly expelled from Headquarters, and Joy and Sadness are left to wander around the labyrinthine field of Riley's Long-Term Memory trying to find their way back. Without her core memories and with both Joy and Sadness in exile, Riley's Islands of Personality begin to collapse: Riley fails her hockey tryout, fights with her parents, and (stealing her mother's credit card) decides to run away back to Minnesota. Joy and Sadness will only find their way back to Headquarters—and Riley will only be able to adjust to her new home and stop behaving badly—once everyone comes to terms with the fact that Sadness has a role to play in Riley's well-being. As the film's narrative makes explicit, our sadness allows others to comfort us. The recognition of what we have lost also allows us to grow: we help others because we have been sad, too. "Sadness or pain are feelings aroused by evils afflicting a man's own self," Aquinas long ago recognized, "and so sadness over another's misfortune is measured by the extent to which we see another's misfortune as our own."[2] Our sadness allows us to empathize with others.

Critics routinely note that *Inside Out* draws on the latest research in the science of emotion and neurophysiology—Docter consulted with University of California psychologists Dacher Keltner and Paul Ekman in making the film—and tout the lessons that the film can deliver about the role emotions play in defining our identities. However, its literary debts have not been so widely recognized, as seen in this *New York Times* review:

> This is a movie almost entirely populated by abstract concepts moving through theoretical space. This world is both radically new—you've never seen anything like it—and instantly recognizable, as familiar aspects of consciousness are given shape and voice. Remember your imaginary childhood friend? Your earliest phobias? Your strangest dreams? You will, and you will also have a newly inspired understanding of how and why you remember those things. You will look at the screen and know yourself.[3]

The "radically new" world created by the film, is, of course, not new at all: it is a twenty-first-century version of a medieval personification allegory.

Just as with the medieval morality play, the film testifies to the endurance of a conception of language where our understanding of a meaning of a word arises through human interactions. At the beginning of the film, Joy recognizes Fear's and Disgust's roles in keeping Riley safe and Anger's role in protecting her against injustices (they unite against eating broccoli), but she is uncertain what role Sadness—which in her view just makes Riley feel bad—might possibly play in Riley's well-being. As becomes apparent, although we might fear sadness because it is painful, when we fail to acknowledge our sadness we become angry and act badly. It will be part of the work of the film to unfold how its characters' (and audience's) understanding of the meaning of "sadness" changes. Keltner and Ekman describe the adjustments to its understanding of sadness the film's audience is asked to make:

> You might be inclined to think of sadness as a state defined by inaction and passivity—the absence of any purposeful action. But in "Inside Out," as in real life, sadness prompts people to unite in response to loss. We see this first in an angry outburst at the din-

ner table that causes Riley to storm upstairs to lie alone in a dark room, leaving her dad to wonder what to do. . . . "Inside Out" offers a new approach to sadness. Its central insight: Embrace sadness, let it unfold, engage patiently with a preteen's emotional struggles. Sadness will clarify what has been lost (childhood) and move the family toward what is to be gained: the foundations of new identities, for children and parents alike.[4]

Keltner and Ekman deliver their views about how best to support the emotional life of a preteen emphatically and didactically: "Embrace sadness!" they suggest. In contrast, although containing a clear moral "lesson" about our emotional lives, the film largely avoids the pitfall of didacticism. It dramatizes the blind spots that the film's version of "vice" presents as both attractive and human: *If you and I can keep smiling, it would be a big help.* The film also makes palpable the costs of such errors. We discover the meaning of "sadness" through the human interactions that show us the price of its dismissal, as allegorized by Joy's and Sadness's expulsion from Headquarters and realized in Riley's subsequent breakdown.

The film also allegorizes the dangers of turning its personified characters into abstractions. In one of the film's most inventive scenes, Abstract Thought is imagined as an industrial building complex with a vast, white space inside. Trying to find their way back to Headquarters, Joy and Sadness discover Riley's childhood imaginary friend, Bing Bong, an elephant-cat-dolphin made of pink cotton candy, who is wandering around, half forgotten, in Riley's Long-Term Memory. Bing Bong advises them to catch the "train of thought" that will carry them back to Headquarters. The nearest train station, however, is in Imagination Land, and Bing Bong urges Joy and Sadness to take a "short cut" through Abstract Thought. Against the better judgment of Sadness — who already knows both intellectually and experientially what it is like to be turned into an abstraction — the three friends enter. Meanwhile, Riley sits sad and alone eating lunch on the playground of her new school. A couple of Mind Workers approach the complex: "What abstract thought are we going to try to comprehend today?" asks one. The other worker checks his clipboard: "Loneliness." Noticing something inside the building, the Mind Workers close the door, turning Abstract Thought "on" for a minute to "burn out the gunk." Trapped inside, Joy, Sadness, and Bing Bong begin to "abstract." Abstraction proves to be a terrifying de Manian process of defacement, disfiguration, and destruction. As they begin to transform into Picasso-like figures, Sadness, who has done her homework on the "Four Stages of Abstraction," tells her friends that they are entering stage one, Nonobjective Fragmentation. When they begin to enter the next stage, Deconstruction, Bing Bong warns that "what is important is that we all stay together!" immediately before they begin to break apart into pieces. Two-dimensionalization follows. "We're lacking in depth!" Bing Bong shouts, making the dangers of abstraction explicit, as the white space of the screen contracts, compressing him, Joy, and Sadness into thin colored lines. In the final stage, the three friends break down into monochromatic shapes, narrowly escaping out the door and into Imagination Land. To contemplate joy, sadness, loneliness, or the products of our imagination in the "abstract," the film seems to suggest, is to deny them of all things that give them "life"—that is, to divest them of the humanity and complexity that gives our lives with signs meaning. They only exist—they only "live"—within the context of lived experience and embedded in human activity and exchange.

Like a medieval morality play, the tensions of the film resolve through a redemptive, quasi-penitential narrative in which the characters' literal and figurative falls will in turn be the catalysts of their redemption. Here Riley's "fall" into wrongdoing (stealing her mother's credit card and running away) is figured by Joy's betrayal of Sadness and literal fall into an abyss. As everything in Riley's life falls apart, the Islands of Personality collapse, and even the ground below Riley's Long-Term Memory begins to crumble. In an act of desperation, Joy attempts to escape with Riley's core memories to Headquarters through a "recall tube," abandoning Sadness, who she fears will forever taint Riley's memories, to fend for herself in the wreckage. When the recall tube shatters as the ground gives way beneath it, Joy and Bing Bong are plunged into the Memory Dump, a vast, dark chasm containing Riley's forgotten memories. Trapped in the dump, with no hope of salvation, Joy feels sorrow and, for the first time, understands Sadness's value. Joy realizes that the most jubilant of Riley's core memories—when after a game her entire hockey team lifted her up into the air in celebration— could only occur because Riley first expressed her sadness. Remembering Sadness's earlier words, Joy recalls that, just before this triumphant moment, Riley had been heartbroken after missing the winning shot and losing the playoff: it had been her sadness that allowed others to help her.

Significantly, in *Inside Out*, the seat of morality is not God but cognitive processes and emotions. The "ghost in the machine" is a remarkably mechanistic one: Riley's interior is imagined as a futuristic industrial landscape. Riley's moral behavior is produced through a system of sprawling storehouses, hydraulic lifts, conveyer belts, pneumatic tubes, front loaders, cranes, and an electric rail line. (Yet even in this very secular production, metaphysical mysteries still reassert themselves: From whom *do* the Mind Workers take direction?) In contrast to the morality plays, communal reconciliation occurs not through the ritual recognition of sin and grace of divine forgiveness but through a balanced emotional life that recognizes a positive role for sadness. Returning home, Riley is worried that her parents will be angry not because she's done wrong (stolen a credit card and run away), but because she is sad. In a modern twist to penitential contrition, her confession is to sadness itself: "I know you don't want me to, but I miss home. I miss Minnesota. You need me to be happy, but I want my old friends and my hockey team. I want to go home. Please don't be mad." God's mercy is replaced by human empathy: "You know what? I miss Minnesota, too," her father replies. Here the divine Father has been superseded by a fallible, human one whose computer-generated form foregrounds human rather than divine creativity. For Augustine, the self is only fully constituted in God as one is united to him in a bond of love. In contrast, in the twenty-first century, it is human emotions that need to be recognized and acknowledged rather than divine presence: to empathize with others, to feel their pain, and thus become one with them is both at the heart of moral rectitude and key to self-actualization. Joy's contrition does not result in a plea for forgiveness (she never tells Sadness she's sorry) but instead produces acts of recognition that acknowledge the value of sadness itself.

I have argued throughout that the medieval morality plays' investigation of language and penitential practice allows us to understand more fully the role of theatricality in medieval notions of the self, wherein even our language for our most individual experiences relies on communal processes of generating meaning. *Inside Out* shows us how the morality play's penitential trajectory and communal meaning-making are still current and powerful narrative forms. We still conceive of human development through penitence and sacrifice: indeed, in keeping with the penitential trajectory of *Inside Out*, Riley's redemption will only be possible through the self-sacrifice of innocence, as Bing Bong, staying behind in the Memory Dump, dies so that Joy can live. My point here is not to argue that Bing Bong is a Christ figure or that the creators of *Inside Out* intentionally modeled their film on a medieval morality play. Indeed, the fact that we are not encouraged to wonder whether there will be consequences, either immediate or eternal, for the stolen credit card marks our distance from the medieval plays. Instead, I wish to suggest that it is still possible, through a very new, digitally animated and cinematic version of a very old theatrical form, to recognize and to know ourselves.

NOTES

INTRODUCTION

1. Augustine, *City of God* 19.3, as quoted in Aquinas, *Summa Theologiae* 1a.75, 4.

2. Aquinas, *Summa Theologiae* 1a.76, 1.

3. For recent studies that seek to correct the critical tendency to impose modern ideologies of the self onto medieval texts, see, in particular, Crane, *The Performance of Self*; Little, *Confession and Resistance*; and Spearing, *Textual Subjectivity*, and Spearing, *Medieval Autographies.*

4. In his narrative of emergent consciousness in *The Philosophy of History* (1837), Hegel establishes a decisive break between the medieval and early modern, identifying the Reformation with the "meditative introversion of the soul upon itself" (421). I discuss Burckhardt's infamous and influential denial of interiority to medieval human consciousness in *The Civilization of the Renaissance in Italy* (first published in English in 1878) in chapter 4. De Grazia, "World Pictures, Modern Periods, and the Early Stage," provides a helpful overview of the history of periodization as it relates to early English theater.

5. Aers, "A Whisper in the Ear of Early Modernists"; Patterson, "On the Margin," quotation at 99–100.

6. See Butler, *Gender Trouble*, esp. 34, 185–93, 193–99.

7. The only surviving text of the play was written onto a parchment account roll for the years 1343–44 for the Priory of the Holy Trinity in Dublin. The manuscript was lost in the explosion and fire that destroyed the Public Record Office housed at the Four Courts Building in Dublin in 1922. Our knowledge of the play today is based on a description and transcription made for the Royal Society of Antiquaries in 1891 by James Mills, the deputy-keeper of the Public Records. For a description of the manuscript history, see Davis, ed., *Non-cycle Plays and Fragments*, lxxxv–lxxxvi. Davis's volume also includes the play's text; hereafter, references to *The Pride of Life* are to Davis's edition and are cited parenthetically by line number.

8. The play opens with the King of Life, attended by his knights Strength and Health, boasting of his power, bragging that there is "no man of woman

iborre" (122) whom he cannot destroy, and rebuffing his queen and bishop when they implore him to remember his death and make a good end. The text breaks off just as the king sends out his messenger, Mirth, to search out and challenge Death to a fight. A full description of the play's plot is included in its banns, indicating that the missing parts of the play dramatize the ensuing battle between the King of Life and Death, Death's inevitable triumph, the devil's seizure of the king's soul, and the Virgin Mary's intercession on his behalf.

9. The Macro plays are difficult to date with any precision. Here I follow Eccles, ed., *Macro Plays*, xi, xxx, xxxviii. But also see the attempts to connect the plays to specific political events by Gibson, "The Play of *Wisdom* and the Abbey of St. Edmunds," who suggests that *Wisdom* may have been performed on the occasion of the Edward IV's visit to the abbey in 1469, and by Brantley and Fulton, "*Mankind* in a Year without Kings," who argue that *Mankind* was most likely written in 1471 during the period in which Edward IV was temporarily deposed.

10. For overviews of theories about the staging of the morality plays, see Twycross, "The Theatricality of Medieval English Plays"; Southern, *Medieval Theatre in the Round*, and Southern, *Staging of the Plays before Shakespeare*; Tydeman, *Medieval English Theatre*; Riggio, "The Staging of *Wisdom*"; and Clopper, *Drama, Play, and Game*. For the argument that the morality plays were put on by parishes, see White, *Drama and Religion*, 10–12, 35–37.

11. References to a "hostler" (722) and a "tapster" (725) suggest that *Mankind* was written to be performed in an inn yard or inn. However, as Clopper remarks, such references may suggest the playing area is simply being *imagined* as one, and the play may have been performed in any number of indoor settings, including a manor house, public hall, or church (Clopper, *Drama, Play, and Game*, 191–92). All references to the *Castle*, *Mankind*, and *Wisdom* are to Eccles's EETS edition of the Macro Plays and are cited parenthetically in the text by line number; stage directions are noted as "sd" with reference to the preceding line.

12. For a side-by-side edition of the two plays, see Davidson et al., eds., *Everyman and Its Dutch Original, Elckerlijc*.

13. *Everyman*, ed. Cawley; further citations refer to this edition and are given in the text by line numbers. As Katherine Little notes, *Everyman* is the only play among what are commonly called medieval morality plays that describes itself as a moral play; for the argument that *Everyman* is better understood in the context of sixteenth-century English humanism rather than medieval drama, see Little, "What Is *Everyman*?"

14. According to Bevington, the *Castle* is written in the dialect of Norfolk, with a northern influence, and *Wisdom* and *Mankind* use the dialect of Norfolk and Suffolk (Bevington, ed., *The Macro Plays*, vii–viii). *Mankind* contains references to Bury (274) and places in Cambridgeshire and Norfolk (505–15). A reference to the gallows of Canwick (2421), which stood just outside the town of Lincoln, suggests that the *Castle* may have been performed in, or originally been a product of, Lincolnshire.

15. On the variety of medieval East Anglian theater, see Coldewey, "The Non-cycle Plays and the East Anglian Tradition"; Coletti, *Mary Magdalene*; Gibson, *Theater of Devotion*; and Scherb, *Staging Faith*.

16. Gibson, *Theater of Devotion*, chap. 5, makes the argument for a Bury provenance. See also Baker et al., eds., *Late Medieval Religious Plays*, xiv. Horner, "The King Taught Us the Lesson," describes Benedictine opposition to lollardy.

17. See Beadle, "Monk Thomas Hyngham's Hand," and Griffiths, "Thomas Hyngham, Monk of Bury." For the earlier argument that the monk Hyngham was Richard Hyngham, who became the abbot of Bury St. Edmunds in 1474, see Baker and Murphy, "The Late Medieval Plays of MS Digby 133."

18. For a discussion of the auspices of the Digby *Wisdom*, see Baker and Murphy, "The Late Medieval Plays of MS Digby 133."

19. I do not include a discussion of *The Pride of Life* in the chapters that follow, as the play does not explicitly dramatize the sacrament of penance and a significant portion of its text is missing.

20. Foucault develops the argument for the importance of the institution-alization of confession in the thirteenth century in the emergence of the modern self as subject in Foucault, *The History of Sexuality*, 1.18–21, 58–67. For more recent arguments that the requirement of annual auricular confession shaped in-dividual medieval (and modern) discourses of the self by mandating a program of self-scrutiny and self-revelation, see Patterson, *Chaucer and the Subject of History*, chap. 8; and Lochrie, *Covert Operations*.

21. On the sacraments as forms of social relation, see Beckwith, *Signifying God*, and her earlier essays in Beckwith, "Ritual, Church and Theatre," and Beckwith, "Ritual, Theater, and Social Space."

22. Beckwith, "Language Goes on Holiday," 109; see also her account of *Mankind* and *The Castle of Perseverance* in Beckwith, *Shakespeare and the Grammar of Forgiveness*, 117–21.

23. Beckwith, "Language Goes on Holiday," 109.

24. Tanner, ed., *Decrees of the Ecumenical Councils*, 1:245.

25. Shinners and Dohar, eds., *Pastors and the Care of Souls*, 178; for the Latin text, see the *Summula* for the diocese of Exeter (1240 and 1287) in Powicke and Cheney, eds., *Councils and Synods*, 2:1060–77; quotation at 1069.

26. Mirk, *Instructions*, 28/912; hereafter citations appear parenthetically in the text by page and line numbers.

27. Woods and Copeland, "Classroom and Confession," 377.

28. Simmons and Nolloth, eds., *The Lay Folks' Catechism*, 22/66–71.

29. For example, Titivillus (or Tutivillus as he is more often called) appears in *Jacob's Well* as the devil who bears in his sack "sylablys & woordys, ouerskyp-pyd and synkopyd, & verse & psalmys þe whiche þese clerkys han stolyn in þe qweere, & haue fayled in here seruyse" (115/3–5). On medieval references to Tutivillus, see Cawsey, "Tutivillus and the 'Kyrkchaterars'"; Jennings, "Tuti-villus: The Literary Career of the Recording Demon"; and Neuss, "Active and Idle Language," 55–64.

30. Hughes, *Pastors and Visionaries*, 149.

31. Potter, *English Morality Play*, 48.

32. Staley, "The Penitential Psalms," 230. See also the lay perfectionist literature described by Appleford, *Learning to Die in London*, discussed in chapter 4 herein.

33. On the role of loss in the dreamer's education, see Zeeman, *Piers Plowman and the Medieval Discourse of Desire*; and Davis, *Piers Plowman and the Books of Nature*.

34. Weatherly, ed., *Speculum Sacerdotale*, 63/7–8; hereafter cited parenthetically in the text by page and line number.

35. Chaucer, *Pardoner's Tale* and *General Prologue* in *Riverside Chaucer*, quotation at 1.231; further citations refer to this edition and are given in the text by line numbers. See, for instance, Gower's account of the worldliness and materialism of monks, friars, and priests in the *Mirour de l'Omme*, 278–91/20833–21780. Mann, *Chaucer and Medieval Estates Satire*, discusses the representation of ecclesiastical abuses in estates literature; Scase, *"Piers Plowman" and the New Anti-clericalism*, provides an account of the growing concern with ecclesiastical abuses in late fourteenth-century England.

36. Wyclif's views on penance are elaborated in *De Eucharistia* (1380), *De Apostasia* (1380), *De Blasphema* (1381), and the *Trialogus* (1381), and helpfully summarized by Penn, "Wyclif and the Sacraments," 283–89. See also Hudson's discussion of Wycliffite views on penance in her foundational Hudson, *The Premature Reformation*, 294–301; and Hornbeck et al., *A Companion to Lollardy*, 125–26.

37. For an account of lollard writing sympathetic to oral confession, see Somerset, *Feeling Like Saints*, 46–54.

38. Matthew, ed., *English Works*, 328.

39. Ibid., 341.

40. Thorpe, *Testimony*, 82/1897–98; further citations are given in the text by page and line numbers.

41. Swinburn, ed., *Lanterne of Li3t*, 3/25–28; further citations are given in the text by page and line numbers.

42. On Wycliffite understandings of the responsibilities within communities for sin and its repair, see Hornbeck et al., eds., *Wycliffite Spirituality*, 16–18.

43. Catto, "Fellows and Helpers," and Catto, "Wyclif and Wycliffism," discuss of the variety of views held by Wyclif's early followers at Oxford. For reconsiderations of the boundary between heterodoxy and orthodoxy, see Havens, "Shading the Grey Area"; Hornbeck, *What Is a Lollard?*, 10–22; McSheffrey, "Heresy, Orthodoxy, and English Vernacular Religion," and the essays included in *Wycliffite Controversies*, ed. Bose and Hornbeck. On lollard pastoral writings and Wycliffite spirituality, see, in particular, Somerset, *Feeling Like Saints*, and Somerset, "Wycliffite Spirituality," and the introduction and texts included in Hornbeck et al., eds., *Wycliffite Spirituality*.

44. On the limitations of medieval heresy trial records, see, for instance, Aers, "Brut's Theology"; Hornbeck, *What Is a Lollard?*, xi–xviii; Hornbeck et

al., *A Companion to Lollardy*, 167–78; the introduction to *Wycliffite Spirituality*, ed. Hornbeck et al., 45–52; and Strohm, *England's Empty Throne*, chap. 2.

45. Walsingham, *Historia Anglicana*, 2:252. The original passage reads: *Quod septem Sacramenta non sunt nisi signa mortua, nec valent in forma qua eis utitur Ecclesia.*

46. Tanner, ed., *Heresy Trials in the Diocese of Norwich*, 140.

47. Clark, ed., *Lincoln Diocese Documents, 1450–1544*, 93. On the antisacramentalism of East Anglian lollards in the fifteenth century, see Aston, *Lollards and Reformers*, 60–61, 84, 88; Jurkowski, "Lollardy and Social Status"; Nichols, *Seeable Signs*, 90–128; and Thomson, *The Later Lollards*, 127–38.

48. All quotations from the *Canterbury Tales* are taken from *The Riverside Chaucer*.

49. Geertz, "Thick Description."

50. For the argument that the Pardoner's self-aware performance serves to undermine religious authority more broadly, see Aers, *Chaucer, Langland, and the Creative Imagination*, 89–106.

51. Patterson, *Chaucer and the Subject of History*, 385.

52. The critical fascination with the Pardoner's sexuality dates to Curry, *Chaucer and the Medieval Sciences* (1926), 59–70. McAlpine, "The Pardoner's Homosexuality," and Dinshaw, *Chaucer's Sexual Poetics*, chap. 6, have been particularly influential.

53. Most notably, see Patterson's critique of his earlier, highly influential reading of the Pardoner in Patterson, *Chaucer and the Subject of History*, and psychoanalytic accounts of medieval literature more generally in Patterson, "Chaucer's Pardoner on the Couch," and Minnis's reappraisal of the question of the Pardoner's "secret" in light of the Pardoner's more public forms of moral deviancy in Minnis, *Fallible Authors*.

54. Pearsall, "Chaucer's Pardoner: The Death of a Salesman," 361. See also Knight's critique of the modern critical constructions of an "individualized, all-too-human pardoner" in Knight, "Chaucer's Pardoner in Performance," 29.

55. Guillaume de Lorris and Jean de Meun, *The Romance of the Rose*, ed. Dahlberg, 195/11063; hereafter citations appear parenthetically in the text by page and line numbers. References to the French text are quoted from *Le Roman de la Rose*, ed. Strubel.

56. Knight, "Chaucer's Pardoner in Performance," 31.

57. All biblical citations are to the Douay-Rheims version unless otherwise indicated.

58. Augustine, *On Christian Doctrine*, trans. Robertson, 4.15; Ginsberg, "Preaching and Avarice in the Pardoner's Tale," discusses this passage in reference to Augustine. On the use of dove imagery in medieval writing about preaching, see Minnis, *Fallible Authors*, 118–25.

59. Here I seek to draw out some of the implications of Patterson's discussion of the Pardoner's literalism in Patterson, "Chaucer's Pardoner on the Couch."

60. 2 Cor. 3:6.

61. Minnis, *Fallible Authors*, chaps. 1 and 2, provides a thorough discussion of late medieval ideologies of priestly office.

62. Austin, *How to Do Things with Words*, Lectures 2 and 4, discusses sincerity as a criteria for the "felicitous" functioning of performatives.

63. Pearsall, *The Canterbury Tales*, 101.

64. Kempe, *The Book of Margery Kempe*, 28/8; hereafter citations appear parenthetically in the text by page and line numbers.

65. For a critique of progressive accounts of fifteenth-century England (and their reverse), see Sargent, "Censorship or Cultural Change?"

66. Written in 1436, *The Book of Margery Kempe* describes events beginning as early as 1393 with the birth of her first child. The Canterbury visit described here probably happened around 1415. For the evidence for dating the various events Kempe describes, see Meech and Allen's notes in the EETS edition.

67. For an example of a typically dismissive view of the morality play, see Watkins, "The Allegorical Theatre."

68. Emmerson, "The Morality Character as Sign," 203.

69. For discussion of medieval definitions of allegory, see, in particular, Whitman, *Allegory*, 263–68; and Clopper, *Drama, Play, and Game*, 250–51.

70. *Tropus ubi ex alio aliud intelligitur*; Augustine, *On the Trinity* 15.9.

71. Quoted in Whitman, *Allegory*, 266. The original passage can be found in *Enarrationum in Epistolas Beati Pauli Liber XV in Epistolam ad Galatas*, *Patrologiae Cursus Completus, Series Latina*, ed. J. P. Migne, 112, 330C.

72. *Aliud dicitur et aliud significatur*; Hugh of St. Victor, *De Scripturis*; quoted in Whitman, *Allegory*, 266.

73. In *On the Trinity* 15.9, Augustine distinguishes between allegories that are obscure or enigmatic in nature and those "patent to all but the very dull."

74. Whitman, *Allegory*, 2.

75. Tuve, *Allegorical Imagery*, 26.

76. For a discussion of the intersections of personification, penance, and personhood in medieval allegory, which in its poststructuralist and Lacanian orientation is different from my own, see Scanlon, "Personification and Penance."

77. Whitman, *Allegory*, 5.

78. Isidore of Seville defines personification as "when personality and speech are invented for inanimate things" (*Etymologies* 2.8.1).

79. Goethe, *Maxims and Reflections*, no. 1112; as quoted in Abrams, *A Glossary of Literary Terms*, 197.

80. De Man, "Rhetoric of Temporality," 187.

81. De Man, *The Rhetoric of Romanticism*, 76 (italics in original). The latent power of personification to reverse itself has troubled critics since long before de Man; for an account of the eighteenth-century articulation of this problem, see Knapp, *Personification and the Sublime*. Paxon, *Poetics of Personification*, chap. 1, provides a history of personification theory from the classical period through the twentieth century.

82. On reification as "dispersonification," see Paxon, *Poetics*, 39–44.

83. Clopper, *Drama, Play, and Game*, 250.

84. Isidore of Seville, *Etymologies* 2.8.1

85. Geoffrey of Vinsauf, *Poetria Nova* 32; hereafter cited in the text by page number.

86. Wittgenstein, *Philosophical Investigations*, §432 (emphasis in original).

87. Ibid., §431.

88. Ibid., §433.

89. Ibid., §435.

90. It is of course a central project of poststructural criticism to show the inherent instability of divisions between individual and society, inner and outer, public and private, and so on. Neo-Marxist theories expose the central role social and political institutions play in the constitution of seemingly "autonomous" modern subjects. Foucauldian forms of analysis demonstrate how concepts central to our self-understanding are products of social and discursive practices.

91. I argue below that elsewhere in his writing Augustine in fact presents a version of the self much more sympathetic to the one described by the medieval morality play.

92. Augustine, *Confessions* 1.8.13, as quoted in Wittgenstein, *Philosophical Investigations*, §1: "When they (my elders) named some object, and accordingly moved towards something, I saw this and I grasped that the thing was called by the sound they uttered when they meant to point it out. Their intention was shewn by their bodily movements, as it were the natural language of all peoples: the expression of the face, the play of the eyes, and the movement of other parts of the body, and the tone of the voice which expresses our state of mind in seeking, having, rejecting, or avoiding something. Thus, as I heard words repeatedly used in their proper places in various sentences, I gradually learnt to understand what objects they signified; and after I had trained my mouth to form these signs, I used them to express my own desires."

93. Wittgenstein, *Philosophical Investigations*, §1.

94. Ibid., §32 (emphasis in original).

95. Wetzel, *Parting Knowledge*, 237.

96. Ibid., 235.

97. On this point, see Kerr, *Theology after Wittgenstein*, 58.

98. Wittgenstein, *Philosophical Investigations*, §2.

99. Ibid., §6.

100. Ibid., §5.

101. Ibid., §693.

102. See ibid., §305.

103. Ibid., §244 (emphasis in original).

104. Ibid., §244.

105. Ibid., §305.

106. Ibid., §244.

107. Ibid., §245.

108. Cavell, *Claim of Reason*, 341.

109. For the argument that Wittgenstein gives voice to and then frees himself from a deconstructive account of how signs express meaning, see Stone, "Wittgenstein on Deconstruction."

110. Burckhardt, *Civilization of the Renaissance in Italy*, 1:143.

111. McCabe, *On Aquinas*, 39.

112. See, for instance, Aquinas, *Summa Theologiae* 3a.77, 2; and Brower, "Matter, Form, and Individuation." I discuss individuation in the morality play and its ethical implications in chapter 4, on *Everyman*.

113. On the transformation from a medieval sacramental theater of signs to a reformed theater of dissimulation and disguise, see Beckwith, *Signifying God*, chap. 7; and Beckwith, *Shakespeare and the Grammar of Forgiveness*, chap. 1.

114. Wittgenstein, *Philosophical Investigations*, 2. 4.

115. Cavell, *Claim of Reason*, 369.

116. Hilton, *Scale of Perfection*, 2.30; hereafter cited parenthetically in the text by book and chapter numbers. I take up the relation between medieval contemplative traditions and the morality play at greater length in chapter 2, on the morality *Wisdom*.

117. Kerr, *After Aquinas*, 27; McCabe, *On Aquinas*, 133; and O'Grady, "McCabe on Aquinas and Wittgenstein."

118. Admittedly, Wittgenstein's interest in the language learning scene in *Confessions* 1.8.13 is far more complex than a simple correction of what he views as a misleading picture of language and the self. On Wittgenstein's engagement of the conversion narrative and confessional mode of the *Confessions*, see Eldridge, *Leading a Human Life*, chap. 5; and Wetzel, *Parting Knowledge*, chap. 13.

119. For the argument that Augustine held that a material existence is necessary to vision of God, see Barnes, "Exegesis and Polemic."

120. Augustine, *On the Free Choice of the Will*, trans. Williams, 3.23; cited in Hanby, "Augustine and Descartes," 471.

121. Hanby, *Augustine and Modernity*, 161.

122. Augustine, Ninth Homily on the First Epistle of John (1 John 4:19), in *Ten Homilies on the First Epistle of John*; quoted in Hanby, *Augustine and Modernity*, 28–29.

123. Hanby, *Augustine and Modernity*, 91. Hanby earlier argues that for Augustine "personhood is *constituted* not primarily as substance but precisely in the *act* of reciprocated giving" (53; emphasis in original).

124. Hugh of Saint of Victor, *On the Sacraments*, 1.9.3.

125. McCabe, *God Matters*, 118.

126. Shakespeare, *Hamlet*, 1.2.85.

ONE.   *The Castle of Perseverance* and Penitential *Platea*

1. The exact origins of the *Castle* are unknown, but most critics agree that the play is of East Anglian provenance and was written between 1400 and 1425. A reference in the text to "crakows" (1059), the pointed toes on shoes, dates the play to between 1382 and 1425 (Eccles, *Macro Plays*, xi).

2. For the argument that the fifteenth-century controversies centered on questions of practice, see Catto, "Religious Change."

3. Here I reproduce Hudson's punctuation in *Selections*, 116–17. As Swinburn and Hudson both note, the source of this metaphor is pseudo-Chrysostom's *Sermons on Matthew, Homily 43*.

4. As I discuss shortly, Somerset, *Feeling Like Saints*, chaps. 6 and 7, describes the use of architectural metaphors in lollard writing.

5. As translated in Lahey, *Philosophy and Politics*, 181. The original passage can be found in Wyclif, *Tractatus de Civili Dominio*, 1.39.288: *domus spiritualis ecclesie edificata habet pro fundamento fidem Christi pro parietibus spem vite, et pro tecto caritatem*.

6. On lollard critiques of late medieval devotional practices surrounding the Eucharist, see Catto, "John Wycliff and the Cult of the Eucharist"; and Rubin, *Corpus Christi*. On the lollard critique of images, see Aston, *Lollards and Reformers*; and, more recently, Gayk, *Image, Text, and Religious Reform*.

7. Hudson, ed., *Selections*, 27/121–25.

8. Davidson, ed., *Tretise of Miraclis Pleyinge*, 94/59–60.

9. Poem 23/1–8, in Barr, ed., *Digby Poems*.

10. "Lore is ȝouen to cristen men: / Into flesch passeþ þe bred, / As holy-chirche doþ vs kenne" (Poem 23/41–43).

11. Barr, introduction to *Digby Poems*, 26. See also Barr's argument that the Digby poet "silences the Lollards by building a reformed church . . . out of penitence, sacramentalism, liturgy, biblical preaching, and purification" (Barr, "The Deafening Silence of Lollardy," quotation at 245).

12. In the Macro manuscript and most modern editions of the play, Humanum Genus is referred to by his Latin name when designating the name of the speaker and as "Mankynde" in the dialogue of the play itself. I use the more inclusive term "Humankind" instead of Humanum Genus throughout this book to distinguish him from the title character of *Mankind*.

13. See Davidson, *Visualizing the Moral Life*, 48.

14. For Eccles's transcription of the stage diagram, see Eccles, ed., *Macro Plays*, 1.

15. On the play's use of theatrical space, see, in particular, Potter, *English Morality Play*, 32–37; King, "Spatial Semantics," and King, "Morality Plays"; and Davidson, *Visualizing the Moral Life*, chap. 2. The location of the physical features indicated in the play's diagram, and especially the location of the moat, have been the subject of some critical controversy. Southern, *Medieval Theatre in the Round*, argues that the play was modeled on Cornish theater in the round and that the circle in the play's diagram represents a barrier around the entire theater. Schmitt, "Was There a Medieval Theatre in the Round?," critiques Southern's view, and Belsey, "Stage Plan," defends it.

16. On the diagram's resemblance to *mappae mundi*, see Belsey, "Stage Plan," 128–31. On the influence of medieval world maps on English theater more generally, see Stevens, "*Mappa mundi*."

17. Davidson, *Visualizing the Moral Life*, 48, 52.

18. Fischer-Lichte, *Semiotics of Theater*, 99. Weimann, *Shakespeare and the Popular Tradition in the Theater*, is the classic study of the relation between audience member and stage character in medieval and early modern drama.

19. King, "Spatial Semantics and Theatre," 47.

20. On the play's diagram, a caption written between the two circles surrounding the castle indicates the presence, and limits the number, of crowd marshals: "Þis is þe watyr abowte þe place, if any dyche may be mad þer it schal be pleyed, or ellys þat it be strongely barryd al abowt, and lete nowth ouyrmany stytelerys be wythinne þe plase." The diagram further indicates that whereas the *platea* was made available to audience members, other parts, and the castle in particular, are restricted. A caption above the castle of perseverance warns that "no men" should "sytte þer, / for lettynge of syt, for þer schal be þe best of all." The notion that the castle is reserved for only the most virtuous is reinforced throughout the play; see, for instance, 1546–58.

21. King, "Spatial Semantics and Theatre," 52.

22. Watson, "Censorship and Cultural Change."

23. Watson, "Censorship and Cultural Change," 823–24n4, discusses his decision to omit drama. For critiques of Watson's thesis, see, for example, the responses to his essay collected in *English Language Notes* 44, no. 1 (2006); and, in particular, Crassons, "Performance Anxiety," and her discussion of the implications of Watson's omission of drama.

24. Catto, "After Arundel," 43; and Gillespie, "Chichele's Church." On early fifteenth-century constructive projects of reform, see also Catto, "Shaping the Mixed Life," and Catto, "Religious Change under Henry V"; and Harriss, *Shaping the Nation*, 317–19.

25. As quoted in Catto, "Shaping the Mixed Life," 104–5. The original passage can be found in Wilkins, *Concilia*, 3:318.

26. Catto, "Religious Change,"109.

27. See Gillespie, "Chichele's Church."

28. On the play's adaptation of penitential manuals, see Hildahl, "Penitence and Parody."

29. Love, *Mirror*, 90/39–40. For discussion of Love's methodology, see in particular Beckwith, *Christ's Body*, 63–70; and Hudson, *Premature Reformation*, 437–40.

30. Love, *Mirror*, 91/12, 16–19.

31. On Netter's emphasis on the external dimensions of Christian belief, see Alban, *Teaching and Impact*.

32. "*Non est ecclesia ubi non est confessio vera*"; as quoted in Alban, *Teaching and Impact*, 194. For the original passage, see Netter, *Doctrinale*, 5.137.

33. Alban, *Teaching and Impact*, 4.

34. On the play as a reflection of contemporary antifeudalist and antimercantilist sentiments, see Clopper, *Drama, Play, and Game*, 254; and Riggio, "The Allegory of Feudal Acquisition."

35. Clopper, *Drama, Play, and Game*, 253.

36. Here I draw on Bell's description of ritual's differentialization of the sacred from the profane; see Bell, *Ritual*, 156–57.

37. See Emmerson, "The Morality Character as Sign," 198–203, for a discussion of the signifying functions of World.

38. On World's use of the language of feudal patronage here and elsewhere in the play, see Riggio, "The Allegory of Feudal Acquisition."

39. For example, the *Speculum Sacerdotale*, 67/36–68/3, chastises parishioners who "comeþ now to you in Quadragesime, but noȝt in the firste weke comenly, ne in the secounde, ne in the þridde, but in the vi. weke and in Good Friday and on Paske Day more for schame and custome kepynge þen att sterynge of compunccion or contricion." Mannyng, *Handlyng Synne*, 159/4783–85, offers a similar admonition.

40. See Emmerson, "The Morality Character as Sign"; Beckwith, "Language Goes on Holiday"; and Clopper, *Drama, Play, and Game*, chap. 7.

41. Owst, *Literature and Pulpit*, attributes the origin of such castle imagery to the description of Jesus's entry into Bethany to visit Mary and Martha, rendered as "intravit Jesus in quoddam castellum" (Luke 10:38), a reference that is in turn interpreted figuratively as the Incarnation (77–85). For discussion of the castle topos in medieval writing, see also Cornelius, *Figurative Castle*; Schmitt, "Was There a Medieval Theatre in the Round?," 134–38; Wheatley, *Idea of the Castle*, chap. 2; and Whitehead, *Castles of the Mind*, chap. 6.

42. From *The Castle of Love* (Vernon MS) in Grosseteste, *Chateau d'Amour*, 282/670.

43. Mirk, *Festial*, 228/33–230/23; hereafter cited parenthetically in the text by page and line numbers.

44. Somerset, *Feeling Like Saints*, chap. 7.

45. Quoted in ibid., 232, from Oxford, Bodelian Library, MS Laud Misc. 23, fols. 61r–v. A modernized text is available in Hornbeck, Lahey, and Somerset, eds. and trans., *Wycliffite Spirituality*, 276–90.

46. Somerset, *Four Wycliffite Dialogues*, 3/14–15; 12/329–31. Cited by page and line numbers.

47. Somerset, *Feeling Like Saints*, 231.

48. Whitehead, *Castles of the Mind*, 113 (emphasis in original).

49. On an audience's perception of its exclusion, see Whitehead, *Castles of the Mind*, 116. The problematic nature of the model of church as fortress is rigorously explored in the apocalyptic conclusion of Langland's *Piers Plowman* (ca. 1370–87); see Aers, *Beyond Reformation?*, 32–37, 53–60, 91–94, and 141–43; and Whitehead, *Castles of the Mind*, 110.

50. Covetousness's prominence in the play may also reflect the tenor of the times: Huizinga, *Waning of the Middle Ages*, famously observes that "a furious chorus of invectives against cupidity and avarice rises up everywhere from the literature of that period," a predilection he attributes to the rise of a money economy (28).

51. Brandeis, ed., *Jacob's Well*, 117/13–17; hereafter cited parenthetically in the text by page and line numbers.

52. On the *ars moriendi* tradition, see, for example, Appleford, *Learning to Die*; Ariès, *Hour of Our Death*, 107–10; Binski, *Medieval Death*, 33–60; and Duffy, *Stripping of the Altars*, 313–27.

53. Hudson, ed., *Selections*, 27/23.

54. The debate of the Four Daughters originates in an early twelfth-century commentary of Hugh of Saint Victor and is taken up in a sermon on the Annunciation by Bernard of Clairvaux. Versions appear in a number of later texts, including Grosseteste, *Chateau d'Amour*; the *Cursor Mundi*; the English *Gesta Romanorum*; Langland, *Piers Plowman*; Love, *Mirror*; and the N-Town *Parliament of Heaven*. For the development of this tradition, see Traver, *Four Daughters of God*.

TWO.   A Theater of the Soul's Interior

1. For Dymmok's remarks on the invisible changes effected by the sacraments, see Dymmok, *Liber contra Duodecim Errores et Hereses Lollardorum*, 129–31.

2. In this vein, see also remarks on the pedagogical capacity of penance by Hugh of Saint Victor, *On the Sacraments*, 1.9.3.

3. Forty-two manuscripts containing one or both books survive. See Lagorio and Sargent, "English Mystical Writings," 3075.

4. On *Wisdom*'s use of liturgical symbolism in its costuming, see Nichols, "Costume in the Moralities."

5. On the representation of gender in *Wisdom*, see, e.g., Clark et al., "Se in what stat thou doyst indwell," and Nisse, *Defining Acts*, chap. 6.

6. On medieval uses of the word "enfourme" to designate both artistic and pedagogic shaping, see Simpson, *Sciences and the Self*, 1–10.

7. Wittgenstein, *Philosophical Investigations*, §23.

8. Cavell, *Claim of Reason*, 177–78.

9. For a discussion of *Wisdom*'s provenance and relation to both the Abbey of St. Edmunds and late medieval East Anglian religious culture more generally, see Gibson, "The Play of *Wisdom* and the Abbey of St. Edmunds," and Gibson, *Theater of Devotion*, chap. 5. For evidence of Wycliffite activity in eastern England in the latter part of the fifteenth century, see Thomson, *The Later Lollards*, 132–38.

10. For the argument that in the third quarter of the fifteenth century East Anglia and the other areas of England that had seen the greatest amount of Wycliffite activity saw an increased interest in orthodox artistic productions of the sacramental system, see Nichols, *Seeable Signs*, chap. 2.

11. For histories of the controversies surrounding penance, see Tentler, *Sin and Confession*; Frantzen, *Literature of Penance*; and Myers, *"Poor, Sinning Folk."*

12. Tentler, *Sin and Confession*, 30–31.

13. See Little, *Confession and Resistance*, chap. 2.

14. Ibid., chaps. 3 and 4.

15. The judicial role of priests and the self revealed in confession are of course the aspects of medieval penance emphasized by Foucault, *The History of Sexuality*, vol. 1 (see, in particular, 18–21, 58–67). For a critique of the Fou-

cauldian prioritization of the confessing self, see Little, *Confession and Resistance*, 3–15.

16. This is, of course, Gregory the Great's famous justification of the use of images in his letter to Bishop Serenus of Marseilles.

17. Hudson, ed., *Selections*, 83–84.

18. For Wycliffite use of this term, see, for instance, ibid., 84.

19. For an overview of the play's sources and contexts, see Riggio, ed., *Wisdom*, 25–77, 181–310; and Eccles, ed., *Macro Plays*, xxxiii–xxxiv, 203–16. Smart, *Some English and Latin Sources*, provides the earliest detailed account of *Wisdom*'s sources.

20. Notably, the lines of the play in which Wisdom discusses the nature of the human soul (103–70) draw for the most part from the early sections of book 2 of the *Scale*, in which Hilton is concerned with the sacrament of penance. Significantly, whereas Hilton provides a *description* of what happens to the soul as it is reformed through penance, Wisdom identifies such knowledge (of the nature of the soul and its parts) as a kind of knowledge that will lead one toward knowledge of God.

21. Hilton, *Scale*, 2.5–17.

22. Molloy, *Theological Interpretation*, argues for a Thomistic reading of the play. For accounts of the play's relationship to Augustinian and contemplative traditions, see Gatch, "Mysticism and Satire in the Morality of *Wisdom*"; Hill, "The Trinitarian Allegory"; Riehle, "English Mysticism"; and King, "Morality Plays." For discussion of the play's use of visual imagery, see Bevington, "Blake and wyght"; Davidson, *Visualizing the Moral Life*, 83–111; and Scherb, *Staging Faith*, 106–8, 130–45.

23. Bevington, "Blake and wyght," 20.

24. In this vein, see Riehle, "English Mysticism," 202–3.

25. Hill, "Trinitarian Allegory," 125–26; Hill's quotation of Augustine is taken from *The Trinity*, trans. McKenna, 513.

26. See Nisse, *Defining Acts*, chap. 6.

27. Pseudo-Bernard, *Meditationes Piissimae*, 485.

28. *Medytacōns of Saynt Bernarde*, A3.

29. I am paraphrasing the characterization of this tradition in Voaden, *God's Words, Women's Voices*, 10.

30. Augustine develops his notion of a divine trinity in the human mind consisting of memory, understanding, and will in *On the Holy Trinity*, bk. 10, in *Nicene and Post-Nicene Fathers*, ed. Philip Schaff, 3:134–43.

31. Ibid., 10.8.11.

32. Smart, *Sources and Parallels*, 24.

33. Augustine, *On the Holy Trinity*, 10.5–8. See also Hilton, *Scale*, 2.30.

34. For a pointed late medieval critique of the dangers of reading spiritual language literally, see *The Cloud of Unknowing*, 52–53.

35. See, for instance, Hilton, *Scale*, 2.33. Turner, *The Darkness of God*, esp. 19–49, discusses this tension in contemplative literature more broadly.

36. Augustine, *On the Holy Trinity*, 10.9.12; emphasis mine.

37. For an account of the Augustinian self and the important ways in which it differs from the post-Cartesian self, see Hanby, *Augustine and Modernity*, and Hanby, "Augustine and Descartes."

38. Augustine, *City of God*, 14.28.

39. Here I draw on remarks on Wittgenstein's vision of language in Cavell, *Claim of Reason*, 184.

40. For Hilton's articulation of such dangers, see *Scale*, 2.30.

41. For the English *Orologium*, see K. Horstmann, "*Orologium Sapientiae*," quotation at 331; hereafter cited in the text by page number.

42. Compare Hilton's description of a mode of contemplation that lies principally in "affeccioun, withoute undirstondynge of gosteli thynges" rather than in cognition (*Scale*, 1.5).

43. I draw again on Cavell, *Claim of Reason*, 184.

44. The mights' costume changes as they fall also suggests such a false likeness; see King, "Morality Plays," 253.

45. Davenport, "Lusty fresche galaunts," 120.

46. For examples of this concern, see Hilton, *Scale*, 1.11; and Julian of Norwich's advice to Margery Kempe in *The Book of Margery Kempe*, 42–43. For an account of the broader context and significance of such warnings, see Voaden, *God's Words, Women's Voices*.

47. See Hilton, *On the Mixed Life*, 1:269; and Smart, *Sources and Parallels*, 27.

48. Riggio, "The Staging of Wisdom," 4.

49. For the sacramental character of *Wisdom*'s social vision, see Cox, *Devil and the Sacred*, 46–48.

50. The varying meaning of these words are outlined in the glossary of Riggio's edition of *Wisdom*, 347, 350, and 351, respectively.

51. Smart, *Sources and Parallels*, 12.

52. Of course the presence of Wisdom, who is a figure for both Christ and prevenient grace, is also key.

53. See *Mankind*, 151–84.

54. Christ's expulsion of the devils (described in Mark 16:9 and Luke 8:2) from Mary Magdalene is dramatized in two other fifteenth-century East Anglian dramas: the N-Town *Passion Play* I, and the Digby *Mary Magdalene*. See *N-Town Play*, 1.270–71/659–64; and *Mary Magdalene*, 1.14.691sd (in Furnivall, ed., *Digby Plays*, 53–136). For a discussion of the play's identification of Anima with the Magdalene, see Coletti, *Mary Magdalene*, 84–90.

55. Nichols, *Seeable Signs*, suggests that contemporary East Anglian baptismal fonts show a similar focus upon the essential action of penance (173–77; 222–41).

56. *Quid retribuam Domino pro omnibus que retribuit mihi? Calicem salutaris accipiam et nomen Domini inuocabo* (What shall I render to the Lord, for all the things he hath rendered unto me? I will take the chalice of salvation; and I will call upon the name of the Lord; Ps. 115:12–13).

57. Connerton, *How Societies Remember*, 58.

THREE.   Speaking for Mankind

1. Coogan, in her 1947 dissertation, *An Interpretation of the Moral Play, "Mankind,"* 1, proposes identifying Mercy as a priest.

2. For instance, quoting Mark 16:15, the author of *City of Saints* explains that Christ orders priests to "preach the gospel, not rhymes and fables and chronicles and poesies or tales from Rome" (Hornbeck et al., *Wycliffite Spirituality*, 283/21–22). On Wycliffite views on preaching, see Hudson, *Premature Reformation*, 351–56.

3. Spencer, *English Preaching*, 132.

4. *"Quod non placet faciliter despicitur"* (Cambridge, University Library, MS Kk.4.24, f. 128vb); cited and translated in Wenzel, *Latin Sermon Collections*, 343. For the argument that in the early fifteenth century there arose after Wyclif within orthodoxy a "new emphasis on preaching as the primary medium of scriptural instruction and exposition," one that was accompanied by a renewed concern with quality of preaching, which encompassed an attentiveness to the needs and capacities of their audiences, see Gillespie, "Chichele's Church," 30. Wenzel, *Latin Sermon Collections*, 393, is less confident that late fourteenth- and fifteenth-century concern with preaching is attributable to lollardy.

5. *"Qui ea docet que ab auditoribus intelligi non possunt, non eorum vtilitatem querit set sui ostensionem facit"* (Cambridge, University Library, MS Ii.3.8, f. 44); cited and translated in Wenzel, *Latin Sermon Collections*, 343.

6. Dillon, *Language and Stage*, 68. See also Forest-Hill, *"Mankind* and the Fifteenth-Century Preaching Controversy,"* for a reassessment of *Mankind*'s treatment of virtuous and sinful language in the context of orthodox responses to the lollard movement.

7. Cavell, *Claim of Reason*, 326.

8. What Nowadays refers to by "thys" is ambiguous. The editors of the Arden edition of the play suggest that the vices are protesting that Mercy's line "Do wey" does not appear in the script (Bruster and Rasmussen, eds., *Everyman and Mankind*, 88n84). In either reading, the joke remains a metatheatrical one that imagines the vice's "pley" as an alternative to the one offered by, or for the benefit of, Mercy.

9. "But I say unto you, that every idle word that men shall speak, they shall render an account for it in the day of judgment" (Matt. 12:36).

10. Ashley, "Titivillus and the Battle of Words in *Mankind*," gives an account of the confrontation between good words and bad.

11. Arnold, ed., *Select English Works*, vol. 3, 144/23; hereafter cited in the text by page and line numbers.

12. Todd, ed., *Apology for Lollard Doctrines*, 32/27–28.

13. For Wycliffite writing on preaching, see Arnold, ed., *Select English Works*, vol. 3, 143/25–145/8, 228/24–229/5, 464/6–465/17; and Matthew, ed., *English Works*, 109/1–113/13; 117/1–17; 188/1–190/1.

14. Matthew, ed. *English Works*, 441; hereafter cited in the text by page numbers.

15. "For if you have ten thousand instructors in Christ, yet not many fathers. For in Christ Jesus, by the gospel, I have begotten you" (1 Cor. 4:15).

16. For contemporary accounts of the "occupational hazards" of preaching posed by unregenerate medieval audiences, see Spencer, *English Preaching*, 1–3.

17. The Middle English text of *A Dialogue between a Wise Man and a Fool* appears under the title "Cambridge Tract XII," in Mary Dove, ed., *Earliest Advocates of the English Bible*, 130–42; for a modern English translation, see Hornbeck et al., *Wycliffite Spirituality*, 248–68.

18. Coogan, *An Interpretation of the Moral Play, "Mankind,"* 10–56, discusses the play's Lenten themes. On Wycliffite use of exegesis and interpolation in their writing, see Hornbeck et al., *Wycliffite Spirituality*, 23–24.

19. Eccles, "Introduction," *Macro Plays*, xlv.

20. Scanlon, "Personification and Penance," 3.

21. Goethe, *Maxims and Reflections*, no. 1112, as quoted in Abrams, *Glossary of Literary Terms*, 197.

22. Cavell, *Claim of Reason*, 326. I also draw on Cavell's critique of Charles Stevenson's elision of morality and propaganda at 286–91.

23. De Man, *Rhetoric of Romanticism*, 75. The latent power of personification to reverse itself has troubled critics since long before de Man; for an account of the eighteenth-century articulation of this problem, see Knapp, *Personification and the Sublime*. Paxon, *Poetics of Personification*, chap. 1, provides a history of personification theory from the classical period through the twentieth century.

24. The phrase is from Kathleen Ashley, "Titivillus and the Battle of Words," 131. Ashley herself critiques the view that the vices divert an audience's attention from the play's moral purposes, instead showing how the vices contribute to the play's broader concern with words "as vehicles to salvation or damnation" (129).

25. Watkins, "Allegorical Theater," 772.

26. Gash, "Carnival against Lent," 94.

27. Gash, "Carnival and the Poetics of Reversal," 99.

28. On the subversive content of the play, see Gash's two important and influential essays, "Carnival and the Poetics of Reversal" and "Carnival against Lent," and Robertson, *Laborer's Two Bodies*, chap. 5.

29. Coleridge, *Statesman's Manual*, in *Critical Theory since Plato*, ed. Adams, 476.

30. De Man, "Rhetoric of Temporality," 187.

31. Neuss, "Active and Idle Language," 45.

32. Robertson, *Laborer's Two Bodies*, 155.

33. Ibid., 157.

34. Wittgenstein, *Philosophical Investigations*, §432.

35. In Emmerson, "Morality Character as Sign," 201, the author explains that in the *Castle* when the vice World appears on stage with Covetousness, the "unlimited semiosis" of World is "temporally narrowed" so that the "wide range of concepts associated with *worldliness* . . . becomes focused . . . primarily upon those that overlap with the range of concepts associated with *covetousness*" (emphasis in original).

36. Job 34:15.

37. Ps. 17:26–27.

38. Gash, "Carnival against Lent," 95. For the articles against William and Richard Sparke, see Clark, ed., *Lincoln Diocese Documents: 1450–1544*, 91, 93.

39. On *Mankind*'s representation of the sin of despair, see Beckwith, "Language Goes on Holiday," 111–14.

40. On the vices' attempt to cast Mercy into this role, see Robertson, *Laborer's Two Bodies*, 162–63.

41. Smart notes that statutes issued in 1463 and 1482 forbade gowns, jackets, and coats that did not cover one's "privy members and buttocks," in Smart, "Some Notes on 'Mankind'—(Concluded)," 304–5.

42. Gash, "Carnival against Lent," 88.

43. Robertson, *Laborer's Two Bodies*, 177 (emphasis in original). For the political implications of the trial scene, see also Brantley and Fulton, "*Mankind* in a Year without Kings"; and Murakami, *Moral Play and Counterpublic*, chap. 1.

44. For instance, witness Mercy's affectionate words to Mankind early in the play when he exclaims: "Kysse me now, my dere darlynge. Gode schelde yow from yowr fon!" (307).

45. Wittgenstein, *Culture and Value*, 86.

46. Beckwith, "Language Goes on Holiday," 111.

47. Ibid., 114.

48. Kerr, *Theology after Wittgenstein*, 69.

49. I discuss the Augustinian version of selfhood in the introduction.

FOUR.   *Everyman* and Community

1. Paxson, *Poetics of Personification*, 46.

2. See Kolve's discussion of how the play's grammatical ambiguity serves to implicate the audience both individually and collectively (Kolve, "*Everyman* and the Parable of the Talents," 82–84).

3. On the communal and public dimensions of medieval penance, see Bossy, *Christianity in the West: 1400–1700*, and Bossy, "The Social History of Confession in the Age of the Reformation"; Mansfield, *Humiliation of Sinners*; Myers, "*Poor, Sinning Folk*"; and Beckwith's reading of the York cycle as an exploration of penitential community, in Beckwith, *Signifying God*.

4. Beckwith, *Signifying God*, 92–95, discusses the emphasis on communal reconciliation in medieval penitential manuals. For the early history of this classificatory scheme, see Mansfield, *Humiliation of Sinners*, 41–49.

5. Mirk, *Instructions*, 63–65.

6. Appleford, *Learning to Die in London*, chap. 1, discusses the "A" and "E" versions of *The Visitation of the Sick*; she extends her discussion of the communal dimensions of London death culture to consider lay bequests for charitable foundations and other civic projects, including the famous *Dance of Death* mural at Saint Paul's Cathedral, in chap. 2.

7. For descriptions of the *ars moriendi* tradition, see Mâle, *L'Art religieux*, 412–22; O'Connor, *The Art of Dying Well*; Beaty, *The Craft of Dying*; Ariès, *The Hour of Our Death*, 106–32, 300–305; Duffy, *The Stripping of the Altars*, 301–37; Binski, *Medieval Death*, 33–47; Cressy, *Birth, Marriage, and Death*, 389–93; Houlbrooke, *Death, Religion, and the Family in England*, 183–219; and Appleford, *Learning to Die in London*.

8. *Book of the Craft of Dying*, in *Yorkshire Writers*, ed. Horstmann, 2:418.

9. Duffy, *Stripping of the Altars*, 317–18.

10. On the corporate and communal nature of medieval and early modern commemorative practices, see Geary, *Living with the Dead*, chap. 4; Binski, *Medieval Death*, esp. 21–28, 70–122; Cohn, "The Place of the Dead"; Burgess, "Longing to Be Prayed For"; and Appleford, *Learning to Die in London*.

11. Duffy, *Stripping of the Altars*, 474–75.

12. Ibid., 475. For arguments about the influence of the abolition of the doctrine of purgatory on early modern drama, see, e.g., Neill, *Issues of Death*, and Greenblatt, *Hamlet in Purgatory*.

13. Appleford, *Learning to Die in London*, 99.

14. Ibid., 103 (emphasis in original).

15. Quoted in ibid., 161.

16. Ibid., 154.

17. Ibid., 143. She also argues that the lay spiritual community described in the *Craft of Dying* also takes over many functions traditionally performed by the priesthood, including the recitation of important liturgical prayers, and thus performs "the equivalent of a sacramental role" (150).

18. Spivack, *Shakespeare and the Allegory of Evil*, 226.

19. For the argument that the abstract, allegorical personifications of the medieval morality play progressively develop into the concrete, individualized characters in early modern drama, see, in particular, Spivack, *Shakespeare and the Allegory of Evil*. A number of other critics have variously traced the morality play's influence on Elizabethan dramatic structure, characterization, and stage-craft, including Tillyard, *Shakespeare's History Plays*; Ribner, *English History Play in the Age of Shakespeare*; Bevington, *From Mankind to Marlowe*; Potter, *English Morality Play*; Weimann, *Shakespeare and the Popular Tradition*; and Belsey, *Subject of Tragedy*.

20. Belsey, *Subject of Tragedy*, 43 (emphasis in original).

21. Kolve, "*Everyman* and the Parable of the Talents," 74. Watkins, "The Allegorical Theatre," 774, cites this passage as an instance of a larger critical tendency to incorporate *Everyman* into a progressivist literary history.

22. Spinrad, *The Summons of Death*, 68.

23. Ariès, *Hour of Our Death*, 112.

24. See, in particular, ibid., 107–18. Appleford, *Learning to Die in London*, challenges Ariès's characterization of these traditions.

25. The narrative of the rise of the individual is thoroughly critiqued in Patterson, "On the Margin"; and Aers, "A Whisper in the Ear of Early Modernists." For important challenges to the morality theory, see Wasson, "The Morality

Play"; Norland, *Drama in Early Tudor Britain*; and Cartwright, *Theatre and Humanism*.

26. Watkins, "The Allegorical Theatre," 773.

27. Rowan Williams provides a particularly illuminating account of how the picture of a private, interior self emerges through human interactions in Williams, "Interiority and Epiphany," and Williams, *Lost Icons*. See also Cavell's commentary on Wittgenstein and the idea of the privacy of the soul in Cavell, *Claim of Reason*, 329–61.

28. Burckhardt, *Civilization of the Renaissance*, 143.

29. Muldrew, "From a 'Light Cloak,'"159.

30. Mills, "The Theaters of *Everyman*," 128. For the argument that *Everyman*'s translator has emended the original Dutch play for a reading audience, see Vanhoutte, "When Elckerlijc Becomes Everyman."

31. For a discussion of the spatial semiotics of medieval theater, see Fischer-Lichte, *Semiotics of Theater*, 93–114.

32. Ryan, "Doctrine and Dramatic Structure," 723.

33. Hunter, "Making Meaning," 83.

34. For a study of the implications of the quite literal ways in which medieval theater put death onstage, see Enders, *Death by Drama*.

35. Other characters refer to Good Deeds using feminine pronouns; see, e.g., 484.

36. The precise doctrinal identity of the character of Knowledge has been the subject of some debate in *Everyman* criticism: for a survey of the critical discussion surrounding the nature of the character Knowledge, see Warren, "Everyman: Knowledge Once More."

37. On Everyman's education as self-knowledge, see, e.g., Jambeck, *"Everyman* and the Implications of Bernardine Humanism"; and Munson, "Knowing and Doing."

38. Munson, "Knowing and Doing," 261.

39. The *ars moriendi* exhibits a similar preoccupation with the solitary character of death. Even as the *Craft of Dying* stresses the responsibilities of the living and the dying to each other, it instructs the dying to renounce inordinate love of temporal things, including love of one's spouse, children, friends, and worldly riches (412). In both *Everyman* and the *ars moriendi*, this isolation is necessary to recognizing one's correct relationship to the world of others.

40. Munson, "Knowing and Doing," 261.

41. Ibid., 266–67. Munson's reading of this moment in the play is by no means pervasive. Contrast it, e.g., with Ryan, "Doctrine and Dramatic Structure," 730–35; and Kolve, *"Everyman* and the Parable of the Talents," 81.

42. See Ryan, "Doctrine and Dramatic Structure," 730–35.

43. "A Lytel Treatyse of the Dyenge Creature Enfected with Sykenes Vncurable," as described in Cawley's introduction to his edition of *Everyman*, xvii. Comper, *"The Book of the Craft of Dying*," 137–68, provides an edition of a fifteenth-century manuscript version of the same treatise under the title "The Lamentation of the Dying Creature."

44. The *Legenda Aurea*'s "faithful friend" story is quoted in Cawley's introduction to *Everyman*, xviii–xix.

45. The "faithful friend" tales that identify the Good Deeds figure with Christ can be found in the *Gesta Romanorum*, ed. Herrtage, 131–32. For a more complete description of *Everyman*'s influences and analogues, see Cawley's introduction to his 1961 edition of *Everyman*, xiii–xix; and Kolve, "*Everyman* and the Parable of the Talents," 74–75, 87–88.

46. See 1 John 4:7–21.

47. See Thomas's discussion of the theological virtues in *Summa Theologiae* 1a2ae.62, 1.

48. Langland, *Piers Plowman*, ed. Kane and Donaldson, 15.161-2a. The translation is from Donaldson, trans., *Piers Plowman*, ed. Kirk and Anderson.

49. Mirk, *Mirk's Festial*, 76/22–25.

50. See, e.g., The Last Judgment, in *The Chester Mystery Cycle*, 1:452–84.

51. Cavell, *Disowning Knowledge*, 108–9. I am indebted to Mulhall's lucid discussion of this passage in Mulhall, *Stanley Cavell*, 196–201.

52. See Cavell, *Disowning Knowledge*, 103–5.

53. Here I draw on Cavell, *Claim of Reason*, 361.

FIVE   A New Theater of the Word

1. Udall, *Respublica*, ed. Greg, 85; further citations are given in the text by line numbers.

2. Potter, *English Morality Play*, 58. See also Womack's memorable reading of the departure of the vices in *Godly Queen Hester* as "a witty farewell to the cultural and religious unity which had sustained their dramatic identity" (Shepherd and Womack, *English Drama*, 26).

3. On the "secularization" of the morality play in the sixteenth century, see Bevington, *From Mankind to Marlowe*; Potter, *English Morality Play*; Norland, *Drama in Early Tudor Britain: 1485–1558*, chaps. 3 and 10 to 15.

4. For discussion of the focus on sovereign authority in light of the centralizations of the sixteenth century, see Simpson, *Reform and Cultural Revolution*, 539–53. The political events that occasioned *Magnificence* and *Godly Queen Hester* have been the subject of critical controversy (on the former see note 6, below): I base my dating of these plays on Walker, *Plays of Persuasion*.

5. For instance, in *Respublica*, where the critique focuses upon the economic abuses of the Edwardian administration, the prologue insists that Truth is the daughter of time (27–33), an adage that points to the work of Queen Mary and the inevitable march of history in which Truth will prevail.

6. Critics disagree about to which events in Henry's reign *Magnificence* alludes. In his influential reading in his 1908 edition, Ramsay identifies the character of Magnificence with Henry and dates the play to 1515–16, arguing that the play satirizes Cardinal Wolsey's encouragement of Henry's profligate spending policies in the war against France (ix–xcix). In the introduction to her 1980 edition, Neuss identifies the character of Magnificence with Wolsey rather than

Henry and argues that the play was written sometime between 1520 and 1522, around the same time as Skelton's other satires of the cardinal (1–64). Walker, *Plays of Persuasion*, reads the play as an allegory of the 1519 "Expulsion of the Minions," contending that the play describes the breakdown of the court patronage system when Henry VIII promoted several of his close companions, known for their reckless and extravagant behavior, to the Gentlemen of the Privy Chamber (60–101). Both Neuss and Walker argue that *Magnificence* was originally intended for performance in the hall of a London livery company; see Neuss's introduction to her edition of *Magnificence*, 43; and Walker, *Plays of Persuasion*, 88–90.

   7. Skelton, *Magnificence*, ed. Neuss, 1459–60; further citations are to this edition and are given in the text by line numbers.

   8. Rossiter, *English Drama*, 125.

   9. For analyses of Bale's use of spectacle to critique Catholic practice, see Beckwith, *Signifying God*, 148–52; Hunt, *Drama of Coronation*, 98–110; Kendall, *Drama of Dissent*, 114–22; Shepherd and Womack, *English Drama*, 140–53; Simpson, "John Bale's *Three Laws*"; Walker, *Plays of Persuasion*, 190–94; and White, *Theatre and Reformation*, 34–41.

   10. Hunt, *Drama of Coronation*, 110.

   11. Sargent, "Censorship or Cultural Change?," 60–61.

   12. Tyndale, *Obedience of a Christian Man*, 115; hereafter cited in the text by page number. See also the preface to Tyndale's 1534 translation of the New Testament, "W. T. Unto the Reader," in *Tyndale's New Testament*, ed. Daniell, 9–10.

   13. Lloyd, *Formularies*, xxvi. On the concessionary nature of the Ten Articles, see Haigh, *English Reformations*, 128–32; and MacCulloch, *Cranmer*, 161–66.

   14. Williams, ed., *English Historical Documents*, 5.815.

   15. *Book of Common Prayer, 1549*, in Cummings, ed., *Book of Common Prayer*, 25.

   16. *Homily of Repentance*, ed. Griffiths, 541.

   17. Robinson, ed., *Original Letters*, 2.535–36; quoted in Haigh, *English Reformations*, 179.

   18. Brokaw, "Music and Religious Compromise."

   19. *Homily of Repentance*, ed. Griffiths, 531.

   20. Hooker, *Of the Laws of Ecclesiastical Polity*, 5.57.2; hereafter citations are given parenthetically in the text by book, chapter, and section number.

   21. Bale, *King Johan*, in *The Complete Plays*, ed. Happé, 496; further citations are given parenthetically in the text by line numbers.

   22. Although the play's auspices are uncertain, Cromwell's accounts indicate two payments made to "Balle and his fellowes," the first in September 1538 and the second in January 1539. In addition, a transcript of testimonies in relation to the inquisition of a man named Henry Totehill describe "an enterlude concernyng King John" performed at Christmastime at Cranmer's residence. The witnesses' description of the play performed at the archbishop's house are in keeping with the content and themes of Bale's play. One remarks that "King

John was as noble a prince as ever was in England" who was "the begynner of the puttyng down of the Bisshop of Rome, and thereof we myght be all gladd." Walker cites these documents in *Plays of Persuasion*, 172–73.

23. Walker, *Plays of Persuasion*, 195.

24. White, *Drama and Religion*, 15–27.

25. For an account of the political and religious contexts in which the play was first performed, see Walker, *Plays of Persuasion*, 194–200.

26. Ibid., 210.

27. The extant text of *King Johan* is a composite of two versions of the play written at different periods. The first, known as the A-text, is a nearly complete scribal manuscript (copied sometime after 1538) that was later revised by Bale himself. The A-text breaks off after King Johan's death (although two leaves of the original scribal manuscript have been subsequently recovered). The B-text, written in Bale's own hand, picks up just before Bale's revisions to the A-text leave off. References to Elizabeth and the prosecution of the Anabaptists date the B-text to sometime after 1560. For a detailed discussion of the extant manuscript and its provenance, see Pafford, ed., *King Johan*, vi–xxix. See also Happé's account of the extant text in his edition of the *Complete Plays*, 1:9–16.

28. But in the case of Bale's biography the two processes may not finally be distinguishable: Bale began his career as a Carmelite friar and only later converted to the new religion.

29. Shepherd and Womack, *English Drama*, 27.

30. Beckwith, *Signifying God*, 151, 152 (emphasis in original).

31. White, *Theatre and Reformation*, 35 (emphasis in original).

32. Here I draw on Hunt's argument that Bale in his plays does not reject ceremony outright, but rather seeks to use theater to expose fraudulent ones: "While Bale's *King Johan* constitutes a devastating critique of the illegitimate and untruthful drama of the Roman Church, it uses the stage to pit corrupt ceremonies against correct ones and therefore attempts to teach a way of re-reading ceremonies and to recuperate their correct authority" (see *Drama of Coronation*, 98–110; quotation at 109).

33. Morison, *Discourse*, 179; hereafter cited parenthetically in the text by page number.

34. White, *Theater and Reformation*, 14.

35. Cavell, *Claim of Reason*, 369.

36. Austin, *How to Do Things with Words*, 9–10.

37. Ibid., 10 (emphasis in original).

38. Wittgenstein, *Philosophical Investigations*, §249.

39. On Medwall's use of disguise, see Alford, "My Name Is Worship."

40. Medwall, *Nature*, in *The Plays of Henry Medwall*, ed. Nelson, 1.938–41; hereafter cited in the text by line number.

41. For Aristotle's account of *clerus*, see *History of Animals*, Books *VII–IX*, 195. For a recent discussion of the lollard complaint that the covetousness of the church injures the poor, see Crassons, *The Claims of Poverty*, chap. 3.

42. Womack, *English Drama*, 28.

43. Hutson, *The Invention of Suspicion*, chap. 1, discusses *Mankind*'s Titivillus as Mercy's carnivalesque inversion or "double" and as a figure who anticipates the masquerading vices of sixteenth-century plays.

44. On *Magnificence*'s use of doubling, see Neuss's introduction to her edition of the play (47–50). See also Dutton's comments on Skelton's use of doubling and her account of her own marvelous staging of the play in Maria Sachiko Cecire and Mike LaRocco's documentary *Magnyfycence: Staging Medieval Drama* (2011).

45. For an account of Wager's critique of idolatry, see Badir, "To allure vnto their loue"; and Badir, *Maudlin Impression*, chap. 1.

46. Most critics have seen the function of the conversion and postconversion scenes as primarily expository, where stage picture functions simply to heighten the psychological effect: see, e.g., White, *Theatre and Reformation*, 86–87; King, *English Reformation Literature*, 315–18; and Dessen, *Elizabethan Drama*, 134–35. Badir reads the final scenes as an ultimately unsuccessful attempt to privilege word over image: "As the almost verbatim transcription of Calvin's *Institutes* in Faith's long speech suggests, Wager's finale conceives of the stage as book, the figures upon it as sermonizers, and the action behind it, the washing of Christ's feet, as appropriately controlled illustration" (*Maudlin Impression*, 43).

47. My discussion of Calvin's views on theater and theatricality is indebted to Bouwsma's discussion of Calvin's dramatic metaphors in *John Calvin*, chap. 11. Diehl, *Staging Reform*, discusses Calvin's theatrical metaphors in relation to Shakespearean drama and the exploration of Calvinist themes in *The Duchess of Malfi*, chaps. 3 and 7.

48. Calvin, commentary on Jeremiah 9:17–18, in *Commentaries on Jeremiah and Lamentations*, vol. 1; quoted in Bouwsma, *John Calvin*, 178.

49. Calvin, *Commentaries on Daniel*, 1.4:27; quoted in Bouwsma, *John Calvin*, 62.

50. Calvin, *Commentaries on Daniel*, 1.4:27.

51. On Calvin and self-examination as a means to counteract hypocrisy, see Bouwsma, *John Calvin*, 179–80.

52. Calvin, commentary on Exodus 10:16, in *Commentaries on the Four Last Books of Moses*; quoted in Bouwsma, *John Calvin*, 179.

53. Calvin, *Institutes*, 2.7.6.

54. Ibid., 2.7.7.

55. Ibid., 2.7.6.

56. Ibid., 1.1.1.

57. Ibid., 1.1.2.

58. Calvin, *Commentaries on Hebrews*, 11:3. See also Steinmetz's consideration of this passage in relation to Calvin's treatment of the question of whether a fallen human race can have natural knowledge of God in *Calvin in Context*, 30.

59. Calvin, *Institutes*, 2.6.1. See also, e.g., 1.5.8.; 1.6.2.

60. Calvin, *Commentaries on Hebrews*, 11:3.

61. Calvin, *Institutes*, 1.5.8.

62. For a discussion of the vices' use of disguise, see White, *Theatre and Reformation*, 84.

63. Badir, *Maudlin Impression*, 38.

64. Diehl, *Staging Reform*, chap. 7, describes a similar process in *The Duchess of Malfi*.

65. Wager, *Life and Repentaunce of Mary Magdalene*, ed. White, 1189, 1202, 1198; further references are to line numbers in this edition and will be given parenthetically in the text.

66. *Mary Magdalene*, 1.14.691sd (in Furnivall, ed., *Digby Plays*, 53–136).

67. Coletti, "Curtesy Doth It Yow Lere," 18. See also Coletti's discussion of the Digby play's ambivalence about its own use of theatrical spectacle in Coletti, *Mary Magdalene and the Drama of Saints*, 192–97.

68. Wager follows medieval tradition, but not Calvin, in assuming that the sinful woman of Luke 7 is Mary Magdalene.

69. Luke 7:47 (KJV).

70. Luke 7:49 (KJV).

71. Luke 7:50 (KJV).

72. Calvin, commentary on Luke 7:41, in *Commentaries on a Harmony of the Evangelists: Matthew, Mark, and Luke*, vol. 2. Calvin also discusses the implications of Luke 7 for a Reformed soteriology in the *Institutes*, 3.4.37.

73. Calvin, commentary on Luke 7:48.

74. Calvin, commentary on Luke 7:44.

75. Ibid.

76. Calvin, commentary on Luke 7:36.

77. Ibid. (emphasis in original).

78. Ibid.

79. Calvin, commentary on Luke 7:49.

80. The stage directions indicate that before anointing Christ's feet Mary should "creepe under the table . . . and doe as it is specified in the Gospell" (see 1828sd).

81. Calvin imagined reprobation as an "empty show" of virtue. See Calvin, commentary on Matthew 13:12, in *Commentary on a Harmony of the Evangelists: Matthew, Mark, Luke*, vol. 2: "The reprobate are endued with eminent gifts, and appear to resemble the children of God: but there is nothing of real value about them; for their mind is destitute of piety, and has only the glitter of an empty show."

82. Indeed, it is a critical commonplace to announce *Faustus*'s debt to the morality play as long-acknowledged, as seen, for instance, in Bevington, *From Mankind to Marlowe*, 245.

83. Marlowe, *Doctor Faustus* (A-text), 1.1.41; hereafter citations appear parenthetically in the text by act, scene, and line number.

84. Here I draw on Shepherd and Womack's observation that Faustus's shows are for Mephistopheles "explicable as part of the project to distract, and retain, Faustus" (*English Drama*, 60).

85. Ibid., 60.

86. Hugh of Saint of Victor, *On the Sacraments*, 1.9.3.

CONCLUSION

1. Notably, the projects of personification allegory and poststructural performativity have different goals. For instance, whereas the medieval morality plays and *Inside Out* emphasize the redemptive power of performance and the role of human interactions in the creation of meaning, for Judith Butler the recognition of the performative nature of the self and the constructed nature of identity serve as important means of challenging oppressive gender and social norms. On gender performativity, see, in particular, Butler's landmark book, *Gender Trouble.*

2. Aquinas, *Summa Theologiae* 2a2ae.30, 2.

3. Scott, "Review: Pixar's 'Inside Out.'"

4. Keltner and Ekman, "The Science of 'Inside Out.'"

WORKS CITED

Primary Sources

Aquinas, Thomas. *Summa Theologiae.* 61 vols. London: Blackfriars, 1964–81.

Aristotle. *History of Animals: Books 7–10.* Edited and translated by D. M. Balme. Loeb Classical Library 439. Cambridge, MA: Harvard University Press, 1991.

Arnold, Thomas, ed. *Select English Works of John Wyclif.* Vol 3. Oxford: Clarendon, 1871.

Augustine. *The City of God.* Translated by Henry Bettenson. New York: Penguin, 1972.

——. *Homilies on the Gospel of John, Homilies on the First Epistle of John, Soliloquies.* In *Nicene and Post-Nicene Fathers,* 1st ser., vol. 7. Edited by Philip Schaff. Peabody, MA: Hendrickson, 1995.

——. *On Christian Doctrine.* Translated by D. W. Robertson. Upper Saddle River, NJ: Prentice-Hall, 1997.

——. *On the Free Choice of the Will.* Translated by Thomas Williams. Indianapolis: Hackett, 1993.

——. *On the Holy Trinity.* In *Nicene and Post-Nicene Fathers,* 1st ser., vol. 3. Edited by Philip Schaff. Peabody, MA: Hendrickson, 1995.

——. *The Trinity.* Translated by Stephen McKenna. Washington, DC: Catholic University of America, 1963.

Baker, Donald C., John L. Murphy, and Louis B. Hall Jr., eds. *The Late Medieval Religious Plays of Bodleian MSS Digby 133 and E Museo 160.* EETS o.s. 283. Oxford: Oxford University Press, 1982.

Bale, John. *The Complete Plays of John Bale.* 2 vols. Edited by Peter Happé. Cambridge: D. S. Brewer, 1985–86.

Barnum, Priscilla Heath, ed. *Dives and Pauper.* 2 vols. in 3 parts. EETS o.s. 275, 280, 323. London: Oxford University Press, 1976–2004.

Barr, Helen, ed. *The Digby Poems: A New Edition of the Lyrics.* Exeter: University of Exeter Press, 2009.

Bevington, David, ed. *The Macro Plays: The Castle of Perseverance, Wisdom, Mankind: A Facsimile Edition with Facing Transcriptions.* Washington, DC: Folger Shakespeare Library, 1972.

Bible. The Douay-Rheims Version.

Bible. The King James Version (KJV).

Book of Common Prayer: The Texts of 1549, 1559, and 1662. Edited by Brian Cummings. Oxford: Oxford University Press, 2011.

Brandeis, Arthur, ed. *Jacob's Well.* EETS o.s. 115. London: Kegan Paul, Trench, Trübner, 1900.

Bruster, Douglas, and Eric Rasmussen, eds. *Everyman and Mankind.* Arden edition. London: Methuen Drama, 2009.

Calvin, John. *Commentaries on Daniel.* Edited and translated by Thomas Meyers. 2 vols. Grand Rapids, MI: Eerdmans, 1948.

——. *Commentaries on the Four Last Books of Moses Arranged in the Form of a Harmony.* Edited and translated by Charles William Bingham. Grand Rapids, MI: Eerdmans, 1950.

——. *Commentaries on a Harmony of the Evangelists: Matthew, Mark, and Luke.* Edited and translated by William Pringle. 3 vols. Grand Rapids, MI: Eerdmans, 1949.

——. *Commentaries on Hebrews.* Edited and translated by John Owen. Grand Rapids, MI: Eerdmans, 1948.

——. *Commentaries on Jeremiah and Lamentations.* Edited and translated by John Owen. 5 vols. Grand Rapids, MI: Eerdmans, 1950.

——. *The Institutes of the Christian Religion.* Translated by Ford Lewis Battles. Edited by John T. McNeil. 2 vols. Philadelphia: Westminster, 1960.

Cawley, A. C., ed. *Everyman.* Manchester: Manchester University Press, 1961.

Chaucer, Geoffrey. *The Riverside Chaucer.* 3rd ed. Edited by Larry D. Benson. Boston: Houghton Mifflin, 1987.

Clark, Andrew, ed. *Lincoln Diocese Documents, 1450–1544.* EETS o.s. 149. London: Kegan Paul, Trench, Trübner, 1914.

Compston, H. F. B., ed. "The Thirty-Seven Conclusions of the Lollards." *English Historical Review* 26 (1911): 738–49.

Davidson, Clifford, ed. *A Tretise of Miraclis Pleyinge.* Kalamazoo, MI: Medieval Institute Publications, 1993.

Davidson, Clifford, Martin W. Walsh, and Ton J. Broos, eds. *Everyman and Its Dutch Original, Elckerlijc.* Kalamazoo, MI: Medieval Institute Publications, 2007. http://d.lib.rochester.edu/teams/publication/davidson-everyman-and-its-dutch-original-elckerlijc.

Davis, Norman, ed. "The Pride of Life." In *Non-cycle Plays and Fragments,* 90–105. EETS s.s. 1. London: Oxford University Press, 1970.

Dean, James, ed. *Medieval English Political Writings.* Kalamazoo, MI: Medieval Institute Publications, 1996.

Dove, Mary, ed. *Earliest Advocates of the English Bible: The Texts of the Medieval Debate.* Exeter: University of Exeter Press, 2010.

Dymmok, Roger. *Liber contra Duodecim Errores et Hereses Lollardorum.* Edited by H. S. Cronin. London: Kegan Paul, Trench, Trübner, 1922.

Eccles, Mark, ed. *The Macro Plays: "The Castle of Perseverance," "Wisdom," "Mankind."* EETS o.s. 262. London: Oxford University Press, 1969.

Furnivall, F. J., ed. *The Digby Plays.* EETS e.s. 70. 1896. Reprint, London: Oxford University Press, 1967.

Geoffrey of Vinsauf. *Poetria Nova.* Translated by Margaret F. Nims. Toronto: Pontifical Institute of Mediaeval Studies, 1967.

Gower, John. *The Complete Works of John Gower.* Edited by G. C. Macaulay. 4 vols. Oxford: Clarendon, 1899–1902.

——. *Mirour de l'Omme (The Mirror of Mankind).* Translated by William Burton Wilson, revised by Nancy Wilson Van Baak. East Lansing, MI: Colleagues Press, 1992.

Greg, W. W., ed. *A New Enterlude of Godly Queene Hester.* Louvain: A. Uystpruyst, 1904.

Grosseteste, Robert. *The Middle English Translations of Robert Grosseteste's Chateau d'Amour.* Edited by Kari Sajavaara. Helsinki: Société Néophilologique, 1967.

Guillaume de Lorris and Jean de Meun. *Le roman de la rose.* Edited by Armand Strubel. Paris: Librairie générale française, 1992.

——. *The Romance of the Rose.* Translated by Charles Dahlberg. Princeton, NJ: Princeton University Press, 1995.

Herrtage, Sidney J. H., ed. *The Early English Versions of the Gesta Romanorum.* EETS e.s. 33. London: N. Trübner, 1879.

Hilton, Walter. *On the Mixed Life.* In *Yorkshire Writers: Richard Rolle of Hampole, an English Father of the Church and His Followers,* edited by C. Horstmann. 2 vols. London: S. Sonnenschein & Co., 1895–96; 2nd ed., Rochester: D.S. Brewer, 1999.

——. *The Scale of Perfection.* Edited by Thomas H. Bestul. Kalamazoo, MI: Medieval Institute Publications, 2000.

Hodgson, Phyllis, ed. *The Cloud of Unknowing and the Book of Privy Counselling.* EETS o.s. 218. London: Oxford University Press, 1944.

Homily of Repentance and of True Reconciliation unto God. In *The Two Books of Homilies Appointed to Be Read in Churches,* edited by John Griffiths. Oxford: Oxford University Press, 1859.

Hooker, Richard. *Of the Laws of Ecclesiastical Polity,* Book V. Edited by W. Speed Hill. Cambridge, MA: Harvard University Press, 1977.

Hornbeck, J. Patrick, II, Stephen E. Lahey, and Fiona Somerset, eds. and trans. *Wycliffite Spirituality.* New York: Paulist Press, 2013.

Horstmann, C., ed. *Yorkshire Writers: Richard Rolle of Hampole and His Followers.* 2 vols. London: S. Sonnenschein, 1896.

Horstmann, K., ed. "*Orologium Sapientiae* or *The Seven Poyntes of Trewe Wisdom,* aus MS Douce 114." *Anglia* 10 (1888): 323–89.

Hudson, Anne, ed. *Selections from English Wycliffite Writings.* Cambridge: Cambridge University Press, 1978.

Hudson, Anne, and Pamela Gradon, eds. *English Wycliffite Sermons.* 5 vols. Oxford: Clarendon, 1983–96.

Hugh of Saint of Victor. *On the Sacraments of the Christian Faith (De Sacramentis).* Translated by Roy J. Deferrari. Cambridge, MA: Medieval Academy of America, 1951.

Inside Out. Directed by Pete Docter and Ronnie del Carmen. Emeryville, CA: Pixar Animation Studios, 2015.

Isidore of Seville. *The Etymologies of Isidore of Seville.* Translated by Stephen A. Barney, W. J. Lewis, J. A. Beach, and Oliver Berghof. Cambridge: Cambridge University Press, 2006.

Kempe, Margery. *The Book of Margery Kempe.* Edited by Sanford Brown Meech and Hope Emily Allen. EETS o.s. 212. London: Oxford University Press, 1940.

Lancashire, Ian, ed. *Two Tudor Interludes: The Interlude of Youth, Hick Scorner.* Baltimore: Johns Hopkins University Press, 1980.

Langland, William. *Piers Plowman: The B Version.* Edited by George Kane and E. Talbot Donaldson. London: Athlone, 1975.

———. *Piers Plowman: An Alliterative Verse Translation.* Translated by E. Talbot Donaldson. Edited by Elizabeth D. Kirk and Judith H. Anderson. New York: W. W. Norton, 1990.

———. *Piers Plowman, the C-Text.* Edited by Derek Pearsall. Exeter: University of Exeter Press, 1994.

———. *The Vision of Piers Plowman: The B-Text.* Edited by A. V. C. Schmidt. London: J. M. Dent, 1978.

Lloyd, C., ed. *Formularies of Faith Put Forth by Authority during the Reign of Henry VIII.* Oxford: Clarendon, 1825.

Love, Nicholas. *Mirror of the Blessed Life of Jesus Christ: A Reading Text.* Edited by Michael G. Sargent. Exeter: University of Exeter Press, 2004.

Lumiansky, R. M., and David Mills, ed. *The Chester Mystery Cycle.* 2 vols. EETS s.s. 3, 9. London: Oxford University Press, 1974–86.

Mannyng, Robert (of Brunne). *Robert of Brunne's Handlyng Synne.* Edited by Frederick J. Furnivall. EETS o.s. 119, 123. London: Kegan Paul, Trench, Trübner, 1901, 1903.

Marlowe, Christopher. *Doctor Faustus, A-Text.* In *Doctor Faustus and Other Plays,* edited by David Bevington and Eric Rasmussen, 137–83. Oxford: Oxford University Press, 1995.

Matthew, F. D., ed. *The English Works of Wyclif Hitherto Unprinted.* 2nd rev. ed. EETS o.s. 74. London: Trübner, 1902.

Meditationes Piissimae de Cognitione Humanae Conditionis. In *Patrologia Latina,* edited by Jacques-Paul Migne, vol. 184. Paris, 1856.

Medwall, Henry. *The Plays of Henry Medwall.* Edited by Alan H. Nelson. Cambridge: D. S. Brewer, 1980.

Medytacōns of Saynt Bernarde. Westminster: Wynkyn de Worde, 1496; facsimile, Norwood, NJ: Walter J. Johnson, 1977.

Mirk, John. *Instructions for Parish Priests.* Edited by Edward Peacock. EETS o.s. 31. London: Kegan Paul, Trench, Trübner, 1902. Reprint, New York: Greenwood, 1969.

——. *Mirk's Festial: A Collection of Homilies.* Edited by Theodor Erbe. EETS e.s. 96. London: Kegan Paul, Trench, Trübner, 1905.

Morison, Richard. *A Discourse Touching the Reformation of the Laws of England,* Cotton. MS. Faustina. C ii, fols. 5–22. In Sydney Anglo, "An Early Tudor Programme for Plays and Other Demonstrations against the Pope." *Journal of the Warburg and Courtauld Institutes* 20 (1957): 176–79.

Netter, Thomas. *Doctrinale Antiquitatum Fidei Catholicae Ecclesiae.* 3 vols. Edited by B. Blanciotti. Venice, 1757–59; facsimile, Farnborough: Gregg, 1967.

Powicke, F. M., and C. R. Cheney, eds. *Councils and Synods with Other Documents Relating to the English Church.* 2 vols. Oxford: Clarendon Press, 1964.

Rastell, John. *Four Elements.* In *Three Rastell Plays,* edited by Richard Axton, 29–68. Cambridge: D. S. Brewer, 1979.

Riggio, Milla Cozart, ed. and trans. *The Play of "Wisdom": Its Text and Contexts.* New York: AMS Press, 1998.

Robinson, Hastings, ed. *Original Letters Relative to the English Reformation.* Vol. 2. Cambridge: Cambridge University Press, 1847.

Redford, John. *Wit and Science.* In *English Morality Plays and Moral Interludes,* edited by E. T. Schell and J. D. Shuchter, 201–34. New York: Holt, Rinehart, and Winston, 1969.

Shakespeare, William. *Hamlet.* Edited by Ann Thompson and Neil Taylor. Arden Shakespeare Third Series. London: Thompson Learning, 2006.

Shinners, John, and William J. Dohar, eds. *Pastors and the Care of Souls in Medieval England.* Notre Dame, IN: University of Notre Dame Press, 1998.

Simmons, Thomas Frederick, and Henry Edward Nolloth, eds. *The Lay Folks' Catechism.* EETS o.s. 118. London: Kegan Paul, Trench, Trübner, 1901.

Skelton, John. *Magnificence.* Edited by Paula Neuss. Baltimore: Johns Hopkins University Press, 1980.

——. *Magnyfycence.* Edited by R. L. Ramsay. EETS e.s. 98. London: Oxford University Press, 1908.

Somerset, Fiona, ed. *Four Wycliffite Dialogues.* EETS o.s. 333. Oxford: Oxford University Press, 2009.

Spector, Stephen, ed. *The N-Town Play.* 2 vols. EETS s.s. 11–12. London: Oxford University Press, 1991.

Swinburn, Lillian M., ed. *Lanterne of Liʒt.* EETS o.s. 151. London: Kegan, Paul, Trench, and Trübner, 1917.

Tanner, Norman, ed. *Decrees of the Ecumenical Councils.* 2 vols. London: Sheed and Ward, 1990.

——. *Heresy Trials in the Diocese of Norwich, 1428–31.* London: Offices of the Royal Historical Society, 1977.

Thorpe, William. *The Testimony of William Thorpe*. In *Two Wycliffite Texts*, edited by Anne Hudson. EETS o.s. 301. Oxford: Oxford University Press, 1993.

Todd, J. H., ed. *An Apology for Lollard Doctrines*. London: Camden Society, 1842.

Tyndale, William. *The Obedience of a Christian Man*. Edited by David Daniell. London: Penguin, 2000.

——. *Tyndale's New Testament*. Edited by David Daniell. New Haven, CT: Yale University Press, 1989.

Udall, Nicholas. *Respublica: An Interlude for Christmas 1553*. Edited by W. W. Greg. EETS o.s. 226. London: Oxford University Press, 1952.

Wager, Lewis. *The Life and Repentaunce of Mary Magdalene*. In *Reformation Biblical Drama in England*, edited by Paul Whitfield White, 1–66. New York: Garland, 1992.

Walsingham, Thomas. *Historia Anglicana*. Edited by Henry Thomas Riley, 2:1381–1422. London: Longman, Green, Longman, Roberts, and Green, 1864.

Weatherly, Edward H., ed. *Speculum Sacerdotale*. EETS o.s. 200. London: Oxford University Press, 1936.

Wilkins, David, ed. *Concilia Magnae Britanniae et Hiberniae*. 4 vols. London: 1737. Reprint, Brussels, 1964.

Williams, C. H., ed. *English Historical Documents*, 5:1485–1558. London: Eyre and Spottiswoode, 1967.

Wyclif, John. *Tractatus de Civili Dominio*. Edited by Reginald Lane Poole. London: Wyclif Society, 1885.

Secondary Sources

Abrams, M. H. *A Glossary of Literary Terms*. 4th ed. New York: Holt, Rinehart and Winston, 1981.

Aers, David. *Beyond Reformation? An Essay on William Langland's "Piers Plowman" and the End of Constantinian Christianity*. Notre Dame, IN: University of Notre Dame Press, 2015.

——. "Brut's Theology of the Sacrament of the Altar." In *Lollards and Their Influence in Late Medieval England*, edited by Fiona Somerset, Jill C. Havens, and Derrick G. Pitard, 115–26. Woodbridge: Boydell, 2003.

——. *Chaucer, Langland, and the Creative Imagination*. London: Routledge and Kegan Paul, 1980.

——. "A Whisper in the Ear of Early Modernists." In *Culture and History 1350–1600: Essays on English Communities, Identities and Writing*, edited by David Aers, 177–202. Detroit: Wayne State University Press, 1992.

Alban, Kevin J. *The Teaching and Impact of the "Doctrinale" of Thomas Netter of Walden (c. 1374–1430)*. Turnhout: Brepols, 2010.

Alford, John A. "'My Name Is Worship': Masquerading Vice in Medwall's *Nature*." In *From Page to Performance: Essays in Early English Drama*, edited by John A. Alford, 151–77. East Lansing: Michigan State University Press, 1995.

Appleford, Amy. *Learning to Die in London, 1380–1540*. Philadelphia: University of Pennsylvania Press, 2015.

Ariès, Philippe. *The Hour of Our Death*. New York: Knopf, 1981.

Ashley, Kathleen. "Titivillus and the Battle of Words in *Mankind*." *Annuale Mediaevale* 16 (1975): 128–50.

Aston, Margaret. *Lollards and Reformers: Images and Literacy in Late Medieval Religion*. London: The Hambledon Press, 1984.

Austin, J. L. *How to Do Things with Words*. 2nd ed. Cambridge, MA: Harvard University Press, 1975.

Badir, Patricia. *The Maudlin Impression: English Literary Images of Mary Magdalene, 1550–1700*. Notre Dame, IN: University of Notre Dame Press, 2009.

———. "'To allure vnto their loue': Iconoclasm and Striptease in Lewis Wager's *The Life and Repentaunce of Marie Magdalene*." *Theatre Journal* 51 (1999): 1–20.

Baker, Donald. "Is *Wisdom* a 'Professional' Play?" In *The "Wisdom" Symposium*, edited by Milla Cozart Riggio, 67–86. New York: AMS Press, 1986.

Baker, Donald C., and J. L. Murphy. "The Late Medieval Plays of MS Digby 133: Scribes, Dates, and Early History." *Research Opportunities in Renaissance Drama* 10 (1967): 153–66.

Barnes, Michel René. "Exegesis and Polemic in Augustine's *De Trinitate* I." *Augustinian Studies* 30, no. 1 (1999): 43–59.

Barr, Helen. "The Deafening Silence of Lollardy in the *Digby Lyrics*." In *Wycliffite Controversies*, edited by Mishtooni Bose and J. Patrick Hornbeck II, 243–60. Turnhout: Brepols, 2011.

Beadle, Richard. "Monk Thomas Hyngham's Hand in the Macro Manuscript." In *New Science Out of Old Books: Studies in Manuscripts and Early Printed Books in Honour of A. I. Doyle*, edited by Richard Beadle and A. J. Piper, 315–41. Aldershot: Scholar Press, 1995.

Beaty, Nancy Lee. *The Craft of Dying: A Study in the Literary Tradition of the Ars Moriendi in England*. New Haven, CT: Yale University Press, 1970.

Beckwith, Sarah. *Christ's Body: Identity, Culture, and Society in Late Medieval Writings*. London: Routledge, 1993.

———. "Language Goes on Holiday: English Allegorical Drama and the Virtue Tradition." *Journal of Medieval and Early Modern Studies* 42, no. 1 (2012): 107–30.

———. "Ritual, Church and Theatre: Medieval Dramas of the Sacramental Body." In *Culture and History 1350–1600: Essays on English Communities, Identities and Writing*, edited by David Aers, 65–89. Detroit: Wayne State University Press, 1992.

———. "Ritual, Theater, and Social Space in the York Corpus Christi Cycle." In *Bodies and Disciplines: Intersections of Literature and History in Fifteenth-Century England*, edited by Barbara A. Hanawalt and David Wallace, 63–86. Minneapolis: University of Minnesota Press, 1996.

——. *Shakespeare and the Grammar of Forgiveness*. Ithaca, NY: Cornell University Press, 2011.

——. *Signifying God: Social Relation and Symbolic Act in the York Corpus Christi Plays*. Chicago: University of Chicago Press, 2001.

——. "A Very Material Mysticism: The Medieval Mysticism of Margery Kempe." In *Medieval Literature: Criticism, Ideology, and History*, edited by David Aers, 34–57. Brighton: Harvester, 1986.

Bell, Catherine. *Ritual: Perspectives and Dimensions*. Oxford: Oxford University Press, 1997.

Belsey, Catherine. "The Stage Plan of *The Castle of Perseverance*." *Theatre Notebook* 28 (1974): 124–32.

——. *The Subject of Tragedy: Identity and Difference in Renaissance Drama*. London: Methuen, 1985.

Bevington, David M. "'Blake and wyght, fowll and fayer': Stage Picture in *Wisdom*." In *The "Wisdom" Symposium*, edited by Milla Riggio, 18–38. New York: AMS Press, 1986.

——. *From Mankind to Marlowe: Growth of Structure in the Popular Drama of Tudor England*. Cambridge, MA: Harvard University Press, 1962.

——. "'Man, Thinke on Thine Ending Day': Stage Pictures of Just Judgment in *The Castle of Perseverance*." In *Homo, Memento Finis: The Iconography of Just Judgment in Medieval Art and Drama*, edited by David Bevington, 147–77. Kalamazoo, MI: Medieval Institute Publications, 1985.

Binski, Paul. *Medieval Death: Ritual and Representation*. Ithaca, NY: Cornell University Press, 1996.

Bose, Mishtooni, and J. Patrick Hornbeck II, eds. *Wycliffite Controversies*. Turnhout: Brepols, 2011.

Bossy, John. *Christianity in the West: 1400–1700*. Oxford: Oxford University Press, 1985.

——. "The Social History of Confession in the Age of the Reformation." *Transactions of the Royal Historical Society* 25 (1975): 21–38.

Bouwsma, William J. *John Calvin: A Sixteenth-Century Portrait*. Oxford: Oxford University Press, 1988.

Boyle, Leonard E. "The Fourth Lateran Council and Manuals of Popular Theology." In *Popular Literature of Medieval England*, edited by Thomas J. Heffernan, 30–43. Knoxville: University of Tennessee Press, 1985.

Brantley, Jessica, and Thomas Fulton. "*Mankind* in a Year without Kings." *Journal of Medieval and Early Modern Studies* 36, no. 2 (2006): 321–54.

Braswell, Mary Flowers. *The Medieval Sinner: Characterization and Confession in Literature of the English Middle Ages*. Rutherford, NJ: Fairleigh Dickinson University Press, 1983.

Brokaw, Katherine Steele. "Music and Religious Compromise in John Bale's Plays." *Comparative Drama* 44 (2010): 325–49.

Brower, Jeffrey E. "Matter, Form, and Individuation." In *The Oxford Handbook of Aquinas*, edited by Brian Davies and Eleonore Stump, 85–103. Oxford: Oxford University Press, 2012.

Burckhardt, Jacob. *The Civilization of the Renaissance in Italy*. Translated by S. G. C. Middlemore. Edited by B. Nelson and C. Trinkaus. Vol. 1. New York: Harper, 1958.

Burgess, Clive. "'Longing to Be Prayed For': Death and Commemoration in an English Parish in the Later Middle Ages." In *The Place of the Dead: Death and Commemoration in Late Medieval and Early Modern Europe*, edited by Bruce Gordon and Peter Marshall, 44–65. Cambridge: Cambridge University Press, 2000.

Butler, Judith. *Gender Trouble: Feminism and the Subversion of Identity*. New York: Routledge, 1990.

Cartwright, Kent. *Theatre and Humanism: English Drama in the Sixteenth Century*. Cambridge: Cambridge University Press, 1999.

Catto, Jeremy. "After Arundel: The Closing or the Opening of the English Mind?" In *After Arundel: Religious Writing in Fifteenth-Century England*, edited by Vincent Gillespie and Kantik Ghosh, 43–54. Turnhout: Brepols, 2011.

———. "Fellows and Helpers: The Religious Identity of the Followers of Wyclif." In *The Medieval Church: Universities, Heresy, and the Religious Life*, edited by Peter Biller and R. B. Dobson, 141–61. Woodbridge: Boydell, 1999.

———. "John Wyclif and the Cult of the Eucharist." In *The Bible in the Medieval World: Essays in Memory of Beryl Smalley*, edited by Katherine Walsh and Diana Wood, 269–86. Oxford: Oxford University Press, 1985.

———. "Religious Change under Henry V." In *Henry V: The Practice of Kingship*, edited by G. L. Harriss, 97–115. Oxford: Oxford University Press, 1985.

———. "Shaping the Mixed Life." In *Image, Text, and Church, 1380–1600: Essays for Margaret Aston*, edited by L. Clark, M. Jurkowski, and C. Richmond, 94–108. Toronto: Brepols, 2009.

———. "Wyclif and Wycliffism at Oxford, 1356–1430." In *The History of the University of Oxford*, vol. 2, edited by J. I. Catto and T. A. R. Evans, 175–261. Oxford: Oxford University Press, 1992.

Cavell, Stanley. *The Claim of Reason: Wittgenstein, Skepticism, Morality, and Tragedy*. Oxford: Oxford University Press, 1979.

———. *Disowning Knowledge: In Six Plays of Shakespeare*. Cambridge: Cambridge University Press, 1987.

Cawsey, Kathy. "Tutivillus and the 'Kyrkchaterars': Strategies of Control in the Middle Ages." *Studies in Philology* 102, no. 4 (2005): 434–51.

Clark, Marlene, Sharon Kraus, and Pamela Sheingorn. "'Se in what stat thou doyst indwell': The Shifting Constructions of Gender and Power Relations in *Wisdom*." In *The Performance of Middle English Culture: Essays on Chaucer and the Drama in Honor of Martin Stevens*, edited by James J. Paxson, Lawrence M. Clopper, and Sylvia Tomasch, 43–57. Cambridge: D. S. Brewer, 1998.

Clopper, Lawrence M. *Drama, Play, and Game: English Festive Culture in the Medieval and Early Modern Period*. Chicago: University of Chicago Press, 2001.

Cohn, Samuel K., Jr. "The Place of the Dead in Flanders and Tuscany." In *The Place of the Dead: Death and Remembrance in Late Medieval and Early Modern Europe*, edited by Bruce Gordon and Peter Marshall, 17–43. Cambridge: Cambridge University Press, 2000.

Coldewey, John C. "The Non-cycle Plays and the East Anglian Tradition." In *The Cambridge Companion to Medieval English Theater*, edited by Richard Beadle, 189–210. Cambridge: Cambridge University Press, 1994.

Cole, Andrew. *Literature and Heresy in the Age of Chaucer*. Cambridge: Cambridge University Press, 2008.

Coleridge, Samuel Taylor. *Statesman's Manual*. In *Critical Theory since Plato*, edited by Hazard Adams, 467–68. New York: Harcourt, Brace, Jovanovich, 1971.

Coletti, Theresa. "'Curtesy Doth It Yow Lere': The Sociology of Transgression in the Digby 'Mary Magdalene.'" *English Literary History* 71 (2004): 1–28.

———. *Mary Magdalene and the Drama of Saints: Theater, Gender, and Religion in Late Medieval England*. Philadelphia: University of Pennsylvania Press, 2004.

Comper, Frances M. M. *"The Book of the Craft of Dying" and Other Early English Tracts Concerning Death*. New York: Arno Press, 1977.

Connerton, Paul. *How Societies Remember*. Cambridge: Cambridge University Press, 1989.

Coogan, Sister Mary Philippa. *An Interpretation of the Moral Play, Mankind*. Washington, DC: Catholic University of America Press, 1947.

Cornelius, Roberta D. *The Figurative Castle: A Study in the Mediaeval Allegory of the Edifice with Especial Reference to Religious Writings*. Bryn Mawr, PA: Bryn Mawr College Press, 1930.

Cox, John D. *The Devil and the Sacred in English Drama, 1350–1642*. Cambridge: Cambridge University Press, 2000.

Crane, Susan. *The Performance of Self: Ritual, Clothing, and Identity during the Hundred Years War*. Philadelphia: University of Pennsylvania Press, 2002.

Crassons, Kate. *The Claims of Poverty: Literature, Culture, and Ideology in Late Medieval England*. Notre Dame, IN: University of Notre Dame Press, 2010.

———. "Performance Anxiety and Watson's Vernacular Theology." *English Language Notes* 44 (2006): 95–102.

Cressy, David. *Birth, Marriage, and Death: Ritual, Religion, and the Life-Cycle in Tudor and Stuart England*. Oxford: Oxford University Press, 1997.

Curry, Walter Clyde. *Chaucer and the Medieval Sciences*. New York: Oxford University Press, 1926.

Davenport, Tony. "Lusty fresche galaunts." In *Aspects of Early English Drama*, edited by Paula Neuss, 110–28. Cambridge: D. S. Brewer, 1983.

Davidson, Clifford. *Visualizing the Moral Life: Medieval Iconography and the Macro Morality Plays*. New York: AMS, 1989.

Davis, Rebecca. *Piers Plowman and the Books of Nature*. Oxford: Oxford University Press, 2016.

de Grazia, Margreta. "World Pictures, Modern Periods, and the Early Stage." In *A New History of Early English Drama*, edited by John D. Cox and David Scott Kastan, 7–21. New York: Columbia University Press, 1997.

de Man, Paul. *The Rhetoric of Romanticism*. New York: Columbia University Press, 1984.

———. "Rhetoric of Temporality." In *Interpretation: Theory and Practice*, edited by Charles S. Singleton, 173–209. Baltimore: Johns Hopkins University Press, 1969.

Dessen, Alan. *Elizabethan Drama and the Viewer's Eye*. Chapel Hill: University of North Carolina Press, 1977.

Diehl, Huston. *Staging Reform, Reforming the Stage: Protestantism and Popular Theater in Early Modern England*. Ithaca, NY: Cornell University Press, 1997.

Dillon, Janette. *Language and Stage in Medieval and Renaissance England*. Cambridge: Cambridge University Press, 1998.

Dinshaw, Carolyn. *Chaucer's Sexual Poetics*. Madison: University of Wisconsin Press, 1989.

Duffy, Eamon. *The Stripping of the Altars: Traditional Religion in England, 1400–1580*. New Haven, CT: Yale University Press, 1992.

Eldridge, Richard. *Leading a Human Life: Wittgenstein, Intentionality, and Romanticism*. Chicago: University of Chicago Press, 1997.

Emmerson, Richard. "The Morality Character as Sign: A Semiotic Approach to *The Castle of Perseverance*." *Mediaevalia* 18 (1995): 191–220.

Enders, Jody. *Death by Drama and Other Medieval Urban Legends*. Chicago: University of Chicago Press, 2002.

Fischer-Lichte, Erika. *The Semiotics of Theater*. Bloomington: Indiana University Press, 1992.

Forest-Hill, Lynn. "*Mankind* and the Fifteenth-Century Preaching Controversy." *Medieval and Renaissance Drama in England* 15 (2003): 17–42.

Foucault, Michel. *The History of Sexuality*. Vol. 1, *An Introduction*. Translated by Robert Hurley. New York: Vintage, 1978.

Frantzen, Allen J. *The Literature of Penance in Anglo-Saxon England*. New Brunswick, NJ: Rutgers University Press, 1983.

Gash, Anthony. "Carnival against Lent: The Ambivalence of Medieval Drama." In *Medieval Literature: Criticism, Ideology, and History*, edited by David Aers, 74–98. Brighton: Harvester, 1986.

———. "Carnival and the Poetics of Reversal." In *New Directions in Theatre*, edited by J. Hilton, 87–119. New York: St. Martin's Press, 1993.

Gatch, Milton McC. "Mysticism and Satire in the Morality of *Wisdom*." *Philological Quarterly* 53 (1974): 342–62.

Gayk, Shannon. *Image, Text, and Religious Reform*. Cambridge: Cambridge University Press, 2010.

Geary, Patrick J., *Living with the Dead in the Middle Ages*. Ithaca, NY: Cornell University Press, 1994.

Geertz, Clifford. "Thick Description: Toward an Interpretive Theory of Culture." In *The Interpretation of Cultures*, 3–30. New York: Basic Books, 1973.

Gibson, Gail McMurray. "The Play of *Wisdom* and the Abbey of St. Edmunds." In *The "Wisdom" Symposium: Papers from the Trinity College Medieval Festival*, edited by Milla Cozart Riggio, 39–66. New York: AMS Press, 1986.

———. *Theater of Devotion: East Anglian Drama and Society in the Late Middle Ages*. Chicago: University of Chicago Press, 1989.

Gillespie, Vincent. "Chichele's Church: Vernacular Theology after Thomas Arundel." In *After Arundel: Religious Writing in Fifteenth-Century England*, edited by Vincent Gillespie and Kantik Ghosh, 3–42. Turnhout: Brepols, 2011.

———. "Vernacular Theology." In *Middle English: Oxford Twenty-First Century Approaches to Literature*, edited by Paul Strohm, 401–20. Oxford: Oxford University Press, 2007.

Gillespie, Vincent, and Kantik Ghosh, eds. *After Arundel: Religious Writing in Fifteenth-Century England*. Turnhout: Brepols, 2011.

Ginsberg, Warren. "Preaching and Avarice in the Pardoner's Tale." *Mediaevalia* 2 (1976): 77–99.

Greenblatt, Stephen. *Hamlet in Purgatory*. Princeton, NJ: Princeton University Press, 2001.

Griffiths, Jeremy. "Thomas Hyngham, Monk of Bury and the Macro Plays Manuscript." *English Manuscript Studies* 5 (1995): 214–19.

Haigh, Christopher. *English Reformations: Religion, Politics, and Society under the Tudors*. Oxford: Oxford University Press, 1993.

Hanby, Michael. "Augustine and Descartes." *Modern Theology* 19, no. 4 (2003): 455–82.

———. *Augustine and Modernity*. New York: Routledge, 2003.

Harriss, Gerald. *Shaping the Nation: England, 1360–1461*. Oxford: Oxford University Press, 2007.

Havens, Jill C. "Shading the Grey Area: Determining Heresy in Middle English Texts." In *Text and Controversy from Wyclif to Bale: Essays in Honor of Anne Hudson*, edited by Helen Barr and Anne M. Hutchison, 337–52. Turnhout: Brepols, 2005.

Hegel, Georg Wilhelm Friedrich. *Philosophy of History*. Translated by J. Sibree. New York: Dover, 1956.

Hildahl, Frances. "Penitence and Parody in *The Castle of Perseverance*." In *Early Drama to 1600*, edited by Albert H. Tricomi, 129–41. Binghamton: State University of New York at Binghamton, 1987.

Hill, Eugene D. "The Trinitarian Allegory of the Moral Play of *Wisdom*." *Modern Philology* 73 (1975): 121–35.

Hornbeck, J. Patrick, II. *What Is a Lollard? Dissent and Belief in Late Medieval England*. Oxford: University of Oxford Press, 2010.

Hornbeck, J. Patrick, II, with Mishtooni Bose and Fiona Somerset. *A Companion to Lollardy*. Leiden: Brill, 2016.

Horner, Patrick. "'The King Taught Us the Lesson': Benedictine Support for Henry V's Suppression of the Lollards." *Mediaeval Studies* 52 (1990): 190–220.

Houlbrooke, Ralph. *Death, Religion, and the Family in England, 1480–1750.* Oxford: Clarendon, 1998.

Hudson, Anne. *The Premature Reformation: Wycliffite Texts and Lollard History.* Oxford: Clarendon, 1988.

Hughes, Jonathan. *Pastors and Visionaries: Religion and Secular Life in Late Medieval Yorkshire.* Woodbridge: Boydell, 1988.

Huizinga, Johan. *The Waning of the Middle Ages.* Harmondsworth: Penguin, 1958.

Hunt, Alice. *The Drama of Coronation: Medieval Ceremony in Early Modern England.* Cambridge: Cambridge University Press, 2008.

Hunter, Kathryn. "Making Meaning," interview with David Jays. In *Moral Mysteries: Essays to Accompany a Season of Medieval Drama at the Other Place,* edited by David Jays, 81–92. Stratford-upon-Avon: RSC Publications, 1997.

Hutson, Lorna. *The Invention of Suspicion: Law and Mimesis in Shakespeare and Renaissance Drama.* Oxford: Oxford University Press, 2008.

Jambeck, Thomas. "*Everyman* and the Implications of Bernardine Humanism in the Character 'Knowledge.'" *Medievalia et Humanistica* 8 (1977): 103–23.

Jennings, Margaret. "Tutivillus: The Literary Career of the Recording Demon." *Studies in Philology* 74, no. 5 (1977): 1–95.

Jones, E. A. "Literature of Religious Instruction." In *A Companion to English Literature and Culture: c. 1350–c. 1500,* edited by Peter Brown, 406–22. Malden, MA: Blackwell, 2007.

Jurkowski, Maureen. "Lollardy and Social Status in East Anglia." *Speculum* 82 (2007): 120–52.

Keltner, Dacher, and Paul Ekman. "The Science of 'Inside Out.'" *New York Times,* July 3, 2015, Sunday Review.

Kendall, Ritchie D. *The Drama of Dissent: The Radical Poetics of Nonconformity, 1380–1590.* Chapel Hill: University of North Carolina Press, 1986.

Kerr, Fergus. *After Aquinas: Versions of Thomism.* Oxford: Blackfriars, 2002.

———. *Theology after Wittgenstein.* Oxford: Basil Blackwell, 1986.

King, John N. *English Reformation Literature: The Tudor Origins of the Protestant Tradition.* Princeton, NJ: Princeton University Press, 1982.

King, Pamela. "Morality Plays." In *The Cambridge Companion to Medieval English Theatre,* edited by Richard Beadle, 240–64. Cambridge: Cambridge University Press, 1994.

———. "Spatial Semantics and the Medieval Theatre." *Themes in Drama* 9 (1987): 45–58.

Knapp, Steven. *Personification and the Sublime: Milton to Coleridge.* Cambridge, MA: Harvard University Press, 1985.

Knight, Stephen. "Chaucer's Pardoner in Performance." *Sydney Studies* 9 (1983): 21–36.

Kolve, V. A. "*Everyman* and the Parable of the Talents." In *The Medieval Drama,* edited by Sandro Sticca, 69–97. Albany: SUNY Press, 1972.

Lagorio, Valerie M., and Michael G. Sargent. "English Mystical Writings." In *A Manual of the Writings in Middle English, 1050–1500,* edited by Albert E.

Hartung, 9:3049–3137. New Haven: Connecticut Academy of Arts and Sciences, 1967–2005.

Lahey, Stephen. *Philosophy and Politics in the Thought of John Wyclif*. Cambridge: Cambridge University Press, 2003.

Little, Katherine C. *Confession and Resistance: Defining the Self in Late Medieval England*. Notre Dame, IN: University of Notre Dame Press, 2006.

———. "What Is *Everyman?*" *Renaissance Drama* 46 (2018): 1–23.

Lochrie, Karma. *Covert Operations: The Medieval Uses of Secrecy*. Philadelphia: University of Pennsylvania Press, 1999.

MacCulloch, Diarmaid. *Thomas Cranmer: A Life*. New Haven, CT: Yale University Press, 1996.

Magnyfycence: Staging Medieval Drama. Documentary about Elisabeth Dutton's 2010 Staging of John Skelton's *Magnyfycence* in Henry VIII's Hampton Court Palace. Directed by Maria Sachiko Cecire and Mike LaRocco, 2011. http://stagingthehenriciancourt.brookes.ac.uk/resources/magnyfycence.html; and https://mariacecire.wordpress.com/media-projects/.

Mâle, Émile. *L'Art religieux de la fin du Moyen Âge en France: Étude sur l'iconographie du Moyen Âge et sur ses sources d'inspiration*. Paris: Librairie A. Colin, 1908.

Mann, Jill. *Chaucer and Medieval Estates Satire: The Literature of the Social Classes and the "General Prologue" to the "Canterbury Tales."* Cambridge: Cambridge University Press, 1973.

Mansfield, Mary C. *The Humiliation of Sinners: Public Penance in Thirteenth-Century France*. Ithaca, NY: Cornell University Press, 1995.

McAlpine, Monica E. "The Pardoner's Homosexuality and Why It Matters." *PMLA* 95 (1980): 8–22.

McCabe, Herbert. *God Matters*. London: Geoffrey Chapman, 1987.

———. *On Aquinas*. Edited by Brian Davis. London: Continuum, 2008.

McSheffrey, Shannon. "Heresy, Orthodoxy and English Vernacular Religion, 1480–1525." *Past and Present* 186 (2005): 47–80.

Mills, David. "The Theaters of *Everyman*." In *From Page to Performance: Essays in Early English Drama*, edited by John A. Alford, 127–49. East Lansing: Michigan State University Press, 1995.

Minnis, Alastair. *Fallible Authors: Chaucer's Pardoner and Wife of Bath*. Philadelphia: University of Pennsylvania Press, 2008.

Molloy, John J. *A Theological Interpretation of the Moral Play, "Wisdom, Who Is Christ."* Washington, DC: Catholic University of America Press, 1952.

Muldrew, Craig. "From a 'Light Cloak' to an 'Iron Cage': Historical Changes in the Relation between Community and Individualism." In *Communities in Early Modern England: Networks, Place, Rhetoric*, edited by Alexandra Shepard and Phil Withington, 156–77. Manchester: Manchester University Press, 2000.

Mulhall, Stephen. *Stanley Cavell: Philosophy's Recounting of the Ordinary*. Oxford: Oxford University Press, 1994.

Munson, William. "Knowing and Doing in *Everyman*." *Chaucer Review* 19 (1985): 252–71.

Murakami, Ineke. *Moral Play and Counterpublic: Transformations in Moral Drama, 1465–1599*. New York: Routledge, 2011.

Myers, W. David. *"Poor, Sinning Folk": Confession and Conscience in Counter-Reformation Germany*. Ithaca, NY: Cornell University Press, 1996.

Neill, Michael. *Issues of Death: Mortality and Identity in English Renaissance Tragedy*. Oxford: Oxford University Press, 1997.

Neuss, Paula. "Active and Idle Language: Dramatic Images in *Mankind*." In *Medieval Drama*, edited by Neville Denny, 41–67. London: Edward Arnold, 1973.

Nichols, Ann Eljenholm. "Costume in the Moralities: The Evidence of East Anglian Art." *Comparative Drama* 20 (1986-87): 305–14.

——. *Seeable Signs: The Iconography of the Seven Sacraments, 1350–1544*. Woodbridge, Suffolk: Boydell Press, 1994.

Nisse, Ruth. *Defining Acts: Drama and the Politics of Interpretation in Late Medieval England*. Notre Dame, IN: University of Notre Dame, 2005.

Norland, Howard B. *Drama in Early Tudor Britain: 1485–1558*. Lincoln: University of Nebraska Press, 1995.

O'Connor, Sister Mary Catherine. *The Art of Dying Well: The Development of the Ars Moriendi*. New York: Columbia University Press, 1942.

O'Grady, Paul. "McCabe on Aquinas and Wittgenstein." *New Blackfriars* 93 (2012): 631–44.

Owst, G. R. *Literature and Pulpit in Medieval England*. Cambridge: Cambridge University Press, 1933. Rev. ed., New York: Blackwell, 1961.

Pafford, J. H. Introduction to *King Johan by John Bale*. Oxford: Malone Society Reprints, 1931.

Patterson, Lee. *Chaucer and the Subject of History*. Madison: University of Wisconsin Press, 1991.

——. "Chaucerian Confession: Penitential Literature and the Pardoner." *Medievalia et Humanistica*, n.s., 7 (1976): 153–73.

——. "Chaucer's Pardoner on the Couch: Psyche and Clio in Medieval Literary Studies." *Speculum* 76 (2001): 638–80.

——. "On the Margin: Postmodernism, Ironic History, and Medieval Studies." *Speculum* 65 (1990): 87–108.

Paxson, James. *The Poetics of Personification*. New York: Cambridge University Press, 1994.

Pearsall, Derek. *The Canterbury Tales*. London: Routledge, 1985.

——. "Chaucer's Pardoner: The Death of a Salesman." *Chaucer Review* 17 (1983): 358–65.

Penn, Stephen. "Wyclif and the Sacraments." In *A Companion to John Wyclif: Late Medieval Theologian*, edited by Ian C. Levy, 241–91. Leiden: Brill, 2006.

Potter, Robert. *The English Morality Play: Origins, History, and Influence of a Dramatic Tradition*. London: Routledge and Kegan Paul, 1975.

Ribner, Irving. *The English History Play in the Age of Shakespeare*. Princeton, NJ: Princeton University Press, 1957.

Riehle, Wolfgang. "English Mysticism and the Morality Play *Wisdom Who is Christ*." In *The Medieval Mystical Tradition in England: Papers Read at the Exeter Symposium, July 1980*, edited by Marion Glasscoe, 202–15. Exeter: University of Exeter, 1980.

Riggio, Milla. "The Allegory of Feudal Acquisition in *The Castle of Perseverance*." In *Allegory, Myth, and Symbol*, edited by Morton Bloomfield, 187–208. Cambridge, MA: Harvard University Press, 1981.

——. "The Staging of *Wisdom*." In *The "Wisdom" Symposium*, edited by Milla Riggio, 1–17. New York: AMS Press, 1986.

Robertson, Kellie. *The Laborer's Two Bodies: Literary and Legal Productions in Britain, 1350–1500*. New York: Palgrave Macmillan, 2006.

Rossiter, A. P. *English Drama from the Early Times to the Elizabethans*. New York: Barnes and Nobel, 1950.

Rubin, Miri. *Corpus Christi: The Eucharist in Late Medieval Culture*. Cambridge: Cambridge University Press, 1991.

Ryan, Lawrence V. "Doctrine and Dramatic Structure in *Everyman*." *Speculum* 32, no. 4 (1957): 722–35.

Sargent, Michael G. "Censorship or Cultural Change? Reformation and Renaissance in the Spirituality of Late Medieval England." In *After Arundel: Religious Writing in Fifteenth-Century England*, edited by Vincent Gillespie and Kantik Ghosh, 55–72. Turnhout: Brepols, 2011.

Scanlon, Larry. *Narrative, Authority, and Power: The Medieval Exemplum and the Chaucerian Tradition*. Cambridge: Cambridge University Press, 1994.

——. "Personification and Penance." *The Yearbook of Langland Studies* 21 (2007): 1–29.

Scase, Wendy. *"Piers Plowman" and the New Anticlericalism*. Cambridge: Cambridge University Press, 1989.

Scherb, Victor. *Staging Faith: East Anglian Drama in the Later Middle Ages*. Madison, NJ: Fairleigh Dickinson University Press, 2001.

Schmitt, Natalie Crohn. "The Idea of a Person in Medieval Morality Plays." In *Drama in the Middle Ages: Comparative and Critical Essays*, edited by Clifford Davidson and John H. Stroupe, 304–15. New York: AMS Press, 1982.

——. "Was There a Medieval Theatre in the Round? A Re-examination of the Evidence." *Theatre Notebook* 23 (1969): 130–42; and 24 (1969): 18–24.

Scott, A. O. "Review: Pixar's 'Inside Out' Finds the Joy in Sadness, and Vice Versa." *New York Times*, June 18, 2015.

Shaw, Judith. "The Influence of Canonical and Episcopal Reform on Popular Books of Instruction." In *Popular Literature of Medieval England*, edited by Thomas J. Heffernan, 44–60. Knoxville: University of Tennessee Press, 1985.

Shepherd, Simon, and Peter Womack. *English Drama: A Cultural History*. Oxford: Blackwell, 1996.

Simpson, James. "John Bale, *Three Laws*." In *The Oxford Handbook of Tudor Drama*, edited by Thomas Betteridge and Greg Walker, 109–22. Oxford: Oxford University Press, 2012.

———. *Reform and Cultural Revolution: 1350–1537*. Oxford: Oxford University Press, 2002.

———. *Sciences and the Self in Medieval Poetry: Alan of Lille's Anticlaudianus and John Gower's "Confessio Amantis."* Cambridge: Cambridge University Press, 1995.

Smart, Walter K. *Some English and Latin Sources and Parallels for the Morality of "Wisdom."* Menasha, WI: George Banta, 1912.

———. "Some Notes on Mankind." *Modern Philology* 14 (1916): 45–58; 293–313.

Somerset, Fiona. *Feeling Like Saints: Lollard Writings after Wyclif.* Ithaca, NY: Cornell University Press, 2014.

———. "Wycliffite Spirituality." In *Text and Controversy from Wyclif to Bale: Essays in Honour of Anne Hudson*, edited by Helen Barr and Anne M. Hutchison, 375–86. Turnhout: Brepols, 2005.

Southern, Richard. *The Medieval Theatre in the Round.* London: Faber and Faber, 1957.

———. *The Staging of Plays before Shakespeare.* London: Faber and Faber, 1973.

Spearing, A. C. *Medieval Autographies: The "I" of the Text.* Notre Dame, IN: University of Notre Dame Press, 2012.

———. *Textual Subjectivity: The Encoding of Subjectivity in Medieval Narratives and Lyrics.* Oxford: Oxford University Press, 2005.

Spencer, H. Leith. *English Preaching in the Late Middle Ages.* Oxford: Clarendon, 1993.

Spinrad, Phoebe S. *The Summons of Death on the Medieval and Renaissance Stage.* Columbus: Ohio State University Press, 1987.

Spivack, Bernard. *Shakespeare and the Allegory of Evil: The History of a Metaphor in Relationship to His Major Villains.* New York: Columbia University Press, 1958.

Staley, Lynn. "The Penitential Psalms: Conversion and the Limits of Lordship." *Journal of Medieval and Early Modern Studies* 37 (2007): 221–69.

Steinmetz, David. *Calvin in Context.* New York: Oxford University Press, 1995.

Stevens, Martin. "From *Mappa mundi* to *Theatrum mundi*: The World as Stage in Early English Drama." In *From Page to Performance: Essays in Early English Drama*, edited by John A. Alford, 25–49. East Lansing: Michigan State University Press, 1995.

Stone, Martin. "Wittgenstein on Deconstruction." In *The New Wittgenstein*, edited by Alice Crary and Rupert Read, 83–117. London: Routledge, 2000.

Strohm, Paul. *England's Empty Throne: Usurpation and the Language of Legitimation, 1399–1422.* New Haven, CT: Yale University Press, 1998.

Tentler, Thomas N. *Sin and Confession on the Eve of the Reformation.* Princeton, NJ: Princeton University Press, 1977.

Thomson, J. A. F. *The Later Lollards, 1414–1520.* Oxford: Oxford University Press, 1965.

Tillyard, E. M. W. *Shakespeare's History Plays.* New York: Macmillan, 1946.

Traver, Hope. *The Four Daughters of God*. Bryn Mawr, PA: Bryn Mawr College, 1907.

Turner, Denys. *The Darkness of God: Negativity in Christian Mysticism*. Cambridge: Cambridge University Press, 1995.

Tuve, Rosemond. *Allegorical Imagery: Some Mediaeval Books and Their Posterity*. Princeton, NJ: Princeton University Press, 1966.

Twycross, Meg. "The Theatricality of Medieval English Plays." In *The Cambridge Companion to Medieval English Theatre*, edited by Richard Beadle, 37–84. Cambridge: Cambridge University Press, 1994.

Tydeman, William. *English Medieval Theatre, 1400–1500*. London: Routledge and Kegan Paul, 1986.

Vanhoutte, Jacqueline. "When Elckerlijc Becomes Everyman: Translating Dutch to English, Performance to Print." *Studies in the Humanities* 22 (1995): 100–116.

Voaden, Rosalyn. *God's Words, Women's Voices: The Discernment of Spirits in the Writing of Late-Medieval Women Visionaries*. Rochester, NY: Boydell and Brewer, 1999.

Walker, Greg. *Plays of Persuasion: Drama and Politics at the Court of Henry VIII*. Cambridge: Cambridge University Press, 1991.

Warren, Michael J. "Everyman: Knowledge Once More." *Dalhousie Review* 54 (1974): 136–46.

Wasson, John. "The Morality Play: Ancestor of Elizabethan Drama?" In *The Drama in the Middle Ages: Comparative and Critical Essays*, edited by Clifford Davidson, C. J. Gianakaris, and John H. Stroupe, 316–27. New York: AMS Press, 1982.

Watkins, John. "The Allegorical Theatre: Moralities, Interludes, and Protestant Drama." In *The Cambridge History of Medieval Literature*, edited by David Wallace, 767–92. Cambridge: Cambridge University Press, 1999.

Watson, Nicholas. "Censorship and Cultural Change in Late-Medieval England: Vernacular Theology, the Oxford Translation Debate, and Arundel's Constitutions of 1409." *Speculum* 70 (1995): 822–64.

Weimann, Robert. *Shakespeare and the Popular Tradition in the Theater: Studies in the Social Dimension of Dramatic Form and Function*. Baltimore: Johns Hopkins University Press, 1978.

Wenzel, Siegfried. *Latin Sermon Collections from Later Medieval England: Orthodox Preaching in the Age of Wyclif*. Cambridge: Cambridge University Press, 2005.

Wetzel, James. *Parting Knowledge: Essays after Augustine*. Eugene, OR: Cascade Books, 2013.

Wheatley, Abigail. *The Idea of the Castle in Medieval England*. Rochester, NY: York Medieval Press, 2004.

White, Paul Whitfield. *Drama and Religion in English Provincial Society, 1485–1660*. Cambridge: Cambridge University Press, 2008.

———. *Theatre and Reformation: Protestantism, Patronage, and Playing in Tudor England*. Cambridge: Cambridge University Press, 1993.

Whitehead, Christiania. *Castles of the Mind: A Study of Medieval Architectural Allegory.* Cardiff: University of Wales Press, 2003.

Whitman, Jon. *Allegory: The Dynamics of an Ancient and Medieval Technique.* Cambridge, MA: Harvard University Press, 1987.

Williams, Rowan. "Interiority and Epiphany: A Reading in New Testament Ethics." *Modern Theology* 13 (1997): 29–51.

———. *Lost Icons: Reflections on Cultural Bereavement.* Harrisburg, PA: Morehouse, 2000.

Wittgenstein, Ludwig. *Culture and Value.* Edited by G. H. von Wright and Heikki Nyman. Translated by Peter Winch. Oxford: Blackwell, 1980.

———. *Philosophical Investigations.* Translated by G. E. M. Anscombe. 3rd ed. Englewood Cliffs, NJ: Prentice Hall, 1958.

Woods, Marjorie Curry, and Rita Copeland. "Classroom and Confession." In *The Cambridge History of Medieval English Literature*, edited by David Wallace, 376–406. Cambridge: Cambridge University Press, 1999.

Zeeman, Nicolette. *"Piers Plowman" and the Medieval Discourse of Desire.* Cambridge: Cambridge University Press, 2006.

interiority in, 72–79, 89–90
meaning of words in, 65–66,
  80, 85
overview, 3–4
plot, 64–65
as response to lollard ideas, 67
Wisdom as character, 80–81,
  188n52
Wit and Science (Redford), 140
Wittgenstein, Ludwig
  on body and soul, 1, 5–6, 25

concept of training, 21, 26–27, 33
on experience, 111
language and forms of life, 66–67, 80
on lying, 152
on meaning of words, 25–29
on personification, 23–24
Womack, Peter, 149–50, 154
Wyclif, John, 11, 37–38, 45, 46. *See
  also* lollards

Youth (morality play), 140

JULIE PAULSON
is professor of English at
San Francisco State University.

S

CPSIA information can be obtained
at www.ICGtesting.com
Printed in the USA
LVHW051807010519
616270LV00004B/257